Bento Boxes, Boomerangs & Red Foxes -
travels around the world

Lisa Rose Wright

Bento Boxes, Boomerangs & Red Foxes

ISBN 9798376039892
Copyright © Lisa Rose Wright 2023

The right of Lisa Rose Wright to be identified as the author of this work has been asserted by her in accordance with the Copyright Designs and Patents Act 1988

All rights reserved.
No part of this publication may be reproduced, transmitted, or stored in a retrieval system in any form or by any means, without permission in writing of the author.

Any queries please contact me at
lisarosewright@msn.com

Cover design by Muhammad Salman
https://www.dezzinex.com/

For S

My husband and companion on all our adventures –
wherever in the world we are

Prologue

"That's not my case."

I pointed to an old, scuffed leather suitcase. As I spoke, it whirled away from me.

"So?" asked my husband, Stewart – better known as 'S'. He'd been busy lifting his own, cabin-sized, blue roll-on case off the airport carousel.

"So, why does it have my name on it?"

"I don't know."

"There. It's just coming round again. That battered, mucky-brown one. Look!" I pointed again to the large suitcase circling in front of us. A piece of A4 paper had been taped to it. LISA ROSE WRIGHT, it read in block letters, followed by the Aeroflot logo. It was definitely not my case.

My brain felt soft, like marshmallow – the result of over 24 hours without sleep and crossing numerous time zones since we left our home in beautiful green Galicia two days ago. Or was it three? I'd lost track.

And, it seemed, lost my suitcase too. I just couldn't compute this disaster. I ignored the mysterious case and kept scanning the circling luggage for my bag, a twin to Stewart's but in a smart girly pink. I loved the colour, and the fact that it was easy to spot – usually.

Bento Boxes, Boomerangs & Red Foxes

As the carousel ground to a halt, my foggy brain ground to the inevitable conclusion.

"They've lost it, haven't they?" I asked no-one in particular.

We'd only been in Tokyo forty minutes, and already my months of careful planning were going awry.

§

I've always been an over-the-top planner.

At high school I had my revision schedule written out on pieces of card. When I went back to college to take an ecology degree, as a rather mature student in 2001, I created pages of financial calculations before taking the decision to leave my well-paid sales job for the unknown.

Before we moved to Galicia to live, in 2007, I filled notebooks with pros and cons, and later with things to take and many more things to dispose of. When my mum moved to Galicia to join us in 2015, I had my 'moving list' organised – though I hadn't banked on Mum 'helping' quite so much!

I have a weekly 'things to do' list and a daily 'things to do' list. I even have lists of lists, and single-handedly contribute much to the destruction of forests. (Please note, that last comment isn't true as my lists are generally written on the backs of old envelopes or the extra bits of pointless paper the bank seem to insist on sending us.)

Given my list-making nature, it should come as no surprise that I'd planned this round-the-world trip, our first 'big' holiday in five years, with military precision.

And now it was coming unravelled before my eyes.

In fact, that trip ought to have cured me irrevocably of my organisational nature, as one thing after another caused my carefully arranged schedule to fly apart at

Prologue

the seams. But I'm getting ahead of myself, so let's begin at the beginning. As Maria said in the *Sound of Music*; 'It's a very good place to start'...

Memories

It was spring 2018. We, that is my hubby 'S' and I, had lived in Galicia in the remote northwest of Spain for eleven years. We moved here to live the 'good life', *la vida dulce*, grow our own food and escape the rat race in the UK.

We'd married in our local town of Taboada in 2010, to the delight of our neighbours, and had now renovated two houses in our tiny hamlet of six. The second one was for my mum, Iris, who emigrated here in 2015 at the grand old age of 84 and eleven months. We all loved the area, and the people. We enjoyed our home and our community; life was good.

The following year, 2019, was to be S' 70th birthday and, towards the end of the same year, my 55th. Our last major holiday had been two glorious weeks in Costa Rica for my 50th, in 2014. Seventy years on the planet seemed too important to not celebrate in style and, if I booked early enough, we could still get travel insurance at the cheaper under-70s price. But, where to go?

Many moons ago, S had been a ship's cook in the Merchant Navy. He had travelled the world between the ages of 16 and 19 and, when suitably tipsy, he would regale me with tales of his voyages and adventures on the high seas. Maybe we could visit one of his old haunts for our trip?

I began to quiz my unsuspecting hubby, to get some ideas.

"Where did you go on your first sea trip?" I asked one evening.

"Birkenhead."

"Birkenhead? As in Liverpool?"

"Well, the other side of the river, but yes."

Memories

"I'm not sure that counts."

"It does. It's on my seaman's card. I signed on in Liverpool and the ship sailed across the Mersey to Birkenhead docks before being hauled out for refitting. I had my sixteenth birthday in Birkenhead. Got horribly drunk."

"Nice. But we are NOT holidaying in Liverpool."

"What's this about?"

I ignored the question.

"When you were in the Merchant Navy, how many times did you go through the Panama Canal?" I asked a few days later.

"Eight altogether. Four trips each way."

"Was it exciting?"

"Transiting the canal was interesting. Looking at the jungle and the wildlife in Gatun Lake. The first thing we noticed in Panama were all the little birds. My oppo, Tony, and I saw they were budgies. I thought one had escaped but they were everywhere. All colours.

"It got a bit samey after the third or fourth trip. We couldn't steam through, we were pulled by huge electric locomotives called mules, one on each side like a railway line. Except through the lake which was deep enough to navigate.

"It was a slow process as we had to wait for the locks. Takes all day, I think. We dropped cargo at Cristobal so part of the time was delivering that.

"Also, we were still working, of course, as we transited."

"What were you delivering?"

"It all depended. It was a Colombian company which hired the tramp cargo ship I was on. We went from Europe to South America, down the Pacific coast to Ecuador, Peru, and Chile."

"Great memories."

Could we sail down the Pacific coast in a fabulous recreation of S' past life?

"The fourth trip, we didn't know where we were going. We ended up doing Aruba, Tampa, then through the Panama Canal and up to San Francisco, Seattle and Portland before heading to Japan."

"Ah! That's when you jumped ship?"

Silence.

I continued to ponder the endless possibilities, eventually confiding my thoughts one winter's evening.

"What about Japan? You always say you'd like to go back there, and it's somewhere I've always wanted to go."

"I liked Japan," he said, nodding. "Why?"

"I'm planning a trip for your birthday. I'd like to recreate some of your merchant navy past. I thought we could visit Japan."

"Sounds good to me."

This is my easy-going hubby's standard answer to any question posed. He rarely wants to get involved in my planning activities, and is generally happy to go along with whatever I plan. This is fabulous of course – until one needs some input.

"Where was it you hid out in Japan?"

"I didn't hide. I travelled round and then gave myself up when I'd had enough."

"You did jump ship, though," I persisted.

"I wanted to see more of Japan."

"Tell me about it."

"I'd planned it all for a while. Our last port was Yokohama. I got off the ship and caught the bullet train to Osaka, where I'd left my suitcase. We'd been in dry dock in Osaka so it was easier to sneak it out there. Then I went exploring."

"What was that lake you walked around?"

"Lake Biwa. It's the largest lake in Japan. It was peaceful. I got the train to Otsu – a tiny place about the size of Taboada, or less."

Memories

Taboada was our nearest town – a market town of some 3,000 souls. We didn't have a railway station. I was impressed.

"Which way did you walk?"

"Clockwise." S looked at me.

"Of course. Carry on." Only I habitually walk anticlockwise, apparently.

"I started walking along the lake edge then headed into the hills. After about an hour, the track dead-ended at some terraced paddy fields. I decided to walk along those, but it was a maze as they climbed the hillside. It got narrower and steeper. In the end it started going dark. All the workers were heading home for the night. I found a sort of grass-roofed lean-to on top of the rice. It was only about three foot high and full of straw. It was quite comfy, 'til the mosquitos found me. I put socks on my hands, a bag on my head past my eyes, and pulled my polo neck up over my nose. Still got bitten though.

"In the morning, I decided to walk round the lake instead. The second day I got talking to some lads in a café who insisted on giving me a lift. I didn't want one. I'd already planned on it taking me four days to walk round. I didn't *need* a lift."

Even 53 years later, S sounded agitated at his plans being spoilt. And I thought I was the planner around here.

"So, what happened?"

"They took me along the lakeside, maybe a quarter of the way round. We went through a tunnel. Then I slept on a beach. That was okay except for the snakes."

"Perfect."

"The next night I found a builders' hut. There were some new houses going up. It was quite comfortable. The last night I slept in a shed on a farm."

"Did no one object to you using their huts?" I asked, intrigued.

"I hardly saw anyone. It was so quiet the whole time. I'd like to go back there."

"Hmm, I wonder?"

Now I had the Pacific coast of South America, and Japan, on my possibles list. I needed to think about an itinerary.

I started my research through the same company we had used to plan our Costa Rica trip. Sadly, on this occasion they failed to come up with a feasible proposal, and I realised Japan alone would quickly blow our budget.

I needed to do some lateral thinking to make this trip work.

Working all over the world

"What if we joined Workaway?"

"I thought we were already members?"

"Yes, but as hosts. I was thinking of as helpers. We'd need a separate profile. It would be cheaper than staying in hotels, and more fun too."

We had first come across Workaway, and similar organisations, back in 2007 when we bought our ruined Galician farmhouse, *A Casa do Campo*. A number of our new-found friends in Galicia had volunteer helpers working with them, renovating their houses or tending the garden. In exchange for bed and board, volunteers worked four hours a day at whatever jobs were needed.

We never had helpers whilst we were renovating *A Casa do Campo*. We felt the house, with its lack of toilet or bathroom, was too primitive to foist onto the unwary. I later realised that many hosts offer less salubrious surroundings than we had at the time, but I didn't know that then. To be truthful, we also wanted the satisfaction of doing every bit of the renovations ourselves. Pride, or pig-headedness, had prevented us asking for help.

By the time we bought *A Casita do Campo*, our 'country cottage', to renovate for Mum, we already had a comfortable spare room in our own house. We took the plunge and joined Workaway. We needed any help we could get to turn a second ruin in to a home fit for a rather discerning, almost 85-year-old.

Over the next six years, we invited over 25 people into our home, in pairs or singly, to help with renovations, gardening, and the ongoing bramble bashing. We enjoyed the variety of, mainly young, people we met and loved hearing of their adventures volunteering around the world.

"I wouldn't mind that. I don't fancy spending the holiday lazing about," replied S, to my question about joining Workaway.

"I even found a host near that lake."

"Biwa? You've been looking already?"

"Well..."

Neither of us are beach-bunnies. We enjoy exploring places that we visit and discovering things off the beaten track. One of the most repeated comments from our Workaway volunteers was that they loved the chance to see the 'real' Spain rather than tourist areas. This was a big draw for us too. But should I go with two weeks in South America, or Japan? An impossible choice.

Then one of those lovely miracles happened. Our friend Maria, when I told her of our ideas, offered to come to house and mother-sit whilst we were away. Mum hates long-distance travelling, preferring the comforts of her own home and had point blank refused to join our trip.

"I can stay as long as you want, my gorgeous. Me and Iris will be fine," she said.

With this immensely kind offer in place, I could expand our horizons to incorporate both destinations. Or even...

"I was thinking..."

"Oh no."

"Haha. Very funny. No, I was thinking that now Maria has offered to stay and look after the houses and Mum, we could have a longer holiday."

"How long?" asked S, warily.

I took a breath. "Weeell. A couple of months? After all it seems a long way to go to Japan for just a fortnight and as we'll be half way round the world anyway its almost to Australia so we could maybe visit your cousin in Melbourne. And then, well, you know I hate coming back the same way so I thought we could complete the circle by flying to Central or South America on the way back and visiting more of your old haunts."

"You've obviously been thinking about this," S said.

I didn't deny it.

"If we do Workaway in some places it will keep the budget down, and I sort of promised Jenny we could meet up."

"New Zealand Jenny?"

"Yes."

Some of our Workawayers had become good friends over the years. Tony, our star English builder-come-plasterer-come-chess player, had visited us a couple of times since work had been completed on *A Casita*, and Jenny and I regularly messaged each other across the globe.

We first met Jenny and her daughter, Dakota, in 2017. At the time, Dakota was just eleven years old. We had never hosted a child before but I was fascinated by their adventures, Workawaying around Europe. I figured that so long as mum worked, the kid could chat to my mum and keep her company.

As it happened, we got two very capable and intelligent volunteers in Jenny and Koty. While Koty had a lie-in, Jenny would be up early hacking at brambles. She would meet us for morning tea, covered in scratches and, on one memorable occasion, in stings after inadvertently hacking at a hidden wasps' nest.

The first time I saw Jenny, she was bleeding. I had driven to Monterroso, a nearby town, to meet our new helpers from the bus. Jenny clambered down hung with rucksacks front and back and oozing blood from a gash on her knee.

"She fell over," announced Koty, gleefully.

"What happened?" I asked, wondering if I could reasonably ask this stranger to put something on the car seat so she didn't drip blood on our almost new upholstery.

"I tried to help an old lady with her bags, but I overbalanced and went flying," Jenny explained. Then she started to laugh.

The ice was broken, our new car forgotten, and we became fast friends from then on.

That trip, Koty took it upon herself to look after Mum's tiny courtyard garden at *A Casita* whilst Mum was away on her holidays. She religiously watered and cared for it, even when we had been out for the day. I soon discovered that Koty was also incredibly well-read for a youngster. Like me at her age, she spent every spare minute with her head in a book and introduced me to the delights of Kindle with its almost infinite storage capacity.

"Koty, I need some more names for our chicks. They have to be H's this year. Can you help? I have Holly, Horatio, Honey and Harry. I need two more."

"Hibiscus."

"Oh great, I like flower names for the girls. What about the boy with the withered leg?"

"Hephaestus," Koty replied, without a pause.

"Brilliant." I agreed.

"Who?" asked the others.

"The Greek god of the forge. Equivalent to Vulcan in Roman mythology," I explained. "He injured one of his legs when his father, Zeus, threw him from Mount Olympus. Left him lame for life. It's inspired."

Jenny looked at her daughter. "How do you even know these things?" she asked.

Jenny and Dakota had taken a year out to travel the world. Dakota had schoolwork, but it was obvious how much more she gained from her experiences. I decided every child ought to have the same opportunity. When they went home to Wellington, we agreed to visit them in return one day.

"I did say we'd visit. Maybe we could do New Zealand too," I said to S, humming softly.

Working all over the world

"How long were we planning on being away again?" asked S. "And what on earth are you humming."

"Working all over the world. Mmm good point, though. Maybe they could fly to Oz."

"Rocking, not working." S shook his head.

I grinned and went off to further research our 'round-the-world' trip.

Bento boxes, boomerangs and red foxes

"Stewart?"

"Mmm?"

"Well... I've been looking at flights. You know, planning our trip?"

S sighed.

"Anyway, we can fly direct to Tokyo from Madrid with Iberia, but it's mega expensive. Aeroflot fly to Tokyo via Moscow and it's much quicker than the Mediterranean route because they go the shortest way, apparently."

"Yes, Mercator."

"Um, yes, whatever. Anyway. That's only two hundred euros each in February. I'm looking forward to eating out of those bento boxes."

"What?" S was puzzled at my non-sequitur.

"You know, the food boxes they have in Japan, with separate little compartments. They do them in Lidl."

"Right."

"Anyway. Then I thought we could go to Australia via Singapore. I love Singapore and you've never been, we could do a stopover with Singapore Air if they have any offers on." And, breathe.

I had been, briefly, to Singapore on the way to and from a six-week volunteer placement in Indonesia, in 2003 – part of my ecology degree at Staffordshire University. That had been one of the best six weeks of my life, and I'd fallen for Singapore in a big way.

"And then," I continued, "we could fly to Melbourne to see Gerry. Or maybe to Perth and travel cross country to Melbourne. I fancy that idea.

"What's the first thing that comes to mind when I say Australia?" I said, trying to engage my hubby.

"Boomerangs."

"Trust you. Why?"

Bento boxes, boomerangs and red foxes

"I bought one in Australia, last time I visited. We tried it out on the cricket club field."

"Did it work?"

"Oh yes. It flew out over the fields then back over our heads and in to the crowded car park."

"Oh no!"

"And it hit our car."

"Ha. What are the chances of that?"

"I was relieved, I can tell you."

S had been to Australia years before, for the Millennium celebrations in fact, but neither of us had visited Western Australia.

"WA is the largest of the Australian States," I quoted from Google. "It covers nearly 33% of the country but has only 10% of the population. Wow!"

S looked suitably impressed.

"From Australia we can only fly to a few places in South and Central America directly. Costa Rica would mean a change in LA, bizarrely. I fancy Uruguay. Remember I wanted to move there?"

I don't know why I'd had a hankering for Uruguay. In 2005, when we'd been examining possibilities for emigrating, my rather old atlas told me it had one of the best rates of longevity and the most stable economy in South America. In 2019, it still had a rating of 96.7% from the World Bank Political Stability and Absence of Violence and Terrorism chart. Interestingly the USA had a rating of 33.49% in the same year.

Once I had a list of South American possibilities to fly to, I looked at getting home to Spain to complete the circle.

I knew we could fly directly from Madrid to most South American countries with Iberia, our local (and fairly rubbish, but cheap) Spanish airline. I just had to work backwards to find the best alternative.

"Did you know that prices to Montevideo in Uruguay, and to Buenos Aires in Argentina, are double those to Santiago de Chile?"

"Mmm," replied S, enthralled – in his book rather than my announcement.

"It's weird, don't you think? I mean Santiago is much further, and you have to cross the Andes too."

"Probably get cheap rates at the airport or something."

"True. That reminds me of our tutor at uni who got a job in Santiago and was surprised when the plane landed after only two hours. He thought they were off to Chile, not Galicia."

S mumbled something into his book.

"Did you visit Santiago with the navy?"

"Merchant navy. Santiago's inland; we docked at Valparaíso north of Santiago, and then Concepción, a way south."

"Funny country, isn't it?" I mused. "Did you know that Chile stretches from 55 degrees south to 15 degrees south. That's the equivalent of from Denmark down to the Sudan in Africa in the northern hemisphere. I nearly ended up in Chile, you know – studying red foxes with Oxford University."

S nodded, unimpressed. It didn't matter; I wanted to do more checking on this interesting new possibility.

The only room in our house where we can get a decent signal for the internet is the first-floor sunroom. I had to keep sloping off to check my fares and routes.

"Oh, this is good," I said, returning to disturb my hubby once more. "We can fly from Sydney or Melbourne directly to Santiago de Chile. Looks a good flight too. It's Qantas."

"Never crash," we cried in unison. Qantas lost their 'no crash' status a few years after the film *Rainman*,

Bento boxes, boomerangs and red foxes

with the singular Dustin Hoffman, came out – but they still had good reviews.

"So, Madrid to Tokyo. Tokyo to Singapore. Singapore to Perth. Cross Australia, somehow. Visit your cousin in Melbourne. Melbourne or Sydney to Santiago de Chile. Santiago to Madrid. Easy."

"Mmm," said S.

A vague itinerary in place, I contacted a couple of round-the-world travel agents to see what they could come up with.

I was most disappointed to find that none of the agencies could beat the package I'd tentatively put together myself online. They had their hands tied by the big conglomerates they were affiliated with, whereas I was free to book with whomever I wanted. This meant my final package was quite an eclectic range of airlines…

We began with Aeroflot, the much maligned and joked about Russian airline. I had a stock of Aeroflot jokes ready for onboard entertainment if this indeed proved to be all vodka and shot-put wielding stewardesses. The flight had a brief transit stop in Moscow, gaining me another stamp in my passport. For contrast, we then had Singapore Air, a well-respected airline I'd loved last time I flew with them, from Tokyo to Singapore. After a stopover in Singapore, we continued on to Perth. Once in Australia, we had a month to get cross country, by any means possible, to Melbourne where we were to stay with S' cousin for a few days. Our Qantas non-stop flight to Santiago de Chile left Sydney on the 15th March and, by the miracle of international datelines, arrived in the Chilean capital some two hours before it left. Our final homecoming was to be with the cheap, but unwelcome, Iberia, back to Madrid.

Now all I had to do was join the dots…

Bento Boxes, Boomerangs & Red Foxes

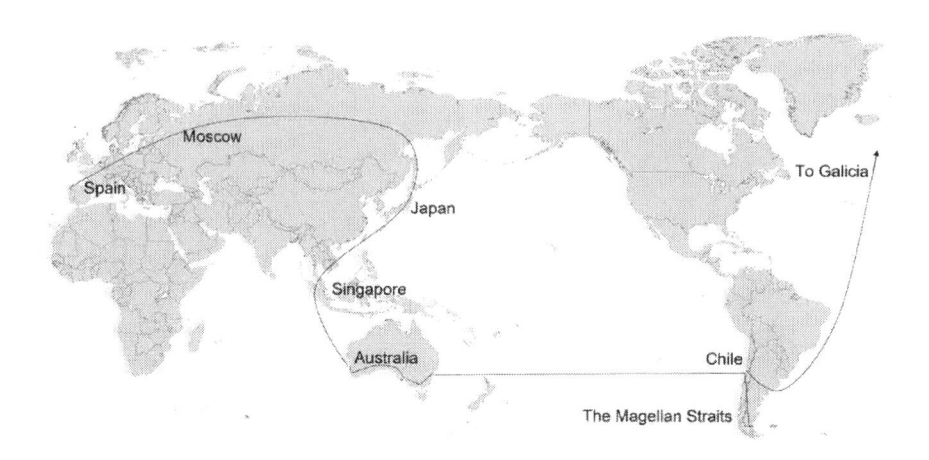

I started a brand-new notebook and wrote down the names of each country we were visiting, on widely spaced pages. Below each country, I wrote a to-do list: book accommodation, find Workaway, get across Australia – those sorts of things.

That was a fun time for me – I was in my element, organising the campaign with precision.

"Packing's going to be tricky," I said, looking up from my notebook. "We're visiting both the northern and southern hemispheres, so we'll have to pack cold and hot weather clothing. It's going to be a pain, keep swapping about."

"I only need two pairs of jeans and a couple of T-shirts, don't I?"

S is nothing if not conservative in his dress.

"Nooo. You'll need shorts in Australia, and Singapore, and a winter jacket in Japan, and south Chile too. The cruise company has a long list of things you have to bring. And you'll need some working clothes."

My pièce de résistance was a four-day cruise along the Magellan Straits. This was to be the highlight and end point of our trip, and my birthday gift to S. The

Bento boxes, boomerangs and red foxes

long clothing list from the company increased our packing two-fold. But I had a plan.

I've always enjoyed packing, and in particular packing into a small space. I know, I'm weird, but everyone has to have a hobby.

When we first moved to Galicia, I actually measured our car, drew up a floor plan of the luggage space, and packaged our belongings for our first few weeks 'camping' in our newly purchased ruin to the millimetre, including an empty box for each of us to be filled as we wished. My box was full of cooking ingredients, pots and pans, and a few garden seeds. S' was full of tools.

This time, I wrote a cold weather and a warm weather list of clothes plus a list of working clothes to be kept separate from the rest. To this, I added the list from the cruise company. (If anyone is really interested, my packing list is in appendix I at the back. It may be useful – or not.)

We were starting from a Galician winter on the first of February 2019 and would be returning home at the beginning of spring. Our dates were determined partly by our friend's house-sitting availability, partly by my needing to be home in time for the spring planting season, and partly by the sights I planned to see on the way.

We were going from cold to hot, hot to cold and back again. From winter to summer, north to south. If anyone ever plans a round-the-world trip, I'd suggest one hemisphere and one bioclimate would make life much simpler – if not so much fun.

Our two larger, cabin-sized roll-on suitcases would initially be full of our hot weather stuff plus the cruise company's list of extra winter gear. Our backpacks would contain the cold weather and working clothes we would need in Japan, plus a small light bag for our two-night Singaporean stopover. We would then repack as and when needed as we travelled around, leaving the unnecessary cases at airports, or at our accommodations.

That was the plan.

Midnight at the lost and found

It was the first of February 2019. The usual 'foreigners' meet up at the monthly market in one of our local towns, Monterroso, had been fun. We'd dropped Mum back home before getting ourselves organised to leave.

For some reason, which now eludes me, we (or rather yours truly, S being in no way responsible) had decided to catch the overnight bus from Lugo to Barajas Airport, Madrid instead of an internal flight from Santiago de Compostela, our nearest airport. It must have had something to do with flight times and price, or maybe long-term parking. Whatever the reason, it was to be a one time, and one time only, experiment.

We left home at six in the evening, after saying our farewells to Mum and our friend, Maria, for the very short drive to Taboada. I'd initially planned to walk the three kilometres into town carrying our luggage, but it was raining quite heavily that evening.

"That messes up my plans," I'd said.

"It's okay, we'll drive."

"We can't leave the car in town for two months, though. Remember when Manuel found that English car here and harangued us for weeks about whose it was? As if we were supposed to know."

"Well, it did have English number plates."

"And we are 'The English'," I replied. "I know."

"I'll drop you and the bags off then drive home and walk back up. It won't take me long."

"That doesn't seem fair. And you'll get wet."

"I'll be fine."

S abandoned me in a café surrounded by our luggage like some kind of bag lady, while he drove home. The rain had slowed to a fine mist and I could see the fog rising over the river Miño as we arrived in our tiny market town.

The café was the one nearest the bus stop. Actually, that's untrue – the café *is* the bus stop. There's no signpost, but everyone knows the Lugo bus stops there.

We thought all the buses stopped there, until one day we were waiting for a bus to Monterroso to collect our car from the garage and were told; "Oh no. *That* bus stops at the other end of the street."

A quick jog past our favourite Scala Bar had found us at the correct stop (still having no sign, of course) with seconds to spare.

I ordered a tea while I was waiting. The new owners of the bar obviously thought I looked suspicious, with my small shop's worth of luggage, and insisted on my paying up front. This is unheard of in our local town. I was so peeved that I declined a second cup.

I spent a worried three-quarters of an hour peering through the steamed-up windows, hugging my empty tea cup, and waiting for my husband to reappear through the gloom of a damp February evening in Galicia. We only had one chance to catch the bus to Lugo – the next one wasn't until the following morning.

Luckily my hero reappeared a few minutes before the Lugo bus arrived and we jumped aboard for the 45-minute ride through the fog.

We were off on the first stage of our adventure.

Midnight at the lost and found

The bus arrived in the Roman city of Lugo three hours before we needed to board our overnight coach to Madrid. I'd already determined that there was a left luggage office, which doubled as a lost and found property office, at the bus station; we stowed our bags and set off for the bright lights of our modest provincial capital (population 75,000). There was only one thing to be done on a cold winter's night in the city of double tapas and cheap wine – go on a pub crawl.

As we wandered into the night, the cold air burnt my cheeks and turned my nose a festive shade of red. Then it began to snow.

"Oh, great. It's freezing. Can we find a bar – quickly?" I mumbled through my scarf. Luckily my hubby understood the muffled moans, or, more likely guessed I was moaning, and dragged me into a likely looking establishment.

I pulled off hat, scarf and gloves, and shook my pony tail free.

"Oh, my glasses have steamed up. *Vino tinto por favor.*" The latter was to the young waiter who had appeared at the table.

"*Dos,*" agreed S.

We soon defrosted with a red wine each, some *jamón serrano* and a warming bowl of soupy *caldo*. We watched snowflakes float to the ground and entangle in the hair of passers-by.

Every now and again a party of youngsters would fly in the door, snowflakes melting in their dark hair, laughing and shaking the moisture from their coats before beginning the ritual kissing and hugging with friends already seated in the warmth. It was a pleasant way to spend an evening.

We arrived back, just before midnight, at the lost and found and left luggage office. The Madrid coach was late due to the weather. We sat, instead, in the café attached to the bus station nursing a thick hot chocolate, surrounded by our bags.

"This weather wasn't part of my plan," I said, sorting through my notebook for my lists.

"Even you can't plan for everything," replied S.

He was right, of course, though at that point I didn't know just how prophetic that statement was.

By the time the coach arrived, the snow had thickened and ice was shimmering in the puddles in the parking area. Thankfully, the coach driver had the heating whacked up to full. I steamed gently – my glasses once more completely opaque.

"This is definitely a blizzard," I said, peering through the windows.

Fat flakes slid down the windscreen, the wipers merely moving them about. I hoped the driver could see more than I could; the way he sliced around roundabouts and bumped through the inevitable potholes, suggested he couldn't.

I decided this was going to be a long, long journey.

Our seats were half-way down, but it was clear from the outset that the coach wasn't going to be packed on an evening such as this one. The first two stops after Lugo produced just one more brave soul, and soon we were on the A6 heading towards Madrid.

The journey to Barajas Airport is six hours, so, once we were on the motorway, I decided to commandeer one of the empty rows of seats in an attempt to get some much-needed sleep. If I'd hoped the red wine would have worked its magic and the gentle movement of the coach would rock me to sleep, I was mistaken. The journey was anything but smooth and the row of seats too short even for my five-foot-two-inch frame. Still, I was tired and I needed sleep. My eyes were closing.

Unfortunately, in my befuddled state I failed entirely to recognise the pungent smell coming from the seat I'd chosen as my bed. In the back of my mind was a

Midnight at the lost and found

thought, but as quick as it appeared it was whisked away before I could catch hold of it.

I'm dreadful at falling asleep in a moving object, be it car, train, or aeroplane, and truly envy people who can just nod off. My brother had a friend who would fall asleep the instant he got in the passenger seat, without fail. I think it's a control thing. Plus, I hate to miss anything. All these thoughts were swirling round my head as I lay semi-conscious, the smell still teasing at the edge of my sleepy mind.

At around three in the morning, the coach pulled in for a rest stop. As I entered the ladies for a much needed wee, my mind cleared and I instantly recognised the smell, now emanating from my favourite jumper - the one I had to wear for the next two days; the one I had to wear until we reached Tokyo.

I stank - of urine.

It seemed some previous occupant of seat 29a had wet him or herself, and I had lain in it for three hours. Now my fluffy, Mexican bought, agave knitted hoodie had soaked up the excess fluid, and aroma. What a perfect travel companion I'd be.

"Dirty git." I stumped back to the coach, muttering the whole way.

"Well, you chose to swap seats," said S, totally unhelpfully - if accurately.

"This wasn't part of the plan."

Back in the (ex)-USSR

Part of my well-oiled plan had included a shower at Moscow Sheremetyevo airport. We had a ninety-minute stopover, and I'd comprehensively Googled facilities there before I even booked the flights. I reasoned that by then we would have been in the same clothes for almost 24 hours and in need of a good wash.

"Look, the showers at Moscow are only 500 roubles each. That's about 5$, and includes soap."

I'd been enthusiastic about my shower plan, and tried to show S the map of Sheremetyevo airport I'd downloaded onto my mobile phone.

"They're even on our way. Look! Here. GettSleep, Terminal D, international departures, near the duty free. That'll be easy to find."

"Bet it's a discus-throwing Russian on the door," was my beloved's reply.

"Yes, whatever. If we pack our travel towels in the top of our rucksacks, we can pop up there on the way to the gate."

"You always know where you are with a towel."

"Haha. It'll be lovely after sitting on a coach and plane for so long." I paused for effect, "Being back in the USSR."

"Huh."

Now, thanks to my unknown 'benefactor', that shower was even more urgent. Maybe I could stuff my ruined jumper in a plastic bag until I had the use of a washing machine? I was sure I had spare clothes in my carry-on bag. It would be better than nothing.

Our Aeroflot flight to Tokyo took off precisely on time. The aircraft was an older Airbus A321, but the staff were friendly and the seats comfortable.

Back in the (ex)-USSR

"I won't be needing my Aeroflot jokes," I said, turning to S, who had the window seat.

"Good."

"Here's one: The Aeroflot stewardess was walking down the plane handing out drinks. A passenger asked for whiskey. 'No whiskey, wodka,' said the stewardess. 'Can I have it with ice?' asked the passenger. 'No ice, wodka,' replied the stewardess. 'Can I have it with water then please?' 'No water, only wodka.'" I grinned.

"Very funny."

"Hey, it's as good as your Terry Wogan jokes."

"Yeah, I miss Radio Two and old Terry's jokes."

"Here's another: Aeroflot only used to have one pilot crewing. On this occasion he needed a pee. He leaves the plane on autopilot and makes his way down the plane, propping the flight deck door open with a shoe. The plane hits some turbulence and the door swings shut. Next thing, the passengers see the pilot running up the aisle carrying an axe which he proceeds to use to hack his way in to the cockpit."

"You are dreadful at joke telling, you know," said S. "And that shot-putter-come-stewardess can hear you."

"Where?" I looked around in terror. S laughed and I hit him, none too gently. "Idiot."

"Actually, there's not a scary Russian in sight," admitted S.

Aeroflot had come a long way in escaping their (possibly uncalled for) reputation. The in-flight meals were excellent; S was particularly taken with the breakfast pancakes slathered in butter. The in-flight entertainment screen was at least seat-back, not a ridiculous small TV screen half-way down the plane which we'd suffered on our last flight with Iberia, and the choice of films was good.

S listened to an eclectic range of music while I decided to teach myself Cyrillic, using the bilingual in-flight magazine as my teacher. By the time we descended towards the bright lights of Moscow, I'd written out the entire alphabet and learnt to spell my name.

"That'll be useful for finding your shower place," said S, when I proudly showed him my doodles.

"Hmm. You'll be pleased if I have to navigate us through Moscow."

"Oh, no. I hope not."

As we came in to land at Sheremetyevo airport, I stared at the pristine piles of snow higher than the aircraft. Marshmallow mounds sat on the edge of the tarmac, where they had been shovelled from the runways. No problem with snow on the tracks in Russia, it seemed.

"Okay, so once we get into the terminal, look for GettSleep. It's opposite the duty-free shop in departures." I was already planning my much-needed shower as we taxied to a halt amidst the heaps of snow.

"We have to get off first," replied S. "The seat belt sign hasn't even gone out and everyone is queueing in the aisles."

It seemed to take for ever to get the exit steps into position. We eventually jumped on the transit bus, me checking my phone every few minutes.

"Still time, still time… Oh, no!"

The terminal building was heaving. Every. Single. Square. Inch. was covered with bodies, baggage, and irate officials. And everyone was being pushed through customs irrespective of their status. It looked like a badly organised cattle market.

"But we're in transit," I said, staring at my phone for the hundredth time. "There must be a transit queue."

Apparently not. We had to queue, with seemingly the entire population of Moscow, around an impossibly complex route. We were herded along with no possible chance of deviation to take in a shower, or even a comfort break.

As we were pushed into an ever-smaller space, I bumped into the man in front.

"Sorry. Look, I don't suppose we can push in at all, only our onward flight leaves in fifteen minutes."

"So does mine," he answered, grimacing.

"Mine leaves in five," a tall man wearing a Stetson said in a Texan drawl.

"Mine was due to lift off ten minutes ago," shouted a plummy English voice from up ahead somewhere. I saw an arm raised in greeting before he was pushed unceremoniously to one side as more bodies joined the pulsing throng.

"This is ridiculous."

"They're passing all the hand luggage through the x-ray machine."

"What the hell for, boy? Y'all in transit."

"Bloody reds."

The murmurs were growing and I could see a second, not so cold, war breaking out any moment. Suddenly the line surged forwards and we were carried along. I grabbed hold of my husband's hand, in terror of somehow losing him and being alone in this madhouse.

"They've opened the gates up."

"About bloody time too."

The murmurs had been heard and acted upon. Customs officers abandoned x-raying bags which had already been x-rayed at the departing airport, and pushed everyone straight through the gate as fast as possible. I had my passport out but no one looked; no one cared any more. We were a nuisance, a thorn in their sides, and they wanted rid of this rebellious crowd.

"But, my passport stamp," I wailed, as we were shoved onwards.

We managed to board our Aeroflot flight to Tokyo before it left, and set down at Narita Airport nine and a half hours later. The first part of our journey had been successfully completed, if not quite according to plan.

My one regret, other than still wearing the same stinking jumper after 33 hours of travel, was that my passport remained unstamped. I have no record of that interesting transit at SVO airport, Moscow.

Japanese girl

Now we were standing at the baggage carousel in Tokyo Narita airport, staring at an unknown bag with my name on it.

"They've lost it, haven't they?" I asked again, looking despondently at the brown case, still patiently circling.

"Possibly. The Aeroflot desk is over there."

I stomped off, hoisting my backpack over my shoulder.

"Good morning, can I help you?" the beautiful Japanese girl on the Aeroflot desk asked in English.

How can they always tell?

"There's a bag on there," I pointed at the carousel. "It has my name on it."

"Ah, Risa Rouzu Raito."

"Erm, yeah, I guess. Have you lost my bag?"

"No, no. We know where bag is. Is in Moscow."

"What?"

"I am ve'y sorry. It did not become transferred. Will be here tomorrow. If you give me hotel address, we deliver it there."

"Oh, okay." That wasn't too bad, I guess. "Hold on. What time will it be delivered?"

"It is same flight tomorrow. Eleven thirty. Luggage will be here in afternoon."

"We take the train tomorrow to Nagano. Snow monkeys," I added, inconsequently.

"Ve'y nice. It is okay. We deliver to there. But it will be next day."

What could I say but thank you?

"Why does everything always go wrong?" I moaned, as we walked away.

"It's hardly a disaster, is it?" said S, reasonably. "It's only a day. What do you need?"

"It's not that. It's mainly stuff for Australia and the extra winter gear for the cruise, but I was planning to store it here at the airport.

"I could tell them to keep it here, I suppose. We could pick it up on the way to Singapore; I don't need it in Japan." I was thinking rapidly. "Oh. Yes, I do. There's my toiletries. I was going to swap them into my rucksack when we arrived because of the liquid restrictions. And my trainers. Oh bugger."

I may have stamped my foot. In my defence I was tired, filthy, and still stank of stale pee.

"You can use my diddy bag until it arrives. It's not the end of the world," said S. "Come on, let's find the trains."

"We need to store your suitcase first. That was the whole point of looking for airport storage, so we only had to carry the rucksacks about on our travels."

Our two weeks in Japan involved a fair bit of moving from place to place. I'd planned for us to store the two suitcases at the airport. I'd thoroughly researched the facilities; prices were very reasonable and it would save a lot of hassle catching trains if we were less encumbered.

Now there was only one case and we would have to drag the other around the country with us – once it arrived, of course.

"Come on," said S, after we dropped off his suitcase and collected the luggage ticket. "Everything will work out fine. Now, Miss Planner, where's that train line?"

I smiled at my hubby. He never failed to be practical, even in the face of one of my meltdowns.

I consulted my carefully annotated list and read aloud; "Drop off bags, Huh. Then…" I traced a line. "Ah, here. We need to go to towards the sign for 'trains' and exchange our Japan Rail Pass Exchange Order for an actual, valid rail pass at the information centre. Um, it's next to the Family Mart and Starbucks."

"How very Japanese," replied S.

I've long held a fascination for Japan and all things Japanese. I blame Richard Chamberlain in *Shogun*, myself. Actually, Richard Chamberlain was probably the fascination as much as Japan at the time, but anyway.

Dad also loved all things Japanese. He was a bonsai grower. He and I nurtured miniature oaks and sycamore trees in tiny shallow pots in our garden in the English Midlands. Dad's dream was to visit the Japanese Imperial Gardens and see professional bonsais for himself.

I'm also partial to Japanese food. A serendipitous discovery in Hendon, North London, many moons earlier, led me to a Japanese food mart. The mall held shops selling Japanese delicacies whilst a central food hall was filled with stalls, each selling a different dish. I ate soba noodles, sushi, and sashimi, and I loved it all. I bought one of my first cookbooks there. I would experiment on friends, inviting them for raw fish and miso soup to my tiny bedsit in Muswell Hill, London. They were brave friends – and happy for the free meals.

The first time I asked at the local fish market for something appropriate for eating raw, the fishmonger suggested smoked mackerel. I don't think he quite got the idea. The salmon and tuna I bought were delicious.

The squid, however, was like eating a particularly thick elastic band. My friends gallantly ate the lot.

Now, here I was in Tokyo. A Japanese girl.

Other than my missing suitcase, everything had gone well so far in Narita airport. The customs area was busy, but organised in a way that ought to have made the Russians cringe in embarrassment, had they experienced it. A number of smartly dressed Japanese gentlemen were positioned along the route to the customs desks. They were there to ensure everyone moved along in a perfectly formed line. As the line moved forwards, it split into discrete lanes, one for each desk.

"This is where you find out if you're allowed back into Japan," I said to S.

"I was only banned for a year."

I smiled.

Once at the front of the queue, we had our fingerprints taken and our faces photographed. A polite 'thank you' meant we were outside and ready to go.

"Phew, you made it." I grinned at my hubby.

The information centre proved relatively easy to find, after we had gone up and down the same escalator a couple of times and chatted with the elderly lady who was seeing people on and off the moving staircase. She spoke no English, and my Japanese was rudimentary in the extreme, but I managed to get our need across and she managed to direct us with much bowing and '*arigatos*'.

'Thank you' was to become my most overused word on that trip. The Japanese use it more often than even the British. A well-placed *arigato* meant more than a smile or a nod could ever do, and seemed to break the ice.

I also found that the 'greeters' we had seen at the airport were commonplace throughout Japan; whether in front of a shop, or at a train station, there was always someone whose sole job was to welcome customers. It felt both incredibly polite and somehow stifling.

We took out some Japanese yen using our newly acquired Revolut bank card – a card which allowed me to withdraw cash in currencies around the world without charge. We bought a bottle of water, queued to exchange our rail pass, and booked both the airport train into the city and our train to Nagano the next day.

"Phew, that was easy," I said, as we left the information centre – rail pass and tickets in hand.

The Japan Rail Pass was part of my planning for our travel around Japan. We were staying overnight in the capital before heading out west to Nagano, then Yudanaka and the famous Snow Monkey Park. Another train would take us south along the China Sea coast to Kanazawa. From there we would travel inland to Lake Biwa, the scene of S' trip down memory lane and our first Workaway of the holiday. By the time we returned to Tokyo for our Singapore flight we would have covered almost one and a half thousand kilometres using at least six trains.

The Japan Rail Pass entitled the holder to free travel on most trains and railway lines, and some city buses, for up to two weeks. Although expensive, at 46,000¥ (350$), it worked out much cheaper than the same journeys paid for individually. I was to discover that it also saved time and hassle. We often simply had to flash our passes at the station master to board.

"The train takes an hour into Tokyo, then our hotel is supposed to be just a ten-minute walk from Central Station. I am sooo looking forward to a shower."

Famous last words.

Lost in Tokyo

The train was sleek and immaculately clean. The hordes were kept back from the platform edge by sliding glass gates operated by a railway official in a smart uniform and cap. As the aerodynamic train glided into the station, there was none of the pushing and shoving I associated with trains and tubes in England. Neither was there any of the non-queuing I had become used to in Spain – where a queue is considered far too orderly.

Here in Japan, the train (exactly on schedule) slowed, then eased itself forward until its doors lined up perfectly with the glass gates. Each gate had a number painted on the ground in front of it with a coloured line snaking back, away from the rails. Along this line, perfectly aligned as if someone had measured the distance between them, were the passengers. We joined line six rather bemusedly and watched as the official looked both ways before opening the sliding doors. Still there was no movement, not even a waft of air.

"Wow, look at this," I said in awe, as the passengers began to alight from the carriage and peel off, disappearing into the cavernous space.

Only once they had all left did our line begin to move, and people board the train. Of course, everyone had a numbered seat; there was no standing in the aisles here.

Once the train was boarded, the official pressed a button on his hi-tech console to close the glass gates. Then he turned his head to the left, sighting along his outstretched arm. He repeated the exaggerated gesture to the right then, once he was satisfied no one was about to launch themselves under his train, he gave the signal for it to depart. It was obviously all part of his station guard training and looked very hammy.

"Dead on time," I remarked, looking at the on-board clock.

Lost in Tokyo

The journey to Tokyo Central Station sped by, and I can't honestly remember much of it. I may have drifted. I do remember noticing with relief that both Japanese and Roman script were used on the station platforms. I had learnt the *kanji* for Tokyo, but wasn't convinced of my ability, if push came to shove.

That train ride was the first of many within Japan. Each one was precisely on time, impeccably clean, and eerily quiet. No one spoke, nor played their iPods, nor talked loudly on their mobile phones. It was bizarre, and really quite pleasant.

In contrast to the clean, peaceful and organised calm of the train journey, Tokyo Central Station was a loud, dusty, disorganised, free-for-all. We emerged from our cocoon of sanity to underground chaos.

"Oh my god, look at the crowds. Ouch!"

Someone had just rammed my leg with their suitcase. I was, admittedly, stationary in the centre of a busy underground crossroads. I was also tired, stinky, and overwhelmed. It was now after two o'clock in the afternoon; I hadn't slept more than three hours since we left home, whenever that was, and following directions whilst being pushed from pillar to post was totally beyond me at this point. I felt like crying.

The signs were confusing and I twisted and turned, trying to get an idea of where to go.

I looked around frantically. "We want Yaesu Central exit. Can you see it?"

"Nope. I can see one for Marunouchi, if that helps?"

"Not really. I only wrote down the exit we wanted. I wish we had a map."

Everyone else seemed to know exactly where they were going in the huge concourse of Tokyo's main Japan Rail station. The complex was vast – spread over two floors with numerous gates leading to various other lines, both overground and underground. There were streets (yes, they are genuine streets), with names such as Tokyo Ramen Street and Tokyo Character Street. None of which helped two weary British tourists.

Eventually, after being pushed this way and that at the whim of the crowd, we were deposited, somehow, outside the station facing the multi-lane Tokyo Expressway.

Four or five lanes of small, square cars raced around like some crazy Scalextric track. Some of the vehicles were converted into vans or flat-bed trucks, holding the tools of their owners' trade, others held a chauffeur, complete with peaked cap. Virtually all were truncated, the back squared off.

I stood with my mouth open, until S nudged me to ask which way we needed to go.

"That way. I think," I said, pointing across the road. "I'm trying to imagine Google maps in my head. Or what's left of it," I added.

Sadly, as soon as we left Spain, my roaming SIM had stopped roaming. This was despite my phoning the company before we departed to check that roaming would work in the countries we were visiting. Without wifi, I was now effectively blind. We set off in the direction I thought was correct, only to get totally confused by the crowds and the unfamiliar signposts.

"I think we need to head towards Takaracho underground station."

"Couldn't we have caught a tube from Central Station?" asked S.

"It's not included on our rail pass and I don't think it's on a direct line. Anyway, Google said it was only ten minutes' walk – even if we have been walking half an hour already."

The sun was surprisingly warm – especially as we were dressed for a much colder winter, in thick coats, jumpers, trousers and boots. Eventually, with much asking of directions, and much pulling out of smartphones to show us the way, much bowing, and much 'arigatoing', we arrived at our first Japanese hotel.

"People are so friendly, aren't they?"

"I think they enjoy practising their English," replied S.

"And showing off their smartphones too. Being lost in Tokyo was fun, though."

"France," replied S.

I grinned. "Bonnie Tyler, correct."

The APA Ginza Takaracho, was part of a hotel chain. I'd chosen it primarily for its location, which we discovered really was only ten minutes from Central Station – in a straight line. It was also very cheap for Tokyo, and the rate included breakfast.

"Right, this is our room. Bags first with the shower."

I opened the door to a blast of hot air and promptly tripped over the end of the bed.

"Ah, not a lot of...ouch."

S had followed me into the room, expecting me to carry on. Unfortunately, there was nowhere to carry on to. I fell onto the tiny double bed whilst he wriggled sideways into the space between it and the desk.

"There's a kettle," I said, from my prone position. "It's under the desk. Look."

"Oh, yes. Could be fun trying to get down there to turn it on."

"Good job we're regular Japanese sized, isn't it?"

"And not sumo size, yes. Does this aircon turn down at all?"

"You fiddle with that, I'm off to try the shower," I said, throwing my stinking jumper in a corner and slithering off the end of the bed.

This was a handy manoeuvre as it meant I more or less ended up in the bathroom doorway.

The bathroom was a box around 1.2m (4ft) to a side and less than two metres (6'6") high. There was a tall step up into it, explaining the lack of head height, and the room was entirely cream.

To the left was a cream-coloured toilet, the likes of which I'd never seen before. It looked more like a garish throne, its armrests inlaid with pictograms. Above this was a shelf on which resided anything the traveller may need for an overnight stay; comb, toothpaste, hairbands, etc. The tub, for calling it a bath would be wholly incorrect, was a box shape too. A three-foot square cube, as deep as it was across, it had a low seat towards one end and a shower hose which emerged from the wall. It was so deep that another conveniently positioned step was needed to get in and out. Between toilet and tub was a teeny sink. It was all most bijou, but handy for washing me, and my stinky jumper, at long last.

Refreshed after my bizarre shower-come-bath and a cup of green tea (which was provided along with the kettle), I was anxious to head out into the city.

"Did you try the buttons on the toilet?" I asked S, as we took it in turns to get dressed. There wasn't space for two people to stand at the same time and I was pleased we didn't have mountains of luggage.

"Not yet."

That was a pleasure to come for us both then.

It was late afternoon by the time we left the hotel, orientating ourselves with the help of a map from reception.

"I'm hungry."

S laughed. "Of course you are."

"I need Japanese food."

We walked towards the station once more, hoping to spot a restaurant or noodle bar on the way. But all the eateries we passed were fancy places with table service and smart greeters in front.

"Way out of our budget, methinks," I said, moving along.

Further down the street there was a neatly laid out garden, and next to it a set of stairs heading underground.

"What's this?" I asked, pointing at a board covered in brightly coloured pictures of food. "That looks more like it."

"The arrow points downstairs. I remember in Osaka when I was there, there was a whole street market underground," said S.

But I was already on my way.

Under the busy streets of Tokyo, there really was an entirely new world. Bars and noodle stands cosied up to mobile phone outlets and gaming shops. I was enthralled.

"Wow! Who'd think all this was underground? It's amazing. And look at the range of foods; sushi, noodles, burgers, there's everything."

Eventually, S managed to steer me into making a decision. It was tricky on a number of counts. Firstly, most of the menu boards were in Japanese with pictograms showing, not entirely clearly (to my mind), the dish on offer. Secondly, I tend towards food envy if I make the wrong decision and there was so much to choose from. Thirdly, I was hungry – never the best time to make an important decision.

One tiny café had real, filled bowls of noodles on display to show the customer exactly what they were getting.

That won the day for me.

I did an excellent job of translation; I simply pointed to two different bowls of noodles and a plate of steamed buns. The tiny wizened owner, for her part, waved a hand in front of her mouth and pointed to one of the bowls.

"Ah. That one must be spicy." I put my two thumbs in the air in acknowledgement, and grinned.

Easy, this foreign language lark.

We entered into the dim but spotless interior. There were six tables, each seating four on benches along either side. We were brought hot towels to clean our hands whilst the table was laid with chopsticks, ceramic spoons, and glasses. A jug of water landed on the polished wood top, quickly followed by two deep bowls of noodles and a platterful of steamed buns.

"This is delicious," I said, between mouthfuls. "I wonder if they charge for the water."

"I don't think so. Can I try yours?"

"Mmm. Swap?"

"Have you noticed how noisily they all eat?" S asked, nodding towards a young man opposite who was vigorously slurping his noodles. I'd been carefully trying to roll mine around my chopsticks.

"You'd think in such a polite society it'd be frowned on, but everyone's doing it." I, in turn, nodded towards a family sitting diagonally across from us, also happily slurping. "Oh well," I added, digging into my almost empty bowl, "when in Tokyo and all that."

S laughed at my efforts to out slurp the Japanese but the café owner seemed impressed, I felt.

As we left, I bowed and gave my best Shogun, '*arigato dimaster*' to our hostess. I've since been told that the correct words for 'thank you very much' are '*arigato gozaimasu*', but she smiled and bowed back anyway.

I'd been fed and watered. Now I was ready to explore.

One of the items on my to-see list was to walk to Chioydu, and Tokyo's Imperial Gardens. Sadly, the bridges to the gardens were all closed by the time we arrived. Dusk was falling, as we watched Japanese families walking the gravel paths around the park.

Afterwards, we wandered the streets of Ginza district. The lighted decorations were bright and garish, but fun. We found a popular-looking bar and ordered a dark, Japanese beer, sitting at a long counter alongside young Japanese businessmen, nodding and occasionally answering their questions. The beer was good, the cost almost as much as our noodle dinner.

Lost in Tokyo

On our way back to the hotel, I noticed a couple in traditional Western wedding attire, sitting on one of the stone bridge columns. I nudged S.

"Odd time for a wedding."

"I think they're posing for photographs. Look, there's the photographer."

Sure enough, a man was setting up his tripod in the street. His large retinue was busy arranging the bride's dress and veil and setting up huge arc lamps. Once we'd spotted that first couple, they seemed to be everywhere.

"Sunday must be wedding day in Tokyo," I whispered, as we passed another happy pair, posing in front of one of the trees on the bright street. Those trees were hung with multi-coloured lights and twinkled like many Christmases come together.

By the time we got back to the hotel it was after 10pm and definitely time for bed. But first...

"Aah! That's just weird."

"You've tried the buttons then?" asked S, peering in the bathroom doorway.

"Well, one has to. This one looks like a lady being sprayed from the front, and this one a man being sprayed up his bum."

"And?"

"That's exactly what it does. Most peculiar sensation."

The multiple delights of dinner, a pleasant walk, a comfortable bed, non-stinky clothes, and a thoroughly washed derrière, helped me sleep through the night.

Tea for two

"I want to see the Imperial Gardens this morning. Our train to Yudanaka isn't 'til twelve thirty."

"Okay."

S was in the bathroom; I was sitting on the end of our compact but comfortable bed, waiting for the mini kettle to boil for our morning cuppa.

"Tea's ready."

S came out looking refreshed.

"You tried the buttons, didn't you?"

As breakfast was included in our room price, we made our way downstairs to take advantage of the free food before heading into the city.

In the elevator there was a cleaning lady, together with all her paraphernalia. I smiled and gave her a hearty good morning, executing a little bow in her direction. She, in turn, looked positively stricken, bowing until her thin frame was almost bent double. For the rest of the, thankfully short, ride the cleaner refused to look up from the floor. I was mortified at my obvious *faux pas*.

This was an aspect of Japanese society I found most uncomfortable. In Spain, no one asks, "What do you do?" before deciding if you are worthy to speak to. Judges, doctors, farmers, and street cleaners happily play cards and drink together. Japanese cultural hierarchy smacked of Downton Abbey and the landed gentry in England, and I was totally unprepared.

Breakfast soon pushed etiquette concerns out of my head. It was a fine spread, including both Western and Japanese cuisines. I started with miso soup, rice and pickles, and a delicious piece of grilled mackerel, then quickly followed up with fresh juice and a berry

Tea for two

smoothie, finishing with bread and jam and plenty of green tea. Feeling we'd done justice to our included meal, we set out into a surprisingly warm and sunny Tokyo.

By the time we arrived at the Imperial Gardens, I was far too hot in my winter woollies and fluffy-lined waterproof boots.

"Wish I had my trainers."

"Why didn't you change?"

"'Cos they're in the suitcase, aren't they?"

"Ah, well."

We walked through a park towards the gardens.

"It's not like any park I know," I said.

Instead of green, newly-mown grassland, this 'park' was a sea of browned, dead tufts of vegetation dotted with trees. In between everything was grey – grey, gravel-filled paths were bounded by huge grey boulders which doubled as seats. Above it all rose tall flat-topped evergreen trees.

"These trees make it look more like the Serengeti."

"Except for the high-rise blocks behind," countered S.

"Good point. It's all a bit grey though, isn't it? Let's see what the Imperial Gardens themselves are like. It looks greener over the bridge. And I love that pagoda."

We followed the signs, arriving at another bridge over the moat which encircled the gardens. The green-roofed pagoda I'd admired from the park was replicated on the other three corners. On the gate was a notice which read, in English; 'Closed on Mondays'.

"Is it Monday by any chance?"

"I think so."

"Ah."

After wandering through a small city park – a minimalist space of paving slabs with cut-out beds displaying colourful winter pansies, etched through with tiny rivulets in concrete canals, I was hungry again.

"Let's find a café. It must be tea time."

Opposite Central Station was a small shop. Above the door was a name plate reading 'café' and some Japanese *kanjis*. Inside, I could see tables and chairs.

"Perfect."

As we reached the door, I spied a smaller notice. In English, it read; 'This is not a café, it is a real estate agency'.

"Brilliant! So why call it café?" I exclaimed.

"Maybe it means something different in Japanese."

"Hmm. I'll have to look it up."

"Here's one," said S.

We'd been walking and talking, and arrived at a smart looking building. There was a menu board outside. The photograph behind the glass was running with condensation making identification difficult, but I was looking at a wedge of something caramel coloured with a white blob next to it, and a large mug.

"So. It looks like tea, and cake with cream, maybe? 670 yen. That's not too bad."

"About five pounds," said S, the lightning calculator.

We followed the arrow down an external stone staircase to a rather grand basement doorway. A greeter opened the door to us and I involuntarily choked as a pall of cigar smoke erupted from the interior.

"Non-smoking. Above," she said in English, pointing.

I wondered how often she had to recite that phrase for tourists.

"That's the first time I've seen a smoking club in years."

"Have you noticed the glass smoking boxes too?" asked S.

"On the streets? Yeah. There's quite a few dotted about."

"There are signs saying no smoking on the streets, which is probably one reason it's so clean, but those boxes are like goldfish bowls."

"I know. Everyone inside is on display. Horrid."

"Not that you can see much for the smog in there."

Tea for two

"That's true. No need to smoke in one of those. You'd probably get a nicotine fix from secondary smoking."

By now we'd reached the upper floor of the 'club', as I now thought of Café Renoir. A male greeter opened the door to us this time and escorted us to a small round table flanked by two comfortable looking club armchairs.

I pointed to the menu special we'd seen outside. "*Ni*," I said, holding up two fingers, then settled back to people watch. "It's so quiet, isn't it," I whispered.

"Why are you whispering?"

"I don't know, it just feels wrong to be loud here. It's not like Spain, is it?"

At home, we joke that just one Spaniard in a room sounds like a huge party. Spain is not a quiet country and, to be fair, when we get together with friends we are as loud. It's just the norm. Here, everyone was quietly sipping their tea, working on their laptops or talking, very, very quietly, to their neighbour. It was unnerving.

I looked up as the waiter brought our hot towels and a jug of water.

"Very civilised, isn't it?" I said.

I cleaned my hands, then spoilt the civilised bit by rubbing the cloth over my face.

"Now for my cake," I added, clapping my hands together.

Our waiter returned with two steaming mugs of miso soup. Not quite tea for two, but I love the salty rich taste of miso. I didn't think it would go with cake, though, and was just about to tell the waiter when the 'cake' arrived.

The photograph *had* been rather poor.

The thickest slice of toast I'd ever seen, dripping with rich salty butter, was placed on the table. Sliced bread in Japan, I discovered, comes in four, six or eight slices per standard 500g packet. This must've been from a four-slice packet. Each slice was cut on the diagonal and toasted to perfection. It was accompanied by a perfectly peeled hard-boiled egg.

"Not. What I was expecting. But very tasty." I laughed, my mouth full of toast, golden butter dripping down my chin. "And it goes perfectly with the miso."

"Not quite a morning cuppa," agreed S, "but good, nevertheless."

In the toilets, I got a shock.

You know that feeling when you go into a public toilet and the seat is still warm from the last user? I sat down and quickly jumped back off the seat. This seat was warm. In fact, this seat was heated.

Heated seats were another of those Japanese things; along with taking your own hand towel into the restroom (I had to shake my hands dry as there were no paper towels), having bum squirters as a matter of course, and piped music at the touch of a button to preserve one's dignity in case of flatulence.

It was, all in all, the best fiver I've spent on food.

Our next destination was somewhere I'd long wanted to visit, and the main reason for choosing Japan in winter – the snow monkeys.

Zen and the art of the slipper shuffle

Our train to Nagano left at precisely 1224 hours. As with all Japanese trains, it glided into its allotted space, the doors opened, the passengers disembarked and the new passengers boarded – all with no fuss, no argy-bargy, and in almost total silence.

The journey was comfortable, but the scenery whipped past the Shinkansen train too fast to see. Instead, we played scrabble with our mini 'travel scrabble' and eyed the other passengers. The seats were so far apart there was no danger of kicking the seat in front even if I didn't have ridiculously short legs. At one o'clock, a uniformed waitress came round with a trolley serving tea, coffee, buns and little picnic boxes. It was all terribly civilised.

Heading across Honshu Island, northwest from Tokyo, we had a perfect view of Mount Fuji. Japan's highest peak, at 3,776m (12,388ft) high, was capped by snow. As we headed further cross country, the landscape outside our window changed. Snow lay on paddy fields and the bare branches of fruit trees poked above the all-encompassing white blanket. It was picturesque from the heated comfort of our train, and much more what I expected from winter in Japan.

At Nagano, we had to change trains. The onward service to Yudanaka was a private line, so our Japan Rail passes couldn't be used. I was standing in front of the huge electronic board trying to work out our destination from the *kanjis*, and wondering which button to press, when a hand reached down from on high.

A disembodied voice asked, "Snow monkeys?"

"Aargh! Erm, I mean, yes please."

The rail worker leant out of his window, situated above the electronic board. Upside down, he pressed the relevant buttons for us; I inserted my yen and received two tickets.

"Thank you. *Arigato*," I said, looking up.

There was no one there.

"Well, that was another strange one."

"They probably employ him just for the tourists," replied S.

"Yeah, but to just pop up like that. He nearly gave me a heart attack. Now, to find the line."

I heard an American accent up ahead. "I think it's this one."

Two young people stood peering at the various arrows and lines. The boy was tall and tussle-haired, looking like a surfer dude with his backpack over one shoulder. The girl was shorter with sleek black hair. She seemed in control of the situation.

"Hi," I said. "Are you going to Yudanaka? We're looking for the right line."

"Yeah, that's right. I think it's this one. I'm Aya," said the girl, holding out a slim hand.

"Lisa. And Stewart. I guess you're going to see the snow monkeys too?"

"We are. I'm Alex."

We passed the short journey chatting to our new friends. Aya was part Japanese. She recognised many *kanjis* and could speak some of the language.

"Oh, here's a question you can answer for me. Do the *kanjis* Ca and Fe mean something in Japanese?"

"Yeah, they mean café. Why?" asked Aya.

I related the Tokyo café-which-was-a-realtor story and we all had a good laugh at the incongruity.

Aya and Alex were staying at the hostel in Yudanaka. We, though, were heading further afield to Shibu Onsen. At the station, they set off walking while we waited for our host.

We waited, and waited some more. A chap came to offer us a taxi but as the lift was included in the price of

Zen and the art of the slipper shuffle

our *ryokan* (traditional Japanese inn) we declined. The chap returned, I thought to hassle us. Instead, he showed us to a tourist window where a bilingual lady rang the *ryokan* for us. Ten minutes later a minibus pulled up and our host climbed out.

"Sorry late sorry," he said, smiling and bowing.

We arrived to the snowy town of Shibu Onsen in a few minutes and pulled up outside a low entrance framed by colourful silken drapes. Our host, an elderly gentleman who deserved the '*san*' suffix if anyone did, spoke only a little English. However, he spent considerable time, through tireless mime, demonstrating how to take off our outdoor shoes at the entrance before putting on the traditional Japanese slippers.

In Japan, outdoor shoes are never worn inside a house. Just inside the entrance to the *ryokan*, there was a large wooden cabinet full of pigeonholes. Each numbered pigeonhole held either a pair of slippers or a pair of outdoor shoes. Hopping about in the freezing lobby, trying to take off wet, snowy boots whilst not putting my feet on the cold, damp concrete floor, and avoiding putting the clean slippers onto the 'dirty' area, was a masterful lesson in Zen and the art of the slipper shuffle.

Our host then showed us the free water dispenser, and the *onsen*.

At Daymaru-ya *ryokan* there was a male and a female bathhouse and a separate, outdoor, private *onsen*.

"Outside *onsen*, key!" said our host, miming locking the door behind us. "Only two!"

One of my reasons for choosing Shibu Onsen was that this tiny hot spring resort is home to dozens of *onsen* or hot pools. There is even an Onsen Trail around the various bathhouses.

Japanese society is highly socialised, and bathing is a group activity – much as there used to be public baths in England before everyone had private bathrooms at home. The *onsen* experience was, I felt, essential to understanding a little more of Japan.

Our host explained the rituals of showering before bathing, of using the correct *yukata* robes whether one was indoors or out and a hundred other things which went right over my head.

"I didn't get much of that. Hope I don't mess up," I whispered, as we followed our host at a fair clip down the corridor.

"Don't worry, you'll get the hang of it," replied S, shuffling behind. "Just like these slippers."

Our room was a traditional one. At the sliding entrance door, we had to remove our first level slippers for another pair.

"Use only in room," said our host, as we all danced the slipper shuffle.

Inside said room, there were two futon mattresses on the floor, a low table with dining chairs either side and, incongruously, a sofa.

"The dining chairs have no legs," I whispered.

"They'd look daft with legs, wouldn't they, with the table so low?" replied clever clogs.

Against one wall was a kettle and a fridge, and to one side was a small room with a sink. Beyond was a separate lavatory.

Inside the entrance to the toilet room was yet another pair of slippers. These were bright pink and had a smiling cartoon toilet on them.

"Use only in here!" said our host, helpfully miming to get his point across.

The number of steps from door to toilet bowl itself was less than two. I struggled to understand the pointlessness of all the slipper shuffling, but, of course, we complied.

It was only later that I heard the story of a tourist who had accidently come downstairs in toilet slippers and almost been evicted from their *ryokan*.

Zen and the art of the slipper shuffle

Once we were alone, we changed into our *yukata* robes and made our way to the outdoor private *onsen*. First, though, we separated to our respective bathhouses to shower.

Inside the women's bathhouse, there was a carpeted changing area. I put my *yukata* robe into one of the baskets provided and entered the bathhouse wearing plastic, 'bathhouse' slippers. Inside was a huge tub almost eight feet across and two feet deep, full of steaming water. Around the wall were low stools. Shower hoses protruded from the walls, each a foot above ground level. I found the cramped, squatting shower most uncomfortable, but managed to negotiate the ordeal.

I was ready for the outdoor *onsen* experience.

Using the 'outside *onsen*, key!', I opened up the wooden door and found myself in a tiny open-air changing room with wooden slatted sides and floor. The sky above was ice blue and the air held just the right amount of nip in it for me to hurry. I hung up the *yukata* robe and toed off my slippers before stepping down into a steaming, stone-lined pool. The smell of minerals was strong, the water deliciously hot and soothing.

"This is lovely," I yelled out, as I heard the door opening.

Only after I shouted did I hope it was my S, not a random stranger, come to join me naked in the pool. I had left the door unlocked, after all.

"Is it hot?" asked S, exiting the changing room.

"Very. I'm sure it'll do you good."

"I hope so. I'm fed up moulting everywhere."

Back in December, S had suddenly found himself covered in an angry, red, and incredibly itchy rash. The doctor, after poking him from a distance, diagnosed scabies, likely caught from our animals. She prescribed some deadly cream which peeled his skin off but did nothing to alleviate the itching.

Our doctor had also told S that scabies was extremely infectious, that I should sleep separately, and that we should change and wash the bedding daily. Just what I needed to hear.

I found it odd that this highly infectious condition had not affected me (who had been sleeping with the patient nightly since it began). I did a bit of checking myself online, and came to a completely different conclusion.

Our local indoor pool, where we swam weekly, had recently changed from using chlorine to bromine to disinfect the water. The first week we visited after this change the water had been so turbid that I accidently swam into S, literally not being able see his foot in front of my face.

"I think you're allergic to bromine. Look, this article is talking about the problems with too strong a mixture."

S immediately stopped swimming, but the damage was done.

He had an appointment with a specialist in May, but our holiday arrived first. We took creams and gels with us, and crossed our fingers that his condition would improve before we arrived in a hot country. Poor S looked like he had a bad case of all-over dandruff; everywhere he went, he left piles of white dust behind.

"I hope it doesn't make it worse," he worried, as we sat in the steaming pools.

"Well, if it feels itchy you can always get out, but the minerals in these pools are supposed to be good for skin conditions. It's worth a go."

"Can't be worse than that cream."

We had a good soak in the pool and, rather than feeling itchy, S said that for the first time in months he wasn't desperate to scratch his skin off.

After another shower, we hit the town.

Zen and the art of the slipper shuffle

Shibu Onsen has a long history, going back 1,500 years, as a stop for pilgrims heading to the Zenjoki Temple in Nagano. Now, it also makes tourist dollars from being the nearest town to the Snow Monkey Park.

The main road passes the front of the town, with the Yokoyu River to one side and a bridge over to industrial units and more houses beyond. Our *ryokan* fronted the main road. Behind it was another street with shops, a hostel, restaurants, and *onsen*. There are nine public *onsen* in Shibu Onsen village, and to visit each one is said to bring good luck. The click-clack of wooden clog-like *geta* sandals tapping on the cobbles as tourists and locals alike walked the Onsen Trail in the warmer outdoor *hanten* robes, was quite soothing.

I was keen to eat more delicious Japanese food.

The problem was that despite the snow monkeys, the town did not really cater for Western tourists. Most establishments had their menus (if that's what they were) written in Japanese. This meant I had no idea what was on offer, nor the prices. Much of the time, I didn't know if something was even a restaurant or simply someone's house. By now I could recognise the *kanji* for Tokyo, and its opposite Kyoto, for exit, and for east and west. Nothing terribly useful for ordering food.

Not feeling brave enough to try and negotiate a meal in Japanese, we opted for a local hostel. My sashimi rice bowl was tasty and the chocolate cake was, well, chocolatey. The local dark beer had a good flavour and the ambience was pleasant, but I didn't feel this was a particularly authentic Japanese experience. I vowed to do better tomorrow.

A Bento box

Our second day at Shibu Onsen dawned sunny and bright. The winter sunshine here was quite a contrast to Tokyo, which had felt positively mild in comparison. This brightness was cold and all embracing. It was also rather beautiful. Pristine white snow lay across the river like a goose down quilt and thickly carpeted the roofs. Only the roadway remained clear, where underground vents spouted super-heated air.

When we'd first arrived, our host's wife asked if we wanted Japanese or Western breakfast.
"Japanese please."
"And second day, Western breakfast. Yes?"
"No, Japanese please. Two days. Japanese."
She didn't seem convinced.
"I bring to room. I your *nakai-san*."
I didn't understand *nakai-san* but got the breakfast bit. We sat on the legless chairs opposite each other at our little low table. At 8am the door opened and our hostess came in with two trays. She elegantly toed off one pair of slippers and slid into a second pair without breaking stride. No slipper shuffle for her. I was most envious, and swore to myself that I'd practise harder.

Each breakfast tray was a bento box made of brown lacquered wood with an intricate pattern, and each segment held a different part of the meal. There was a perfectly steamed piece of salmon; a mound of fluffy sticky rice, sprinkled with spices; a heap of piquant pickled ginger in the centre section; some broccoli with ham and a lone tomato; a section containing fresh chopped fruit; and a final one with some marinated brown something – which I failed to identify but tasted good. It was served with a bowl of miso soup and the ubiquitous green tea.

A Bento box

   Our breakfast was truly exquisite, and reminded me of a quote in my Japanese cookbook; 'First you eat with your eyes'. So true.
   "You like?" our hostess asked, later.
   "Yes, very much."
   "Tomorrow, Western breakfast, yes?"
   "No. Japanese please."
   "Oh. You like?"
   "Yes, yes we do."
   This conversation was repeated a number of times over the course of the day. I wondered if most tourists came to Japan to eat Western fare, or if our hosts simply expected them to.
   Whilst we waited for the minibus for our short ride to the Snow Monkey Park, I tried to chat more to our hostess. She spoke little English but loved to practise. Although our conversation was basic, she did have one thing to say which was very clear.
   "This," she pointed at her home and the town. "This, snow monkey." She rubbed her fingers together in the universal sign for money, put her hands together in prayer and smiled serenely. "Thank you, snow monkey."

I first heard of the so called 'snow monkeys' when an article appeared in National Geographic Magazine in 2002. A further article, in 2016 in the same magazine, showed photographs of these large primates – heads and shoulders covered in snow, sitting in outdoor *onsen*. Their fur was ice-rimed, and they were surrounded by the steam rising from their bathing pools. I was fascinated.
   Japanese macaques live the furthest north of any primate, other than man. In the 1960s, some of the macaques began bathing in a series of public *onsen* in the area. Quick to realise the tourist potential, but concerned that the practice of sharing an *onsen* with monkeys was unhygienic, a separate pool was set aside for the macaques to use.

The Wild Snow Monkey Park (Jigokudani Yaen-Koen) first opened to tourists in 1964. There are now over 150 macaques using the pools. Park rangers feed them grains to encourage the animals to stay in the area, and thousands of visitors come to see them.

We were sharing the ride to the park with another resident at the *ryokan*. Jenny was a stunningly beautiful, dark-skinned, dark-haired woman with an immediate presence. She was confident and outgoing and we all got on well. The walk from the park entrance to the pools where the snow monkeys hang out went by in a flash. We never stopped chatting the whole way.

The track was icy underfoot as we wound our way along a narrow strip beneath tall, bare-branched trees. Wrapped in our winter jackets, scarves and gloves, and keeping up a good pace, we soon warmed up.

The snow lay thickly in the woodland either side of us. The track itself was hard packed snow and slippery in places, with a steep drop to the river. Through the trees we caught glimpses of sink holes bubbling and sending out steam into the frigid air. We could easily tell where the thermal waters rose from the earth by the circles of melted snow around each pool. It was a different world.

"Let it snow, let it snow, let it snow," I sang, dancing and trying to catch fat snowflakes on my tongue.

S groaned.

There were macaques everywhere as we neared the pools set aside for them, digging in the snow to find the small grain seeds the rangers feed them. A mum came near carrying a baby, teenagers played tag, and large males preened at the camera-toting humans. With their red faces and thick, woolly, off-white coats they looked so very human.

Although snowy, it was a mild day. The macaques were indifferent to us, busy hunting for grain and refusing to play their part by entering the hot water,

A Bento box

even when the rangers threw some of the grain in for them.

I'm sure the macaques are happier without humans contaminating their *onsen*, but I couldn't help feeling this was a zoo in everything but name. Fencing keeps the macaques close, and a regular food supply ensures they don't wander far afield.

In the minibus on the way back, I mentioned something I'd seen online about a *sake* museum in the town. Jenny was interested, so the afternoon's entertainment was settled.

There were a few false starts finding our venue; the Tamamura museum and gallery was not quite where I thought it was; instead, it was high up on the hill across the river from our *ryokan*.

As we entered the large wooden building, we spotted Aya and Alex, our new friends from the previous day, sitting at a long wooden table sipping *sake*.

"Fancy seeing you two here," I greeted them, before introducing Jenny.

"Look around the museum first," suggested Alex.

"Yes, it's really interesting. Then come and join us for some *sake* tasting."

"That sounds like a plan."

The museum, upstairs, *was* interesting. It held brewing artefacts, and large wooden barrels from the old brewery as well as artwork and silk wall hangings. It also had the most incredible wooden beams overhead, which S and I enjoyed staring at.

"Reminds me of home," I said, slightly wistfully.

"I wonder if these have been repurposed, like ours?" replied S.

Many of our house beams seem to have begun life as something else entirely, and I often imagined their long history from chestnut seedling to darkened sweet chestnut beam.

After a good peruse, we returned to the tasting room.

"There are seven different *sake* on the bar, each one is brewed for a different period and has a different strength. It's best to start with the least alcoholic and work your way up," explained Alex.

"The idea is to buy a bottle or two of the *sake* you prefer," added Aya.

We soon discovered that we all shared interests in the environment and nature, and the same political opinions. The afternoon passed in a blur of chat and alcohol.

As neither S nor I are big drinkers, we had a tiny taste of each one of the bottles before moving on to the locally brewed Shiga Kogen dark porter. The *sake* took my breath away, but the porter was rich and dark.

When we left, the icy air outside made me gulp and the ground spun for a moment.

"Stronger than I thought," I giggled, trying not to slip down the steep snow-covered slope back to the roadway below.

At some point during the afternoon, we'd all agreed to have a late lunch together in Shibu Onsen. Sadly, by the time we left the *sake* museum dusk was falling and everywhere was closed for the afternoon. Instead, we shared Aya and Alex's thoughtfully put together snack-bag of crisps and nuts and agreed to meet for dinner.

Jenny was unable to join us for dinner, having a previous engagement, so it was just the four of us who walked the dark streets of Shibu Onsen looking for a restaurant that night.

"That one's a noodle bar. A ramen bar." Aya pointed at what looked like a shack.

"How do you know?"

"That *kanji* stands for ramen."

"Ah, obviously."

"And that one says female. It's the changing room for the *onsen* there."

A Bento box

The board didn't say 'female' in any script I recognised. "That could have been interesting had we been going hot pooling," I said to myself. Until S' rash cleared, though, we were forfeiting the full round of *onsen*.

Finally, Aya pointed at yet another nondescript building. "Here. This is a restaurant."

"I'd never have known."

Inside the wood-clad building there were piles of shoes beneath flimsy looking paper *shoji* doors raised above floor level.

These traditional Japanese partition doors are made of a wooden latticework frame covered with a translucent white waxed paper. They look flimsy but are surprisingly sturdy and allow light to filter through into different rooms. In a restaurant such as this, they confer privacy; each dining party sits in their own private room.

I hopped on one foot to toe off my outdoor shoes, thankful that my wellie-style boots were oversized and easy to slip off. S had his walking boots on. Whilst unlacing them, he wobbled and put his hand out to steady himself on one of the *shoji* doors, which began to shake. This caused angry mutterings from inside the adjacent dining compartment and giggles from us. I was still enjoying the *sake* high from the afternoon.

Eventually, sock-clad, we crawled into our private, elevated dining compartment. Inside was a low table and padded seats. I was pleased to see that the seats were actually built down below the raised floor, allowing us to sit as normal rather than having to cross our legs or crouch.

"It feels strange to have our waitress crawling along to us," I said to Aya, as we were served the hot towels and jug of water I'd already come to expect in Japan.

"She's called a *nakai-san*. It means attendant service. They're proud to serve us. It's very traditional."

So that's what our hostess had meant when she said she was our *nakai-san*.

Aya helped us choose our dishes from the complex Japanese menu. For S, a large, beautifully grilled mackerel; for me, my favourite, a sashimi bowl with salmon, tuna, and other fish I didn't recognise but enjoyed enormously. There was the ubiquitous and warming miso soup, pickles, and a huge blob of vibrant green wasabi paste – the pungent Japanese 'horseradish'.

Previously, I'd always just dipped my fish in the wasabi, or slathered it on my meal. Aya showed me how to mix it into a small bowl of soy sauce to produce a delicious fiery dip.

Alex ordered more *sake*, this time hot, which warmed our bellies. And, of course, there was green tea. It was the perfect end to the day, and to our time in Shibu Onsen, chatting over dinner with this lovely young couple.

Couchsurfing

Breakfast the next morning, was another delicious bento box; this time with grilled mackerel, rice, fruit, and pickled peppers – though our landlady had added a discreet pile of fries in one corner as a concession to the Western breakfast we didn't want.

Downstairs, I paid our host and thanked him for a lovely stay. Then I presented him with a tiny gift; a small Galician-made pottery owl, the symbol of wisdom, wealth and good fortune, in a tiny purple box. I chose purple as a symbol of nobility and wisdom. I hoped my clumsy intentions would be interpreted correctly.

I was aware of the Japanese tradition of giving and receiving symbolic gifts, thanks to an ex-boss of mine who visited Japan regularly for sales meetings. Malcolm was six foot four and loathed raw fish. He detested going to Japan and I had long (and unsuccessfully) campaigned for him to send me instead.

It was Malcolm who told me that you must never turn up empty-handed to a meeting in Japan and must always accept the gift you are given, graciously. I thought it a lovely tradition, and was pleased to have brought the little owl along.

Our host seemed surprised and delighted, calling his wife over to admire our owl. Their gift to us was a beautifully woven little crane, made of twisted wire. In gold and white, it had a tiny red crest on its head and a long golden beak. Cranes are the symbol of long life, happiness and good luck in Japan. I was touched and honoured to have met this welcoming couple.

Our return journey to Nagano was straightforward, though for some strange reason the ticket cost more than the one out to Yudanaka. Maybe the rail company knew they had a captive audience – the train was the only way out of town.

Our next destination was Kanazawa, south along the Japan Sea coast, but all trains headed inland first to Nagano. There we changed back to the Japan Rail line where we could once more use our rail passes. In Kanazawa we were meeting a Japanese man called Sho who had contacted us through Couchsurfing.

We had joined Couchsurfing a year or so earlier, when I was first organising our trip. It was a strange, but intriguing, 'pay it forward' concept. Hosts would offer accommodation, and often food, to travellers via the online site, or act as sightseeing guides to their locality. In exchange, hosts built up points to make themselves more interesting and visible to other potential hosts when travelling themselves.

Two of our first Couchsurfers had been a couple from Halifax in West Yorkshire. Janice and Peter were aiming to visit every World Heritage Site and had come to Galicia to find more to tick off. We'd hit it off immediately; they loved real ale and our self-sufficient lifestyle. Janice is one of the few people I know to post pictures of the turkey they were about to kill for Christmas dinner and who has made her own haggis using the lights (lungs) from a lamb. They also didn't flinch at eating our rabbits. As I said, we got on famously.

In Lugo, we met Kris, a lovely Vietnamese girl from America. She had asked, through Couchsurfing, if anyone would like to show her around. Kris was working at a local school as an English auxiliary for a year.

"Which school are you at?" I'd asked, as we walked the Roman walls that mild spring day.

"Oh, it's in a tiny town about an hour south of here," she'd replied. "I'm living in Lugo, though; there's more going on."

Couchsurfing

I mused. "Which town? We're south of Lugo."
"Taboada."

S and Mum heard our shouts of laughter from fifty metres back, they said.

Kris became a good friend, visiting us a number of times. Before she left, she cooked us a delicious Vietnamese meal at our house.

Siobhan, another Couchsurfing contact, arrived on a bicycle, in need of a shower and desperate to wash her only set of clothes. She had two panniers fashioned from beer crates, one of which held her acoustic guitar, had lived on a commune as a child, and went 'skipping' on a regular basis.

Up to that moment, I'd never heard of skipping – the practice of checking skips, usually behind supermarkets, for any out-of-date food which has been thrown away. Siobhan told me that one Christmas Eve she'd rescued a dozen frozen turkeys from behind a famous store. They weren't even out of date, but no one wanted turkey after Christmas Day. It was quite an eye-opener for me and I despaired of the waste we create as a species. Siobhan asked me to make up some cake recipes without flour, as they often found eggs and other goodies in the skips. It was a fun request and I enjoyed experimenting, though I've never yet dared to peep in the skip in front of our local supermarket.

Siobhan had asked if she could help us in the garden in exchange for food. I was more than happy to agree. Our Workawayer at the time was the self-titled Sunny, a wholly inaccurate name for the woman herself. Sunny was menopausally inept, and a disaster to work with.

On the second day, Sunny had told me it was too hot to work by noon so she wanted an indoor job. I pointed out that she had come to us knowing that the job we needed help with was bramble clearing, and that maybe she could start work before ten in the morning.

"I can't do that," she said, alarmed. "I don't sleep very well, you see."

When Siobhan arrived, she soon had Sunny toeing the line and working harder than she ever had with us. I could hear Siobhan in the allotment, urging Sunny to cut the brambles, and I watched her patiently showing the less organised woman how to do so efficiently. That girl was a regular miracle worker and always at least one step ahead of any request I had.

"I've emptied the compost bin," she said one day.

"Oh, thanks. It goes on the compost pile over by the *hórreo*," I replied.

"Yes, I've done that. And hosed it out."

"Right, great. S usually lines it with newspaper."

"Like this?" She held up the perfectly lined bin.

We were incredibly sorry when Siobhan moved on.

Sho time

We didn't need a couch to surf on during our trip, but I thought it would be nice to see some sights with the help of a local. Sho was the first person to reply to my online request, and offered to take us around his home town of Kanazawa. He met us at the train station and turned out to be a delightful young man who was desperate to practise his English on us.

"We can exit here the bus," he said, as we careered around a corner on the city bus (free with our rail passes).

"My notes say stop eight, not seven."

"No, here."

I had (of course) already checked online for the nearest stop to our booked *ryokan*, but it was Sho's city so I let it go. Sadly, Sho knew less than the TripAdvisor reviewers. We had a very long walk to the geisha area where our hotel was situated – right next to stop eight.

By now I had been reunited with my girlie pink roll-along case which was left behind in Moscow and then couriered across Japan to us in Shibu Onsen. I'd named her Rosie, in honour of her new status as a well-travelled, independent tourist. From now on, she would be following us around Japan.

By the time we reached the *ryokan*, I was hot and sweaty in my winter gear, and my fur-lined boots were rubbing my heel. Poor Rosie had been bounced around on the uneven pavements and looked quite sorry for herself. Only my S, and the enthusiastic Sho, were still fresh and raring to go.

I quickly forgave Sho his lack of directional sense when he pointed out the *ryokan* for us. The sign for the accommodation was in Japanese, whereas my booking confirmation was written in English. We would never have found it.

In the entrance hall we met our new host, a tall, elderly gentleman who spoke good English. Again, we did the slipper shuffle in the entrance hall before heading to our room. The staircase was steep and my stockinged feet kept slipping out of the too-big slippers. It was a disaster waiting to happen, though our host had no such problems.

A large room with tatami matting on the floor and two made-up futons awaited us. It had a hanging rail for clothes, a kettle, green tea, and a second door opening, bizarrely, half way up the staircase.

"Handy for a quick getaway," whispered S.

The wash room was along the corridor, and there was a toilet block next door. In the doorway of the toilets, I was unsurprised to find a pair of pink 'toilet' slippers. The *onsen*, downstairs, was neither as fancy nor as large as the one at Daymaru-ya but it looked clean, and the water in the tub steamed invitingly.

There was no time to bathe, though. Our own personal guide to the city was waiting for us. We dropped off our bags and rushed back downstairs, me managing to stay on my feet only by surreptitiously discarding the deadly slippers and running down in my socks.

It was Sho time.

Kanazawa is a well-preserved city on the Japan sea, founded in the 14th century as part of the so-called peasants' kingdom. It was one of the few major Japanese cities not destroyed during the Second World War and so has much of its architectural heritage intact. Kanazawa is famous for Kenrokuen Garden, an extensive, landscaped garden of the Edo period (1603-1868), designated a Cultural Property and a National Site of Scenic Beauty, and one of the three 'great' gardens of Japan. Kenrokuen was the main reason I'd chosen Kanazawa as a stop on our Japanese tour.

Sho time

The garden was one of the places Sho promised to take us. But first, we began with coffee and cakes at the Kanazawa 21st Century Museum of Contemporary Art.

The café was certainly modern and contemporary, with floor to ceiling glass windows enclosing the circular building. White leather chairs sat at white counters, hung overhead by white lampshades above a white marble floor. It was all rather snow-blindness inducing. The juice and the cakes were, however, delicious and the prices less eye-watering than I expected.

In the museum there were many Japanese art works but an intriguing sculpture caught my eye.

Across the garden was a swimming pool, and beneath the water were a dozen or more people. One lady held on to the pool steps, ready to climb out. She wore an immaculate skirt suit, high heels, and carried a handbag. Other 'bathers' had cameras slung round their necks. They all looked remarkably dry. They also seemed to have no problem breathing underwater.

The mystery was solved as we made our way down a staircase at the side of the pool.

From below it was clear that the 'pool' was actually a perspex box, approximately a foot deep, filled with water. From the underground room below, we could look up through the swimming-pool-blue water at the gawping tourists above our heads. The bunker room was cleverly designed, with its pool steps, blue paint, and tiny pool tiles, so that it looked authentic from above.

"I want one in the garden," I said to S.

"No."

Our first sight in Kenrokuen Garden was a picturesque Japanese bridge over a lake. In the background was a wooden teahouse, built out over the water. Next to the bridge was a stone Japanese-style lantern. Above, bare-branched acer trees would be full of colour in the spring and autumn. It was all very willow-pattern-plate-like.

The eleven-hectare site was first opened to the public in 1874 following the Meiji restoration, when the feudal shogunate powers declined and practical imperial rule was restored under a single emperor, Meiji Tenno.

Kenrokuen was originally the outer garden of Kanazawa Castle but has been moved, considerably altered and adapted over the four hundred years since its inception. Known for its six attributes of a perfect garden: spaciousness, seclusion, artifice, antiquity, watercourses and panoramas, Kenrokuen was busy with local people and tourists alike.

Around the park I was surprised to see many broad-girthed, ancient-looking trees propped up with bamboo canes. Others had what looked like a maypole surrounding them – many ropes tautly stretched to the ground from a tall central pole.

"The Karasakinomatsu pine trees are many years old," explained Sho. "In winter there is many snow. The *yukizuri*, it protect trees from snow."

"Ah, I see. The tepee thing is a *yukizuri*? It allows the snow to slide off instead of weighing down the branches," I said. "But, Sho. It *is* winter, and there is no snow."

It was true. Once we'd left behind the hills around Nagano, the monochromatic landscape had reverted to sepia – winter browns with not a speck of snow in sight. Kenrokuen, although bare for winter, showed signs of early plum blossom emerging and many birds pecked around our feet as we wandered in the sunshine.

"Yes," replied Sho to my question. "This year ve'y little snow. As child I jump from my bedroom window up here…" he lifted his arms to indicate first floor height, "… on to snow. Always ve'y deep. Many month. Now," Sho shrugged and raised his arms, "no snow."

"Wow. Global warming for real," I replied.

"This tree," continued Sho, "it is called raised root pine. Neagarinomatsu."

Sho time

"Nigar... Oh never mind, I can see how it got its name. Those roots are five foot above ground. But why the props?" I pointed.

"Ah, yes. The tree is many years old. It is, how do you say? Empty inside?"

"Hollow?"

"Yes." Sho smiled. "Without help they break and die. Then, no garden."

Sho was a lively and enthusiastic tour guide. I could have spent a whole day wandering around Kenrokuen Garden, but he had more to show us.

"This is the samurai area. These houses ve'y old," he told us, pointing to what looked like a row of garden sheds raised on concrete pillars. The walls were thin, straw covered panels with bamboo slatted windows below a shallow tin roof. At intervals along the narrow, cobbled street, there were double wooden gateways, often with writing above. They didn't look very Shogun-like to me.

"The house is inside the gate," said S.

He pointed to an open gateway he was busy photographing. Inside was a small, formal garden with a wooden bench and bonsai trees in front of a two-storey, wood-clad house.

"Oops!"

I later read that the size of a samurai house, and the width of its entrance, was determined by income. Wealthier samurais had entrance gates wide and high enough for horses to enter. I also discovered that most of the houses we'd seen were not genuine samurai houses but post-war housing. I enjoyed walking the area, which was certainly atmospheric, whether it was genuine or not.

Our last stop with Sho was a visit to the enclosed Omicho market.

"Wow, look at the colours!" I exclaimed, as we entered the vast, open, concrete floored area.

"The fish pongs a bit," added S.

He was right, we were in an area where fruit and vegetables vied with the aroma of fresh fish and seafood.

"Kanazawa has ve'y excellent seafood," explained Sho, ushering us through puddles and entrails.

"The veg look fresh," said S.

"And well laid out too."

It was a busy market, reminiscent of ones at home in Galicia. Market traders yelled at each other and housewives carrying laden baskets bartered for their daily shopping.

"It's been a fascinating day, Sho. Thank you so much for showing us around." My feet were aching after so much walking and an *onsen* soak beckoned.

"My pleasure."

Sho was a nice lad with a poor sense of direction and slightly unconventional English, which he worked hard to improve. We bid him a fond farewell as he jumped on board the bus at the end of the street, and hoped he would manage to get off at the correct stop.

After Sho left us, we investigated our new accommodation's bathhouse. I was getting used to these amazing communal hot tubs and already planning how we could incorporate one at home. If only S could read my thoughts.

There was a private *onsen* on the ground floor which we decided was perfect for two. It looked like a giant bath and the water was gloriously hot. S enjoyed showing off his new *yukata* robe and slippers.

"Very trendy, dear," I said, trying not to laugh at his posturing. "Not sure the red, scaly skin look is in this year, though."

"It's much better since I've been using the *onsen*. I think it's clearing up at last," he replied.

"Shorts for Singapore then," I said. "Do we pull the plug when we get out?"

"I don't think so. The tub was full when we arrived."

Sho time

"Mmm. I don't think I want to dwell on how many people have bathed in here before us," I said with a shudder.

S laughed. "It's fine. So long as they all showered first."

"And don't have madly shedding skin," I added, peering into the clear depths of the tub."

"Haha."

"Now, food. I can't believe we haven't eaten all day. I must've hinted to Sho numerous times but to no avail."

"Maybe he thought he'd have to pay."

"Mmm. I didn't think of that. I should've said 'our treat'. Never mind. Let's go."

We wandered the geisha district looking for food, and soon came to the main road again. Across the street was a craft brewery.

"That looks like a good stop," said S.

I couldn't have agreed more. Inside was a small, bright bar area and behind was an open brewery full of stainless-steel vats and shining pipework.

We chose two roasted tea stouts to drink with our fried chicken and chips in a basket.

"Delicious," I said, licking salt off my fingers.

"And so Japanese," added S.

"Craft beers are taking off in Japan in a big way, you know. I read it's one of the biggest growth areas. The young prefer it to *sake* and whiskey."

"They have good taste then," said S.

After dinner, we thought we would wander back to Kenrokuen Garden to watch the light show – which ended at the exact moment we reached the gates.

Oh well, it *had* been a busy day.

Not a log cabin

Breakfast the next morning was taken downstairs in the dining room. Against one wall was the obligatory electric rice cooker, whilst against another was a table on which sat a microwave and a toaster. Hanging on the wall above was a bizarre collection of ghoulish masks. The grimacing heads peered down on us as we enjoyed our rice, salmon, pickles, fresh fruit, miso, and green tea.

I decided I could quite easily get used to Japanese breakfasts; the pickles wake up the taste buds and the tea awakens the brain. Perfect.

Our morning walk took in the geisha area of Higashi in which we had been staying. There were a number of ladies wearing kimonos and wooden *geta* sandals, wandering the streets in pairs. Their protruding bustles, at the back of the traditional dresses, looked most uncomfortable.

The traditional geisha or 'tea houses' are two storeys, made of wood and with windows or *shoji* doors at first floor level. Some of the buildings now housed shops or cafes offering tea ceremonies – all at tourist prices.

I imagined the area as it used to be, with pleasure houses, and prostitutes roaming the streets on the arms of wealthy merchants – before the profession was deemed illegal.

"Shall we get some food to take with us from the market?" I asked, after we'd collected our rucksacks and the patient Rosie from the *ryokan*.

"I thought food was included with Workaway," replied S.

"Not in Japan. I didn't see one place that offered food, only accommodation. Mark says they supply Workawayers with the basics, so I'm guessing maybe

Not a log cabin

rice and oil, that sort of thing. But we'll need to stock up. I thought we could get some veg from the market then pop in a supermarket for anything else we need on the way."

"Is there an 'on the way'?" asked S.

"Yes, of course. The train from Kanazawa goes to Kyoto, then we have to change for a local train to Hira. Our train leaves here at 11:24 but the onward one isn't 'til three so we have plenty of time, and it's another lovely day."

"And I presume you've booked the trains already?"

I looked at him. Of course I had.

When we'd joined Workaway, as volunteers rather than hosts, over a year earlier, my first task had been to start sifting through all the thousands of possibilities to find our host families. If I thought it would be difficult to find someone willing to accept a nearly 70-year-old and a 54-year-old, I was happily mistaken. We had offers flying in from all directions and could have easily worked our way around the world for a year or more.

One of the first offers I had was from a 90-year-old American who had been posted to Japan with the peacekeeping force after the Second World War, and had stayed to father an American-Japanese family. He lived near Tokyo and had sounded quite a character. I was disappointed we couldn't fit in a visit, even more so when his profile vanished sometime later. I assume he'd died.

Instead, I focused on the area S had previously visited on his illegal Japanese stopover in 1968 – Osaka and Lake Biwa.

In the end it was easy to find a host. Mark was an Englishman who lived on the shores of Lake Biwa with his Japanese wife and three children. He was looking for people to help in construction and, in winter, snow shovelling, and was rather surprised to receive an email from me a full year before we planned to arrive. He didn't know my organisational aptitude, though.

Mark and I chatted a number of times by email, and quickly came to an arrangement; in exchange for four hours work a day, five days a week, Mark offered us our own self-catering cabin and the chance to explore a totally different area of Japan. The house, as well as being on the shores of one of the most beautiful lakes in Japan, was walking distance to a train station – opening up the possibility of visiting Kyoto and other local areas for free using our Japan Rail passes.

I had visions of us snuggled in a cosy log cabin, waking up to the sun rising over the lake, birds calling, and the lapping of water on the shore. All in all, it sounded perfect.

In Omichi market, I was enjoying looking at the different vegetables and fish on display.

"I think fish might get stinky. I don't even know what cooking facilities there are. Think I'll stick with veggies for now. These leeks look fresh and the green beans are a good price too. Anything else?"

"Fruit?" asked S.

"Good idea, you have a look at that stall, I'm going to buy these and some mushrooms. I can do us a stir fry for tea."

The bullet train glided into Kyoto station on time and silently, as always. I was ruined for catching an English train ever again, with their erratic times and ridiculous excuses. I somehow doubted Japan ever had trains delayed due to leaves on the line.

"Someone would have to clear them up."

"Sorry?" asked S, not party to my inner deliberations.

"Leaves," I replied, cryptically. "Look, we're here. Those *kanji* say Kyoto."

"Mmm. It says Kyoto in English below them too."

Not a log cabin

I didn't fancy dragging Rosie all over town and was pleased to spot a Family Mart, the popular Japanese mini-supermarket with the very Western name, just across the street.

We soon discovered shopping can be tricky in a foreign land.

"What do you think this is?"

"Pass. It's a tin, but could be anything."

"A photo on the can would be useful," I said, turning the offending item round and round.

"I remember trying to buy tins when I was walking round the lake. It was pot luck. I bought corned beef once but it was chicken."

"Mmm. Could've been worse. It might have been dog food. What about noodles? I can see what they are."

"Fine by me."

"Okay, so we have veggies and noodles. That'll do for tonight's stirfry. We can have one of those chewy bars I made for breakfast, then we can do another shop tomorrow afternoon, once we know what's already provided."

Mark had asked that we arrive before four in the afternoon due to the children's timetable. It was two minutes to and already getting dusk when we arrived at the house. The walk from the station had been straightforward, but hard work dragging poor Rosie over the gravelly footpath.

"Great instructions," I said, as we rounded the corner by the Chinese lanterns Mark had used as a landmark, "but Rosie'll need new wheels by the time we get home, poor thing."

"But think of the experiences she's had," joked S.

"Huh."

Mark welcomed us at the gate and introduced us to our accommodation for the week.

It was my fault entirely.

In my mind, a cabin is invariably a log cabin; warm and inviting, with synthetic furs on sagging sofas, and a roaring open fire. This was not a log cabin; it was a prefabricated shed with glass sliding doors and a draught which whistled through the roof space.

Inside the single-roomed twelve by ten-foot space, was a futon which doubled as both sofa and bed, a small dining table and chairs, a sink, kettle, hob, and the ubiquitous electric rice cooker (which I never did figure out how to operate). There was also a small electric fire.

"Don't leave the fire on overnight, or if you're out. It uses too much electric and the switch will trip," Mark warned us.

Our compliance with that rule lasted one night. It was freezing in our shed. I woke up damp and cold and vowed to leave the thing running as long as possible, all day and all night too. I did explain to Mark what we were doing and he seemed resigned rather than annoyed. It was bloody cold after all.

Our bathroom was housed in a separate shed, which was icier than the living quarters and reminded me of the privations of our early life in Galicia. Risking the cold for a wee was punishment enough, no way was I stripping off in there for a shower. Instead, I managed with a strip wash in our marginally warmer kitchen area – until Mark took pity on us and offered us the use of their bathroom one night.

I think Mark rather liked us, to be honest. He said that the family kept themselves to themselves, not socialising with helpers other than during working hours, but the second day their little girl came over with two bowls of delicious miso soup at lunchtime; we shared tea and cake at morning break each day, were offered the use of their computer, and even invited to dinner one night.

In return, we worked hard that week.

Mark had a Japanese work ethic; organised and regimented. One reason we got on well, I think. I like to

Not a log cabin

know what is expected of me so I can endeavour to meet those expectations. And I'm not keen on surprises.

"We start work at eight in the morning. Please don't be late," he'd said on that first day. "I've left a folder in your room. Please read it and ask me any questions tomorrow. There's a calendar of the days I need you to work. One's an afternoon, the rest mornings. Let me know if there are any problems with that."

Inside the thick folder was a calendar with working days crossed off, and our jobs for each day. There was also a comprehensive list of rules of the house, together with a whole pile of local information.

"A man after my own heart," I said, carefully reading through the folder. "Look, he's even written his address in Japanese in case we need it. That's clever."

I was so impressed with Mark's folder that I produced one of my own when we got home. Our Workawayers have told us how useful the local information section is, and we have had no issues with helpers' working days or hours since.

It was Sunny, our menopausal disaster of a Workawayer, who first complained about her days off. She had arrived on a Sunday afternoon and gone with us to a barbecue that evening. She then worked two mornings before needing a rest day as she felt ill. We all went out for another planned day off on the Thursday but on the Saturday, Sunny demanded the weekend off too.

"Look Sunny, you leave on Monday, you arrived last Sunday, and have so far worked three rather short days. That's three working days out of nine, not a good ratio for us."

"But I was ill on Wednesday."

"That's true, but I still made you three meals that day. And you've had two meals out with us too, on non-working days."

"But I should have the weekends off."

79

"Why? We don't," I said, frustrated. "Our agreement was four hours a day, five days a week. *You* start work at ten, have a half hour tea break with us at twelve, and then want to finish at one thirty. That's only three hours a day, even when you are working."

"But it's so hot."

"Yes, it's summer, Sunny. But I do think I need to make it clearer what we expect from our workers."

I was pleased when Sunny left, to be honest.

We have a problem, Houston

Our accommodation might not have been the cosy log cabin I'd imagined, but the sun did rise over the water in front of us, the birds did call, and I could, if I listened carefully, hear the lapping of waves on the shore.

The first morning we were up early.

"Muesli bar?" I asked S, when he returned from the bathroom shed.

"Thanks. These are keeping well."

"The cold's useful for that. I'm glad I made so many now. They're pretty substantial too."

I never journey anywhere without a small stock of food. Aeroplanes don't frighten me, but running out of food on one does. The food on our Iberia flight to Costa Rica had been so bad that we'd lived on my homemade muesli bars and cheese pies. This time I'd made a dozen of the chewy, nutty and fruity bars. They were handy for breakfast, and a good snack if we couldn't get anything to eat.

"We have to eat them all before we get to Australia, anyway. They'll never let us in with these."

At 8am we reported for work.

It was a busy morning; me humping scaffold poles round to the rental house Mark owned whilst S and Mark did the 'technical stuff' – fixing the poles together and erecting the scaffolding for our next task. There was a quick tea and scone break back at the house at ten and we knocked off at exactly noon, as the siren sounded in the town for the workers' lunch break.

After a welcome mug of English tea and some house work – for that read washing out of undies – we set off to explore. Our first stop was the local Weimado supermarket, one station along the line.

Mark had given us a food box when we arrived. There were eggs from their own hens; potatoes, dug from the garden; jam, peanut butter, oil, butter, and some jars of spaghetti sauce. I'd spent the previous evening writing out a menu for the week so I knew what we needed to buy.

"I can do spag bol tomorrow if we get a few carrots and some mince. We've got some leeks and mushrooms left from the market. We can have a Spanish *tortilla* one evening too, with those lovely eggs and potatoes."

I was writing as I was speaking, but I knew S had drifted. Menu planning wasn't his thing. Instead, I let him read in peace whilst I completed my list.

List in hand, we entered the Weimado.

Whilst the Family Mart in Kyoto had been a mini-market, Weimado was a substantial mega-supermarket.

"I think you can tell a lot about a country from its supermarket produce."

"You reckon?" laughed S.

"Yeah. Look at this aisle; it's all sushi, and there's so much fresh fish."

There was a huge section given over to fresh fish and seafood, though it was all more expensive than I was used to at home. There was also an aisle full of giant sacks of rice at incredibly expensive prices.

"I thought the Japanese lived on rice. Why is it so expensive?" I asked S.

"No idea, but we can't eat a whole sack anyway."

"True. Not in a week. What about this one? It's cheaper."

"Is it rice? The grains are a bit big"

"I think so. It's probably like risotto rice."

No, it wasn't.

It was only when I attempted to cook the 'rice' for dinner one day that I realised it was some kind of sticky grain, more akin to barley or tapioca. I decided it was better suited to eating as porridge and we finished it

We have a problem, Houston

over the next few days as a very stodgy but warming breakfast. I never did discover what it was.

That second evening, after dinner, I noticed my phone had a low battery.

"I'd better charge it. I'll need the alarm to make sure we're not late for work."

"Give us time to have breakfast too."

"Don't worry, I will." I laughed. "We're having eggs on toast tomorrow."

I plugged the phone in but was met with a blank screen.

"That's odd, the phone isn't charging up."

"Leave it overnight, it'll probably be okay," said the technician, S.

I tried a few more times during the evening – between scrabble games, and green tea to warm us up, but the screen remained blank.

"We have a problem, Houston."

"Don't worry; we can sort it tomorrow."

"Yes, but we don't have a clock. We won't know when to get up."

Neither of us wears a watch. My smartphone was our only timepiece. It was also my camera, access to the internet, and phone.

A disaster indeed.

Shaka shaka chicken

The following morning, we were out of bed in a rush. We ate our eggs on toast, watching a great orange ball rise over the lake through a gap beneath the house in front. Without that house, the view would be magnificent. I wondered if Mark would consider allowing us to demolish it.

Breakfast over, we stood in front of the glass sliding doors watching for Mark.

"Morning," I yelled, as he appeared around the side of the house.

"You're late," Mark yelled back, carrying buckets and brooms under his arm.

I removed my indoor slippers and pulled on my boots, kept strategically just inside the doorway, rather than outside as convention dictates; no way was I starting the day with frozen feet. Then I ran across the yard.

"What time is it?" I asked. "My phone died last night and it won't recharge. We've been watching for you for ages. Sorry."

"It's eight o five."

Five minutes late. Not bad considering.

Mark forgave us our un-Japanese tardiness, and even promised to look at my phone and see if he could reboot it later. The morning was to be spent cleaning their guest house ready for the next occupants.

"You can do the bathroom," I said to S, as we were given our instructions. "I'm happy cleaning, but I'm not cleaning someone else's loo."

S laughed. He knew my foibles. "I don't mind; it was one of my jobs as cabin boy on my first ship. These can't be that bad."

The morning passed quickly. We worked well as a team, cleaning the house thoroughly from top to bottom. I was fascinated by how many toast crumbs

Shaka shaka chicken

could make their way beneath and all around the toaster, and Mark was mumbling about guests using four toilet rolls over a single weekend. That one I could empathise with; it also intrigued me how many toilet rolls our Workawayers got through – despite having a bidet in the bathroom.

After work, Mark and Kana pored over my phone trying to reboot it. Despite their joint efforts it remained as dead as a dodo. Mark checked the local equivalent of Yellow Pages and found a couple of likely-looking phone shops in Kyoto.

"We'll go and have a see what we can find. It'll be nice to have a better look at Kyoto anyway. And we may as well use our rail passes, now we have them."

"Kyoto is lovely," said Kana. "An historic capital. It's well worth a visit."

Kyoto, meaning Imperial Capital, is Japan's third largest city, after Tokyo (East Imperial Capital) and Osaka, and is one of the oldest. Kyoto, then known as Heian Kyo (Tranquillity and Peace Capital) was founded in 794 and remained Japan's imperial capital for eleven centuries until the restoration in 1869.

As Kyoto was spared both the nuclear bomb meant for it, and much of the general bombing during the Second World War, it still has many historic buildings, temples, and castles. I was looking forward to learning more.

Sadly, that second trip to Kyoto was to be no more a cultural one than was our previous shopping trip. We found the first mobile phone shop that Mark had written down but, as my phone was not registered in Japan, they refused to even look at it.

"But I only want someone to tell me if it can be repaired."

"Sorry. No contract."

The 'man on a corner' type repair shop did not seem to exist in Kyoto. There was no enterprising youngster set up in their bedroom either. Every phone was on a contract, and if repairs were needed it was sent off to a central repair depot. Even if the shop agreed to send it away, it would apparently take two weeks. It all was so different from Galicia, where Paco, our local phone and computer guru, would have taken it in to his back room and poked and prodded until he either fixed it or declared it defunct.

"Well, that's the third shop that's a washout," I said, as we traipsed the streets of Kyoto.

"The tourist office was helpful."

"True, she was lovely. But we still haven't found anywhere to fix the thing. I vote we give up and go exploring before it gets dark."

"How about a tea first? There's a McDonald's."

We generally avoid McDonald's burgers as cheap rubbish with no nutritional value. In Galicia, a local café will inevitably do a much better (and bigger) burger for a similar price. I do, though, have a penchant for their tea; it's a big 'mug' made with boiling water and much cheaper than the likes of Starbucks. Some of the desserts are pretty good too.

"These chocolate pies look interesting," I said, peering at the overhead board. "I've not seen those before. Shall we?"

I also love seeing how each country adjusts its fast-food menus for local tastes. I remember years earlier visiting a Pizza Hut in Makassar, Indonesia, and being shocked at how tiny their individual pizza was. Some of the toppings were a revelation, too. In Japan, McDonald's had teriyaki burgers and something called shaka shaka chicken. Different strokes, as they say.

I couldn't help but think that if our local Galician Big McD in Lugo had *pulpo* burgers for sale, they may do a better trade with the octopus-chomping Galegos. The only customers I ever saw there were British, or teenagers. Even the staff go to the café across the way for their morning coffee.

Shaka shaka chicken

Anyway, I digress. The Kyoto McDonald's chocolate pies were pretty good, and helped me get over being potentially phone (and therefore camera and internet) less until something could be done.

"You'll have to be chief photographer," I said to S, as we walked up the busy street, past temple after temple. "Can we go in?" I added, pointing at a huge, black-roofed pagoda.

"Looks like it," replied S.

There were people milling about in a cobbled courtyard beneath a tall, red painted archway and walking up the steps towards a wooden-sided temple. The gates stood invitingly open, but as we entered the courtyard we were politely turned away.

"Close now," said an official looking guard. "Open morning."

S snapped a couple of quick pictures in the courtyard before the gates closed behind us. "They close early."

"I don't know. I don't have a watch."

"McDonald's had a clock," replied S. "It's just after five."

"Now there's clever. Let's walk up to Nijo Castle, then. It's on my list of things to see," I said, scanning the map we'd picked up in the helpful tourist information centre. "It's not far."

It wasn't far at all. The frontage of the castle grounds took up one whole street. There was a moat and an imposing grey stone wall.

As we approached the gates, my heart sank.

"It says it closes at 5pm," said S, helpfully, as I pointed to the locked gates.

"We're not doing well with temples and castles, are we?"

"Never mind, let's get a warm drink on the way back to the station."

I'd seen just the place – a cosy looking café advertising hot juices. The apple and ginger juice was delicious. It hit the spot perfectly, warming me inside and out – even if the price was twice that of a McDonald's tea and chocolate pie.

On our way back to the station, S spotted an internet café. I paid for ten minutes – just long enough to go on Facebook to warn my family and friends that I'd be incommunicado for a while, and to dash off an email to my Singaporean friend.

"If anywhere'll have a phone repair shop, it has to be Singapore. Ann-Nee will know," I said, confidently. "We'll be there in less than a week."

We had met Ann-Nee, her Spanish husband, and gorgeously attractive five-year-old son on one of our cross-province meetings in Galicia and had become firm friends. She would be bound to know the answer to my dilemma.

When we got back, our shed was toasty warm – due to me having left the heater on all day.

"I wonder why no one else has ever said anything?" I said that night over the scrabble board, replete with stir fried veggies and noodles.

"Mark was saying the other day how unusual the weather is this year. Normally they have snow drifts several feet thick in winter. He showed me a photo of a big van with snow up to the windscreen."

"That's a point. He told me our jobs would be mainly snow clearing at this time of year when I first emailed him. But surely that means it's normally much colder than this."

"Yes. But snow is insulating, remember. If there was a thick layer of snow on the roof and around the walls, it would actually be warmer in here."

"Mmm." I wasn't convinced.

I might have to acknowledge that I was turning into a wimp, or worse, in my Midlands' lingo, someone who was 'nesh'.

Winter wonderland

Sunday was one of our designated days off and we were going on a trip with another new Couchsurfing friend.

When we'd joined Couchsurfing, it had been my hope to meet locals who could introduce us to the areas we were visiting and show us a different aspect to the usual tourist trails. Michiru had been one of two people who had responded to my message about visiting Japan. He had offered to take us around Kyoto prefecture on one of his rare days off.

We were up early on Sunday morning, according to the new clock which Kana had presented to us the evening before. We breakfasted on some of the odd barley stuff we'd bought; boiled with milk, it was warming – and sweet with jam spooned over.

Michi, as he liked to be called, arrived at exactly ten o'clock.

I was just pondering how polar opposite the Japanese and Spanish are over timekeeping, when he pulled up outside. Whilst Spaniards think nothing of arriving an hour later than the given time, and, in fact, to arrive on time is considered rude in Galicia, the Japanese were punctuality personified. I'd still not decided which version I preferred. There were pros and cons to each, depending on if you were the host or the guest.

We liked Michi straight away. He was a fireman and spoke excellent English.

"I like to show people around. When I was young, I decided to cycle across Australia…"

"Cycle?" I interrupted. "Not motorcycle?"

"No, I had a cycle. It didn't look so big on the map." He laughed and raised his hands. "I didn't know it was 5,000 kilometres across. When I found out, I decided to cycle the Gold Coast instead."

"That's still a long way," said S.

"Yes, but I enjoyed it very much. The people were so kind. They gave me food and a bed for the night. I said that when I was able, I would do the same for other people."

"Pay it forward," I mused.

"Yes! That!"

"So now you do Couchsurfing?"

"Yes. I used to welcome people to our home to stay, but my wife," Michi paused, shrugged, "she was not happy. It's not a big house." Michi looked saddened momentarily, but he brightened as he said; "Instead, when I have a day off, I show visitors around the area. I enjoy it."

"And your wife?" I couldn't help but ask, "is she happy with you doing this on your days off?"

Michi shrugged again. "I like to help people."

Michi had planned a perfect day for us.

First, we drove along the edge of Lake Biwa, admiring the scenery as we passed.

"Do you recognise anything yet?" I asked S, more than once.

"Nope. Not a thing. It's all so built up."

I looked around at the peaceful lake with a few scattered houses lining its shores, and at the dense pine forests opposite. "Hardly."

Our first stop was at a Shinto shrine set in expansive forests. The pine needles were thick underfoot and the air smelt fresh and clean. Out in the lake, close to the shore, an iconic Japanese *torii* rose incongruously from the water. The gateway looked magnificent in vermillion red, as if it was floating above the water.

"It is very famous *torii*," said Michi. "Many people come to photograph it."

"But why is it in the lake?"

Michi lifted his hands in the air. "I do not know."

We walked up a slope into the forest. There was a second *torii*, and a large shrine in front of us. Dotted

Winter wonderland

about the forest were dozens more, tiny but perfectly formed, shrines.

"These small shrines often belong to rich people. They pay someone to clean and to pray here," Michi explained.

I turned to S, not wanting to offend our host. "That sounds like cheating, somehow."

"It's only the same as a Catholic priest praying for someone."

"And being paid for it too. Good point."

From Shirahige-Jinja Shrine, we left a cool but dry Lake Biwa to venture into the higher mountains beyond.

"There's a ski station here somewhere, isn't there?" I asked Michi.

"That's right. Biwako Valley. Do you ski?"

"Erm, no. Definitely not. I don't stand upright well on two feet never mind two bits of wood. Was that there when you visited?" I asked, turning to S again.

"I don't think so. I told you there was nothing here."

As we climbed, the snow lay thickly and the road conditions deteriorated. Our host seemed to have no problems negotiating the icy roads and occasional drifts.

"It's a bit of a contrast to the lakeside."

"Yes, we are quite high now. There is much more snow here."

That was an understatement. We hadn't seen this much of the powdery white stuff since Shibu Onsen and the Snow Monkey Park.

We drove through a small, silent village, entirely blanketed in white. The drifts at the edge of the road were three feet thick in places and houses sported fluffy white hats. I was about to ask where we were heading when Michi drew up, seemingly in the middle of nowhere, and stopped the car. I stepped out, straight into a snow drift.

"Oops! Where are we, Michi?"

Our guide pointed through an avenue of low bushes crowned with clumps of snow, to a tall, white triangle. It was the roof of a squat building.

"It is a museum. A traditional Japanese house. You will like it."

"Oh brilliant! Thank you Michi. And what a beautiful spot."

It was. We had passed along a river and through a winter wonderland to arrive at this quiet, serene building at the edge of woodland. The building itself was traditionally built with *shoji* walls and a steep thatched roof, completely obscured by snow. Inside a covered entrance, we were introduced to a tiny, wizened Japanese lady wearing two thick jumpers, a long, padded coat, and thick, woollen trousers. She bowed low and invited us to remove our shoes. A line of the ubiquitous Japanese slippers lay in front of an inner doorway.

Inside, the floors were all dark polished wood buffed to a deep shine – probably from generations of slippered feet shuffling along them. The temperature inside the building was similar to that outdoors, except I no longer wore my fur-lined boots which had kept my toes warm.

There were rooms with low futons on the floor, and ones with equally low coffee tables fashioned from a single piece of thick oak. Alongside were traditional water-colour painted screens, acting as room dividers. My breath huffed out as I spoke to Michi about the building.

I wondered why the Japanese spent so much time low to the floor when it's so cold. The *shoji* sliding doors seemed incredibly thin, and the draught was ice-cold coming both through and around them.

"Ah," said Michi, "but in summer, it is hot. Then the breeze is good."

In a kitchen area there was an eclectic collection of bamboo baskets – from ones I recognised as being used

Winter wonderland

to steam fish and vegetables, to large ones which looked like lobster pots. There was a row of deadly-looking Japanese knives hanging from one wall, a rack for drying fish, or maybe clothes, and many items I couldn't even guess at.

Through another door, I was delighted to feel a surge of heat caressing my icy extremities. My feet had long since gone numb. In the middle of the wooden floor, a section had been cut away and in it was a blazing firepit. The flames leapt a good foot above the floor and were lapping the bottom of an ancient looking cast iron cooking pot resting above the fire on a thick iron tripod. I could feel the warmth seeping up through the soles of my inadequate borrowed slippers and toasting my toesies. Above the fire was a hook, used to hang fish for smoking.

"This must have been a popular area of the house in winter," I murmured to S.

I thought of the dressing room in Mum's cottage, *A Casita*, back in Galicia. When we bought the house in 2014, as a virtual ruin, that room had been used for smoking chorizos. We'd discovered a stone-lined firepit in the centre of the soot-blackened space. The benches around its edges, and the many empty wine bottles lying around, painted a picture of cold evenings spent in front of the warmth of a living flame. There, like here, it could be cold in winter and a roaring fire has a certain attraction on a chilly night.

I was reluctant to move on, but there was more to see and Michi faithfully translated everything the guardian of the museum told us.

Outside there were extensive gardens which, from the photographs in the official brochure, must have looked magnificent in spring when the acer trees leafed up in bronze and gold and woodland bulbs poked through. In winter it was a different magnificence, everything coated in heavy mantles of pristine snow.

Bento Boxes, Boomerangs & Red Foxes

Snow was falling again as I posed for a photo with Michi in front of the museum, laughing as I tried, and failed, to avoid yet another snowdrift.

Oishii

It was lunchtime.

Michi suggested a workingmen's *ramen* café on the edge of the river. Inside it was steamy, the smells comforting. The slightly intimidating owner-chef gave us plastic-coated menus with the usual indistinct pictures on, whilst Michi explained the ingredients and the differing types of noodles.

"Soba noodles are made from a brown wheat," explained Michi. "They are strong flavoured. Udon noodles are thicker. They are very good in winter when it is cold."

"Buckwheat," I said, a foodie memory coming into my head. "That's why soba noodles are brown, I think."

"Udon sound good to me," said S, pointing to a photograph of a bowl filled with noodles, cabbage, meat and eggs.

"Me too," I agreed.

The huge bowls of thick noodles in a rich soup were comfort food at its best. I slurped in time with the other diners, to Michi's delight.

Our filling *ramen* meal, accompanied by the usual green tea, was a surprising 800 yen, or around six dollars, each.

"That was delicious, Michi," I said, as he accompanied me to the till. I needed the presence of another person to face the stern owner. "How do I say 'delicious'?"

"*Oishii.*"

I turned to the owner. "*San,*" I said, holding up three fingers. Then; "*Oishii. Arigato.*" I nodded my head, and the stern face broke into a huge smile.

"*Arigato, arigato,*" she replied.

"You are learning quickly," laughed Michi.

"I wish."

"Have you seen Kyoto?" he asked as we walked back over a small bridge to the car.

I explained our food shopping trip, our abortive trip to find a phone shop, and our failure to visit any temples or castles.

"Then we will go today," he announced.

"But don't you have to get home?" I asked, concerned that this generous man had spent a whole day ferrying us around, for which he would take no petrol money.

Michi smiled. "I enjoy this."

We drove into Kyoto under a huge *torii*.

"Wow! I've never driven under a shrine entrance before, Michi."

"No. This is biggest *torii* in Japan. It is over 24 metres tall and only one with a road through it."

The *torii* spanned the four-lane roadway with ease. I felt quite humble as we passed below the vast, vermillion archway. I guess that's the idea.

"It is the best way to the city for the visitor," said Michi, smiling at us.

"Yes, it really is. Awesome," I added.

"We will walk to the temple of Kiyomizu-dera. It is very good walk, with many shops."

I was going to say I didn't do shopping, when Michi added, "And many sweets to try."

Ah. That sounded more like it.

The six-storey, black-roofed temple dominated the surrounding area, perched at the top of a steep pedestrian street. The lower streets were full of tourists, geisha girls, and touristy shops. Michi saw me looking at the geishas.

"They are not real geisha," he said. "You can rent the costume to wear. Look!"

He pointed at a crowded doorway. Inside, I could make out rows of silken dresses, bustles and wooden clogs.

"Ah, I thought they didn't look as elegant and comported as geishas should. Are they all tourists then? They look Japanese," I said, gesturing around.

"Mainly here they are tourists, yes. They are Chinese tourists."

"Oh, sorry."

Michi laughed. "You know how you can tell they are Chinese?"

"No, go on."

"They are ones buying ice-creams with gold on. Very expensive. Too expensive for Japanese."

I looked about, noticing long queues at the many ice-cream shops. Matcha tea seemed a popular flavour and yes, many of the cones were topped with edible gold leaf. At 800 yen (six dollars) they were the same price as our ramen lunch.

At the base of the steps up to Kiyomizu-dera Temple, slate-grey statues stood guard over many smaller, red-roofed temples and shrines. The three-metre-tall statues were intricately carved with snakes, dragons, fish, and what looked like an octopus around them. They were magnificent, and I coveted one for outside our gate at home – though I'm unsure what the neighbours would have said.

We climbed the long steps up to the temple and watched a steady trail of people queuing to enter. The views from the top were magnificent. We could look down on the city skyscrapers, and the iconic spire of Kyoto tower.

"At night it is lighted with different colours," said Michi, pointing at the tower. "Now, I am hungry." He rubbed his belly. "This way, please."

We reached street level again, and Michi said, "This is Kiyomizu-dera Street. There are many traditional sweet shops here."

"They are so colourful."

"These are *wagashi*. Very traditional in Kyoto. We eat them with matcha tea. They are called works of art."

"They're certainly that."
"Do you want to taste?"
"Of course!"

Michi showed us how to get free samples at every single sweet shop down the long street.

There were many to try.

At the entrance to each shop a pretty greeter stood with a tray, offering tiny cups of matcha tea or miso soup to drink. Inside were glass display counters full of the vibrantly coloured sweets, and in front of each counter were platters of sweets for tasting.

It was a magnificent end to the day. We chomped our way through every flavour and colour of *wagashi* we could – Michi always leading the way and encouraging us to taste 'one more'. We loaded up with red, yellow, and orange sweets for our host family, and presented Michi with bottles of artisan beer we had bought in Shibu Onsen.

Michi wanted to drive us home but it was in the opposite direction for him. As we had our trusty Japan Rail passes, we insisted he leave us at the station.

"Thank you so much, Michi. It's been a fabulous day. I hope you will visit us in Galicia sometime."

"Thank you. But not on a fireman's wages." He smiled sadly, and waved as his ancient red car spluttered away.

Michi had told us during the day how low the wages were for firemen in Japan. It seemed wrong for such a dangerous occupation to be so poorly paid. Michi was the most cheerful and friendly person we could have hoped to meet. We would always remember him and his kindnesses.

Boats and trains

The following day we were working in the afternoon, according to our calendar – now pinned to the wall next to our shiny new plastic clock. Over peanut butter on toast, I asked S what we should do for the morning.

"Let's walk along the lake, it's not too cold. Maybe I'll recognise something."

"Ha. You haven't so far."

Why either of us had expected my hubby to remember somewhere he had visited over fifty years previously, I've no idea. Otsu, where S remembered rice paddy fields and terraces, was now a bustling metropolis called Otsu City; it was nothing like his memories.

Still, it was another pleasant day. We wandered along the lakeside, occasionally having to move away from the shore due to buildings or roads – none of which S remembered.

"Which part did you walk around?"

"I think maybe the other side, but there were no houses at all, only rice paddies and terraces."

"You'd have a job to camp out round the lake now without being spotted," I replied.

The lakeside was dotted with pretty white and blue houses set back from the rocky shoreline, the lake itself dark grey under the low-clouded sky. Palm trees, and the occasional shuttered café, made the place seem seasidey.

After a couple of hours walking, we stopped near Kitakomatsu railway station for a cup of tea. The smiling waitress managed to understand my mangled '*ni cha*' (two tea) and we enjoyed watching the railway workers come in for their breakfasts.

Thick wedges of Japanese style bread were toasted on both sides then spread with butter before being put back under the grill for it to melt and seep into the toast.

The smell was delicious, and I was sorry we'd already eaten.

Our return train took us in to Katata station, another nice easy *kanji* that I'd learnt. From there we had to double back to Hira station as there had been no local train due from Kitakomatsu. I spent the two-way trip memorising the *kanji* for each station.

"I reckon by the time we leave, I'll be able to read every train station on our route in Japanese."

"Very useful."

The afternoon was again spent cleaning the guest house after the weekend visitors had left, and fixing guttering. After a welcome cuppa and cake from Kana, we refixed the scaffolding poles in the freezing early evening air, ready for the next job. I pondered that it was just as well we were not afraid of heights.

That evening Mark kindly offered us the use of their shower, and his computer to log on and check my messages. The shower was a delight after days of strip washes, but best of all was a message from our friend, Ann-Nee.

"Yes, it is very easy to fix the phone in Singapore. Where are you staying? There is a place called Sim Lim Square which has all the mobile phone places you will need."

A quick look on Google confirmed that Sim Lim Square was an easy walk from Orchard Road and our accommodation. Perfect.

Tuesday was our final working day with Mark and Kana. Mark set our work up then went to his own job, leaving us to get on with sanding and repainting the red-coloured shutters from the guest house.

By noon, despite a small flurry of snow we had all the shutters painted and lined up under the eaves drying.

A quick noodle lunch and we were ready to hit the trains again.

Boats and trains

For no particular reason, our trip today was to a port town called Tsuruga in Fukui prefecture.

Tsuruga is a natural harbour between Kyoto and Osaka to the west and Nagoya to the east, according to its tourist brochure. The brochure also said the city flourished because of its key transportational links.

As we stepped off the train, what I saw was a sort of faded prosperity. There were wide streets and lovely temples dotted about but many of the shops were closed and shuttered, and much of the area looked derelict.

It took two changes of train to get to the Japan Sea on which Tsuruga lies, but our trusty railcards meant the trip was free, and we could watch the scenery pass by our (clean) carriage windows. That was another thing I'd never seen on English trains – clean windows. I'm sure they must have started out that way but they were always grubby, as if we still relied on coal-stoked steam engines.

From Tsuruga station, we walked along Tsuruga Symbol Road to Kehi Jingu Shrine, built in the year 702. The eleven-metre-high vermillion *torii* guarding the shrine is, according to the tourist information, one of the three greatest wooden *torii* in Japan.

Tsuruga Symbol Road is lined with bronze statues of strange figures and animals. They are characters from Leiji Matsumoto's Galaxy Express and Star Blazers series and (again according to the tourist blurb) symbolise Tsuruga's close ties with both boats and trains.

The park surrounding Kehi Jingu Shrine was peaceful in late winter. There were ducks and turtles in a pond surrounded by large rocks. Huge pine trees stood sentinel overhead. The shrine itself was stunningly beautiful, polished cherry wood held up by tall vermillion pillars, with what looked like an altar at the far end.

The port when we arrived was huge. Derricks and other 'porty' looking machinery were dotted about. Crates sat on the docks and bright fishing boats of all sizes bobbed at anchor. We continued over a busy road bridge, which was probably not accessible to walkers. But hey – I can't read Japanese, and the cars seemed to manage to avoid two idiot *gaijin* wandering the highway.

Pine Tree Park was, as its name suggests, a park full of pine trees. A gravel path wound beneath the tall trees to a sandy beach. It was peaceful beneath the spreading branches but there was little wildlife in sight. Maybe winter in Japan is not the time for wildlife spotting.

The beach was white sand. The sea looked calm and inviting – until I remembered it was winter in Japan. Maybe not.

On the way back to the station, we passed a cemetery.

In England, cemeteries tend to be set in green spaces on the outskirts of towns. They are places to avoid, unless one is taking flowers to dead relatives' graves or hunting for gravestones. In Galicia, cemeteries are often in the centre of town, set in their own enclosed space. A wall of stone tombs set one above the other are where people often gather to talk to the deceased, especially on the 1st November, All Souls Day.

Here in Tsuruga, cut and carved memorial stones were set in a pyramid shape, topped by a stone lantern and watched over by a stone Buddha. The cemetery was shoehorned into a tiny space, on the street, surrounded by houses. It was peaceful and convenient. And I dare say the dead don't object.

On the way home we stopped at the supermarket for supplies before, another long wait and two trains later, we arrived at Hira station.

Our vegetarian spaghetti bolognese was very welcome that evening as we eased our footsore toes.

Turning Japanese

Wednesday was our final day at Lake Biwa and the second of our designated days off. We had offered to work another morning, as we were of necessity leaving early the following day, but Mark was adamant and we knew enough by now to realise Japanese rules are not made to be broken – even when made by an Englishman.

"Shall we go into Kyoto again?" I asked over the last of our odd rice/barley porridge for breakfast.

"Sounds good to me."

It was another beautiful, bright sunny day. I was happy to wander and soak up the atmosphere. Our time in Japan was coming to an end and I already felt a profound loss. The country had more than lived up to my childhood dreams and my adult expectations. I loved the calm and peace of the temples, the frenetic bustle of the cities, and the serene greeters. I loved the regimented organisation.

It couldn't be more different to our little corner of Spain, in tradition or in character, but I loved it just the same. Maybe Japan fitted in with my contrary nature. Chaos versus order, planning versus spontaneity, tranquility versus clamour. I was a contradiction as much as Japan was.

On this occasion we found the Imperial Palace Gardens in Kyoto were open. The palace itself was, of course, closed, but the gardens around it were divine. Over 900,000 square metres in size, Kyoto Gyoen National Garden is beautifully arranged into discrete areas around the grand façade of the Imperial Palace.

"In the Edo period of the 18th century, the area included many residences of the imperial families and other court nobles. Later, the area was turned into the beautiful parkland for all to share," I read from the

English language brochure I'd picked up. "And there are over 50,000 trees in the park."

"Do you want to count them to be sure?" asked S.

"Haha. I don't know why I try to educate you. Let's sit in this gazebo and watch the birds."

"Your brochure says this is called dragonfly pond," read S.

"Probably more in summer, I'm guessing. I'd love to come back in spring; see the cherry blossom, and the grass growing." I pointed at the brown, bare earth where grass would surely sprout in spring.

The parkland had evocative names such as plum blossom grove, grasshopper field, peach grove and dragonfly pond. It was a lovely day, and I felt I was finally turning Japanese.

That evening Mark and Kana invited us to their house for dinner. This was quite an honour from a reserved Japanese family, and I felt, once more, that we had been appreciated. I left them one of our little Galician owls and took away my name, written in Japanese by one of the children. It is still a treasured possession.

Train travel, Japanese style

"It's snowing," I said the following morning, peering through the glass door at the fat flakes coating the road.

It was the first proper snow we'd seen at the lake. It was pretty, but I wished it hadn't waited for our final day. Wheeling Rosie through a snow drift to the station didn't appeal at all.

Thankfully, Mark offered us a lift – so long as we were ready by eight. After cleaning the shed/cabin and bathroom, and putting our used bedding into the washing machine, we said our goodbyes to Kana and the children and jumped into the car. Our first Workaway had been a great experience. Mark and family, and Lake Biwa, would be a hard act to follow.

Our train back to Tokyo was one of the shinkansen 'bullet trains'. It was waiting on the platform as we arrived and I gasped at the sight of the sleek red and grey locomotive with its aerodynamic, bullet-shaped nose. It was quite literally the most beautiful train I'd ever seen. It was also immaculate, with not a speck of dust to spoil its mirror-like shine.

"I wonder if someone's employed to polish it at each stop?" I said to S, as we stared at the engine.

The two and a quarter hour journey, 445 kilometres (283 miles), to Tokyo on the Komachi Shinkansen was another wonder. The sleek train was almost silent, though the tilting on bends was rather alarming at first. Seats were in a two-by-two layout which meant even more space, and privacy. Each seat had a power point outlet, and the onboard wifi was free.

"The seats are comfy too," said S, as I extolled the virtues of train travel, Japanese style.

"The top speed's 320 kilometres (200 miles) an hour. Without stops we'd be in Tokyo in just over an hour," I said, recalling a fact from my early trip planning. "Impressive, eh?"

Back in Tokyo Central Station we spent an inordinate amount of time hunting for an empty locker for our bags. Not wanting to spend the day carrying all our luggage around, I'd planned to pop them all in one of the large station lockers.

Japan is possibly the only country in the world which still has coin-operated station lockers. In these days of terrorist threats and bombs, a coin-operated locker seems a strange idea at best but here in Tokyo station there were literally thousands of them lining the walls in every available space. There were three locker sizes and three corresponding prices.

Our problem was that lockers were premium space, and finding an empty one was not as easy as we expected. There were even monitors next to the banks of lockers showing the entire (and it is vast) space, with a green dot where a vacant locker might be. We'd dash across a heaving concourse, up stairs and round corners, down stairs and along walkways, avoiding bumping into the thousands of other tourists trying to track down a left-luggage locker, only to find the one we'd spotted on the screen had long since been occupied and the only free locker was now back where we'd started.

Eventually, I got fed up. We stuffed the two rucksacks into a small locker, leaving Rosie to come walkabouts with us.

"At least we didn't get lost this time," said S, cheerfully.

"I'm hungry."

There were plenty of options down here, below Tokyo, and huge billboards advertised lunchtime menu deals.

"That one looks good." I pointed at a billboard advertising a sashimi or tonkatsu (a breaded pork cutlet) meal for just 2,100¥ (18$), for two.

We just had to find the restaurant.

"Excuse me. Do you speak English?" I asked a smartly dressed young woman carrying a briefcase and tap tapping along the concourse in high heels.

"Of course." She smiled at us, waiting.

"Do you know where this restaurant is?" I pointed at the billboard which had taken my fancy.

"Yes, I think so. Follow me."

And off she went, the two of us, and Rosie, trailing behind. We turned a couple of corners and our rescuer stopped.

"No, it is not this way. Come."

By now I was worried we were delaying her. I knew the Tokyo lunchbreak was brief. "Don't worry. We will find it. Please, you will be late."

"It's fine. This way."

And off she went again. Tap, tap, tap.

"Ah. Here we are."

"*Arigato dimaster*," I said with a little bow.

The businesswoman smiled and waved a hand as she tap tapped away.

The restaurant was popular, the lunchtime crowd already busily eating their meals. The food, passing by us in waves, looked delicious. A smiling server escorted us to a table, handing us hot towels and telling us to help ourselves to the jugs of coffee and tea which were provided on a separate table. Our two menus came with rice and pickles, miso, a fermented soy bean mixture which I decided was definitely an acquired taste, and as much tea and coffee as we wanted.

As we wandered back through the underground shopping centre, I looked at S. "Where's Rosie?"

My hubby looked down, then looked at me. "Oops. We must have left her in the restaurant."

Being Tokyo, of course, Rosie was carefully stowed behind the greeter's desk waiting for us when we arrived back at the restaurant in a rush.

"We should have left her there while we walked around the Imperial Gardens," I said, wheeling our obedient 'pet' along the streets. "I do hope they're open this time."

"And that they let us in," added S, pointing at the queue of people being frisked and checked at the gates.

"Oh, heck. I didn't think of that. Maybe they'll let us park Rosie somewhere. They seem to be stopping people with bags."

Oddly enough the guards seemed totally unconcerned by our roll-along hot-pink suitcase, and waved us through. Maybe they thought that someone wanting to cause trouble would have been more subtle in their choice of concealment. Or we simply have innocent faces.

The Imperial Palace in Tokyo is the main residence of the Japanese Emperor, but we saw no signs of royalty as we wandered the quiet pathways around the gardens, dragging Rosie behind us.

The East Gardens, which are open to the public, cover around 210,000 square metres and are a 'special historic relic'. I thought them magnificent and imagined spring, splendid with cherry blossom and woodland bulbs.

Trundling Rosie along cobbled walkways did take the shine off the scenery, though. We soon collapsed on a convenient bench to take in the sights.

"Who knew there'd be so many hills?"

"Or so many cobbles? I'm pulling my arm off."

"It's warm too. I'll buy you an ice-cream?"

"Done."

Our final day in Japan was over. As we sped toward our overnight hotel, near to Narita airport, we shared memories.

"Hot springs and cold sheds."

"Bullet trains and bento boxes."

"Erm, *ryokans* and *yukata* robes."

"That doesn't rhyme. Noodles and 'no monkeys."

"Haha. Politeness."

"Yes, definitely that."

Two drinks in the hotel bar cost a small fortune that evening, but the views out over the twinkling lights of the airport were really rather beautiful through the floor to ceiling picture windows.

Breakfast in the morning was a vast buffet of every kind of Eastern and Western food.

"This is amazing," I said, traipsing along in the wake of hordes of other tourists.

Both Japanese and Westerners queued with laden platters, all filling up before heading for the international airport at Narita.

I had to try everything, and went back and forth collecting smoked fish, rice and pickles, bacon and eggs, sweet buns and toast, and fruit and tea.

"Right, I think I'm ready," I said, holding my swollen stomach. "Good job they don't weigh you before boarding."

At the airport we exchanged our last few Japanese notes for twenty Singaporean dollars, and bought a box of chocolates with the rest of the coins.

"That's us done. Singapore here we come."

Singapore sling

Our next stop was the city state of Singapore. It was one of the few places I'd been to before that S hadn't. I was looking forward to showing him possibly the only large city in the world which I love.

I am, as many of you may know, not a city girl. I was brought up in the English Midlands' countryside in a small village and though I moved to London in my teens, I moved back to the country as soon as I had the Big Smoke out of my system. Our home in Galicia is in a tiny hamlet of six houses, in a municipality of 3,000 souls. Our biggest Galician city has less than 300,000 inhabitants. Oh, yes, and I hate crowds.

So why on earth would I want to go to Singapore, a miniscule city state of 5.7 million people crammed into 719 square kilometres (278 square miles)?

I first visited Singapore in 2002 as a stopover on my way to Indonesia, where I was doing a thesis for my ecology degree. I'd enjoyed 24 hours in a city which never sleeps, alone, unmolested, by turns hot and sticky or soaking wet and steaming. From the opulence of Raffles, where I had a Singapore (virgin) sling, to the alleyways of Chinatown and the bustling quays, and from sudden rainstorms to helpful locals, Singapore was wondrous and exotic.

On my way back from Indonesia, I'd once more stopped in Singapore. The waiter at Raffles remembered not only my order, but where I'd travelled to. The streets were busy but pristine and a local man had pulled me back from crossing on a red light, explaining there was a 50S$ (37US$) fine for jaywalking. I was hooked.

Our flight was late leaving Narita but the Singapore Airlines plane was modern, the Japanese style lunch tasty, and the film selection extensive. I thought, being a daytime flight, that we'd see some interesting islands as we crossed the Philippine archipelago but there seemed to be endless sea below us. Instead, I watched films: *Crazy Rich Asians*, *Ant Man*, and *Bohemian Rhapsody*, and an entire series of my favourite, *Big Bang Theory*.

"When are we landing?"

"I think we're there," replied S from his window seat. "We're circling. Look."

He pointed down to the bay, as we continued in our holding pattern. Singapore looked bigger and more magnificent than ever, and I itched to be on the ground.

Immigration was the first hint that not everything was the same as seventeen years earlier. Then, I'd been waved through on my transit flight, the customs officers happy for me to go and sightsee whilst my luggage stayed behind in the airport. I'd also gone through customs carrying a newly purchased *prang*, or Indonesian machete, with nary a flicker of interest.

This time, long immobile queues snaked along the polished floor. We'd filled in our immigration forms on the plane, where the only pen I happened to have in my bumbag (fanny pack) was green. Green ink was apparently not considered suitable; we were sent off to fill the forms in again.

Singapore sling

I was so not going to go to the back of the queue afterwards. Instead, I hung around near the immigration desk, getting in the way, until the officer called us forwards to the angry murmurs and mutterings of other visitors.

With one thing and another, and a little bit of getting lost, it was 8pm and fully dark by the time we reached the Hotel Mi where I'd booked a two-night stay.

I'd already discovered that my Singaporean dollars from 2002 were no longer valid currency in 2019, which spoilt my plans a bit. The efficient, clean, MRT train had cost us six dollars twenty cents of our twenty Singapore dollars exchanged in Tokyo, and dinner at a large food hall cost us another 11.80S$. That left us with just two dollars until we found a cash point. Still, it was a beautiful, warm sultry evening and we enjoyed simply wandering the streets to Clarke Quay.

"Wow, so much has changed."

"Not you too?" S laughed.

"Mmm, but Singapore has changed in just a few years."

"Seventeen years."

"Okay, point taken. But your memories were over fifty years old."

"Did I tell you? Mark showed me a photo of the lake area from around 1970. There were no houses along that part of the lakeside at all."

"No. I missed that."

"You were probably on the computer, but it shows I wasn't imagining things."

"As if."

"Where now?"

"I don't know, but there's lots of people down there, near the river."

Each year since 2010, Singapore has celebrated its special place in the world with an illuminated art show, i Light Singapore, exhibiting the best in sustainability, and laser art. Unbeknownst to me, 2019 was a special bicentennial festival celebrating not only the two hundredth anniversary of Sir Stamford Raffles arriving in the small port previously known as Temasek, but its origins as a fishing village as far back as the 14th century.

That balmy February evening, lasers lit up buildings, painting them with scenes from Singapore's varied past, while upcycled sculptures abounded in parks and along the bay. Every hour there was a free light show on the Singapore river. We sat on a rock and watched, mesmerised, as with lights and sound, we were immersed in Singapore's evolution from fishing village to global metropolis.

"You did well to book at the right time for the show," said S.

I smiled. "I did, didn't I?"

I love serendipity.

We walked and walked that evening. Then we sat and people watched until I realised it was midnight.

"Pumpkin time! So much for jetlag."

Back at our hotel, the receptionist was fascinated by my ancient two-dollar notes and oddly shaped coins. So much so, that he happily exchanged them all for shiny new ones. We were eight dollars fifty in credit again.

Orchid heaven

The next morning, I was awake early as golden light poured in through our bedroom window.

"That pool down there is calling to me," I said, pulling on bikini and T-shirt.

"Let me know if it's chloriney. I'll join you if not."

S was, unsurprisingly, still wary of chlorine and bromine filled pools. Although the hot springs in Japan seemed to have cured his rash, he didn't want to push his luck.

I raced downstairs, grabbing a fluffy white towel from a large pile near the pool. The water was clear and pure, the pool deserted. I couldn't smell any alkaline gas so stuck my two thumbs up at my hubby, who was looking down from our third storey window.

At least I think it was S that I raised my thumbs to. Without my glasses on, I couldn't actually see the edge of the pool clearly, never mind three floors above me.

One of my must-sees this time round was the botanic gardens, reputedly one of the best in the world. We set off after a quick breakfast of a couple of my homemade muesli bars (which *still* needed eating before our arrival in Australia).

The Singapore Botanic Gardens were founded in 1859 and declared a UNESCO World Heritage Site in 2015, the only tropical garden in the world to be so honoured. The gardens consist of a huge parkland, which was well used by picnicking families, and quieter areas of great beauty. I, though, wanted to see the orchid house.

I love orchids. We have a beautiful *Phalaenopsis* which one of our lovely friends bought for our wedding in 2010. I repot it each year using dried oak and chestnut leaves, and moss. In return, it rewards me with vibrant fuchsia pink blooms virtually all year round.

I remember the first time I transited through Singapore airport there were orchids seemingly hanging all around me. It was less like an international airport and more like a beautiful glass house.

"Guided tours of the orchid gardens are offered four times a day and cost five Singapore dollars. They have over a thousand species of orchids on display and loads of hybrids too."
"Do you know the way, though, Miss Encyclopaedia?"
"Haha. Up here."

"Two please."
"There is a discount for over 65s," replied the lady at the ticket desk, looking at me intensely.
I know I've aged over the last few years, but still.
"Great. One discount and one adult please."
She glared at me, before sighing and ripping off two tickets. "Six dollars please."
"Should I have asked for two discounted ones?" I asked S, as we walked away. "She didn't ask for any proof of age and I'm sure she was trying to get me to say two. Do I look 65?"
Since one of my first ever conversations with my husband-to-be consisted of me guessing he was four years younger than he was and him adding six years on to my age, I was never going to get a satisfactory answer to that question. Move on, Lisa!
The tour of the orchid garden was breathtaking. With Singapore's year-round steamy climate, orchids don't need to be kept under glass and pampered. They grow everywhere. There were orchids in treetops, in cages, and growing in the ground. Special, named hybrids were lined up in pots on antique tables in Burkill Hall – a colonial plantation house built in 1886 and once the home of the director of the botanic gardens.
"I must take a photo of Margaret Thatcher for Debs. Who'd expect her to have such delicate pink blooms?"

Orchid heaven

"Bloomers?" asked S.

"Mum would prefer Andrea Bocelli, I think," I said, snapping another pic using S' camera. "That reminds me, I must get my phone fixed this afternoon."

Orchids bloomed in colours from pure white to fiery orange, and from baby yellow to devil's scarlet. There were bicoloured flowers in pink and white or pale green-yellow with russet centres. I was in orchid heaven.

"You could make me a trellis like that for my orchid." I pointed to a curved, ladder-like structure spanning two trees above our heads and hung with the most delicious lemon blooms.

"Is it lunchtime already?" asked S, steering me away.

We spent the morning wandering the extensive gardens, and admiring the array of flowers.

"In a tropical country everything seems to bloom all the time, doesn't it?" I said. "It's not like the winter bleakness of Japan."

It was intoxicating.

We bought Mum some delicate orchid earrings before walking back towards the city and that appointment to fix my phone.

Sim Lim Square, or Sim City as I had dubbed it from the outset, was exactly as Ann-Nee had promised; a huge six-storey retail complex in central Singapore, not far from our hotel, where large stores rubbed shoulders merrily with tiny pop-up type shacks below. All around were signs declaring; 'phone's freed' 'window package 50S$' 'repair 30 minutes' and other wild and grammatically inaccurate promises.

Sim Lim Square, or SLS, is renowned for scams, and for rip-offs of electronic goods, but it has its share of genuine miracle workers too. I found a small but busy looking stall with a large Indian man standing nearby watching the crowds. Inside a smaller, beturbaned man and a short, rotund lady were working on a collection of phones. Pieces were scattered all around.

"Hello. Can you help?" I asked, easing my way to the counter.

"What is problem?"

I explained what had happened as the man nodded knowledgeably.

"Hard drive needs reboot. It is possible, madam, but will wipe the memory. You have the backup?"

This was my nightmare. I hadn't backed up as I should have and would inevitably lose some data, but there was nothing I could do about it.

"It's no good as it is now," I sighed. "How much?"

"Thirty dollars, thirty minutes."

I couldn't say fairer than that.

Leaving my phone in expert (I hoped) hands, we sat outside at a nearby café, supping colas, people watching, and simply waiting.

"I hope I have all my passwords and stuff or it'll be a disaster," I worried to S, who, not being in the least technologically minded, just shrugged.

After getting my new, rebooted and wiped clean phone back, on schedule and for the agreed 30S$ in cash, it was time to eat.

"Oh good, all my photos are still there on the memory card. I hope you took some in Japan, 'cos I couldn't after Kanazawa."

"A few, I think."

"They are probably of doorknobs and gutterings," I mumbled to myself. Then more loudly; "I fancy a proper noodle bar today. The food hall was nice but I want something tiny and authentic."

I've read that Singapore is one of the most expensive cities in the world. Tokyo too is allegedly expensive, but we'd eaten incredibly well for no more than we'd spend on a meal in England. I was sure the same was true for Singapore.

"There." S pointed to a tiny café beneath the massive arcade of a shopping centre. Inside ran a long counter with people sitting, shoulder to shoulder, all slurping

Orchid heaven

noodles from vast bowls. Beyond was an open kitchen, a fridge with soft drinks, and an elderly, wrinkled Chinese lady serving customers.

"Perfect."

There was a menu of sorts, but I could only guess at the pictures so we ordered a bowl of noodles each.

"*Cha*?" I asked, hoping the universal word for tea would suffice, given my total lack of Chinese and the elderly lady's total lack of English.

She grinned and nodded vigorously, lifting up a huge blackened kettle.

At the counter, a turbaned man moved along, smiling and gesturing for us to sit. We squeezed into the space and slurped along with everyone else. Including our 'cha', the meal cost just 9S$ (less than £5) for the two of us. Who says food has to be expensive to be tasty and filling?

One thing I love about Singapore is the way all cultures seem to mingle and mix. Turbaned Indians, silk clad Chinese, Malaysians and Westerners all appear to live, if not in harmony, then in something approaching acceptance. Our fellow diners, an eclectic bunch of businessmen and women of all races, seemed to epitomise this.

"Look, a juice machine."

We'd been wandering back towards our hotel for a siesta when I spotted a large drinks machine at the side of the road. A clear glass window at the top showed a line of bright oranges running down into a hopper. 'Fresh orange juice' it said on the front. Below were comprehensive instructions in a range of languages.

"Two dollars. Let's try it."

I was like a kid in a sweet shop. I love clever mechanical things. In Galicia we have similar machines which dole out fresh milk into your own bottles.

On this occasion we popped our 'free' paper cups under the spout as directed and watched as the oranges rotated and disappeared into the hopper, emerging a few seconds later as a stream of fresh, fragrant juice into our waiting cups.

"That was worth two dollars for the fun," I said happily, sipping my fresh juice.

Back at the hotel I spent a frustrating hour fiddling with the phone and reloading all my apps, while S had a much more relaxing time snoozing and reading. A quick shower and I was ready to hit the bright lights of Singapore once more.

"Can we have a Big Mac?"

"You hate McDonald's."

"I know. But I have a mission – to check out the menus in each country. They might have those chocolate pies you liked in Japan…"

They didn't. In fact, the Singaporean McDonald's menu looked far more similar to a standard British one than the exoticness I expected from such a vibrant community.

"I think I'll stick to noodles."

I desperately wanted to return to the Raffles Hotel of my previous short visits, but it was being renovated. The courtyard bar, where I had enjoyed not one but two Singapore slings back in 2002, was closed off. A set of stairs rose to the first floor.

"Let's go upstairs to the bar there," I said, leading the way onto an outside terrace above the streets of Singapore.

As I pushed open the door onto a cool, tiled area filled with tables and chairs, a black-and-white clad waiter approached.

"Closed." He said firmly.

"Oh. For renovation?" I asked, bewildered.

"No, for evening. Goodbye."

With that he closed the door and I heard a lock snick. I looked at my newly refurbished phone.

"It's only ten thirty. Bit early."

Orchid heaven

"English closing times," replied S, as we walked back to the stairwell.

At that moment a group of youngsters came around the last bend chattering in English.

"Hi!" said one. "How you doing?"

"It's shut," I replied, pointing to the bolted doorway.

"No way! We've come specially. I'll get them to open up." At this the man began to bang good naturedly on the door.

Amused, we watched for a time then, as it became obvious his tactics were not going to have the desired effect, we withdrew, throwing a 'goodnight' over our shoulders as we left.

Back on the quays we sat and watched the i Light show all over again, sipping a beer on one of the many riverside terraces.

"I think this show is my favourite Singapore memory."

"And not recognising anywhere?"

"Haha. I did so recognise some bits. More than you did in Japan, anyway."

"Well, Perth will be new for both of us," replied S.

Tomorrow was a new country and a new continent, Australia; it would prove to be an adventure for us both.

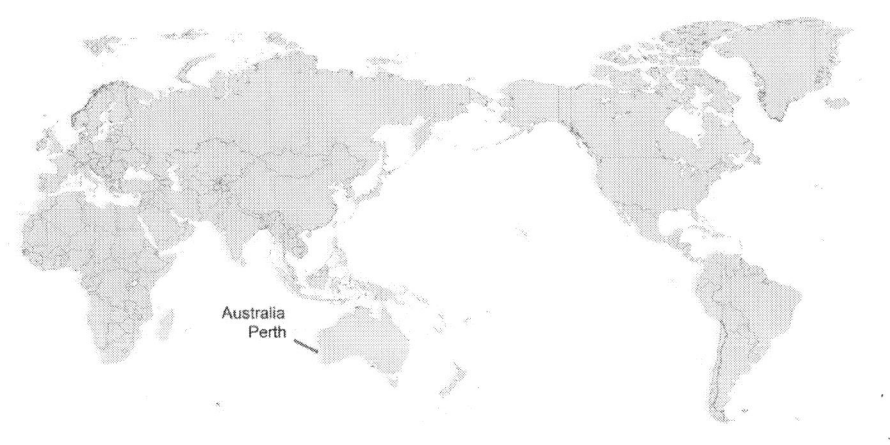

Park life in Perth

"We need to get some money out," I said the following morning.

"I thought we had enough. We'll need Aussie dollars in a few hours."

"I know. I totally forgot to save some Singapore dollars for the MRT to the airport. What an idiot. Can you check out while I go find a cashpoint?"

The MRT fare was six dollars twenty, but the minimum withdrawal at the ATM was ten dollars. At least we could get a drink at the airport with the change. And there were lots of shops to browse if I remembered rightly from my last visit.

I was wrong on both counts.

The airport seemed much more chaotic than I remembered. I recalled a large airy space of peace and harmony; of shops and sweet-smelling flowers. What I got was a long sweaty queue before being pushed and pummelled straight through customs.

"At least we can relax now we're airside," S said.

No, we couldn't.

No sooner had we sat down than the board flashed to make our way to the gate.

"No rest for the wicked," I groaned, standing up. "Want a muesli bar," I added. "We've still two left."

"Thanks."

We took our time, wandering the terminal building and enjoying the last moments of Singapore. Then I saw another huge snaking queue.

"Oh, no!"

This queue seemed to be going through a second customs area.

"That's odd, I thought we were already airside."

"We are. They must just be checking passports."

No, they weren't.

There was a full customs set-up, and all cabin bags were being x-rayed.

"You can't bring that through," snapped a miserable looking customs officer, pointing at my bottle of water.

"Why not? We're through customs."

"No liquids."

It's always pointless arguing with customs officials, or any officials with guns, so I tipped the remains of the water down my throat and threw the bottle heavily into the bin. At least we had enough Singapore dollars left to buy another bottle at a shop on the other side.

Wrong again.

Instead of arcades of shops and cafes, duty frees and entertainments, we were herded into a tiny holding cell. A glassed-in room scarcely big enough to hold a plane load of people was our home for the next hour as we waited for our flight.

"This is ridiculous; there's not even a loo and I'm dying for a wee."

"You shouldn't have drunk all that water," replied S.

"I should've saved the empty bottle as a pee container," I grumbled.

Did I mention, I hate small, crowded spaces?

Park life in Perth

We landed at Perth International airport early afternoon. Our bags took far longer to arrive at the carousel than we did, but at least they all made it together this time. Contrary to expectations (mine), customs on the Australian side was quick and easy. We were soon outside in the late Western Australian summer sunshine, ready for our next Workaway adventure.

I'd seen Paul's profile online months ago, and thought it looked interesting. Before I had time to write, though, he got in touch via our profile and asked if we'd like to Workaway at his home. Serendipity put us together.

At that time, I'd still been pondering how we were going to cross the 3,900 kilometres to Stewart's cousin Gerry's home in Melbourne. I told Paul we'd love to Workaway for him, dependent on our schedule, and we left it at that.

One of my options had been a campervan relocation. Because of the vastness of the Australian continent, many people are unable to return their campervan, or recreation vehicle (RV), to its departure point. This leaves the vehicle stranded thousands of kilometres away from its home base.

There are many websites offering cheap or free relocations of one-way hires in Australia; I joined one called Imoova. I entered our details, requesting a campervan from Perth to Adelaide or Melbourne on or around the 25th February.

In Japan, two days before my phone crashed, I'd received an offer. A six-berth RV was available to return to Melbourne from Perth on Thursday 21st February. It was slightly earlier than I'd planned, but at five dollars a day and eight days to cross the country, I'd snapped it up.

I immediately contacted Paul and we agreed a short stay of four days. We were confident we could do some useful work for him in that time.

"Where now," asked S, as we exited the airport.

"Paul said we should hire an Uber car to get to his house. But I'm sure there'll be a coach we can catch."

There wasn't.

My phone's roaming appeared not to work in Australia either, despite the company's reassurances back home, so I couldn't contact Uber anyway. We were forced to ask a taxi driver to take us.

"How much?" I gasped.

"It's a fair old way. You'd be better using Uber," he replied, helpfully.

"Great. We'll take it."

The driver was chatty and pointed out landmarks to us on the hour's drive to the suburb of the city where our host lived. He might have been pricey, but he was an interesting tour guide.

It was already early evening by the time we pulled up on a wide, tree-lined avenue. Once more we had been travelling for the best part of a day.

The single storey Art Deco style house was set in its own grounds behind a high wall. The front porch was flanked by unusual corner windows – diamond shaped panes of glass sat in flaking, green painted, wooden frames. These must have looked beautiful once; now, the paint was peeling, the wood soft. Because the windows were set on a diagonal, the wooden filets between the panes had collected rainwater and rotted in the corners. Despite the damage of time, the overall effect was still one of elegance.

Paul welcomed us warmly and showed us around. Inside, an open-plan living area led up two steps to an office-come-dining-room. Beyond was a large kitchen, and behind that were a couple of bedrooms and a bathroom.

"This is you," Paul said, showing us into a large room looking out onto a swimming pool in the back.

Park life in Perth

"Wow! That's a bit different to the last place," I said, smiling, as I took in the light, high-ceilinged room. "Thank you, Paul."

"Warmer too," added S.

Whilst Paul prepared dinner, his lovely dog, Luna, took us for a walk to the park at the bottom of the road. Luna was a mongrel of multiple breeds. Brindle coated, she had the head and deep chest of a Staffordshire bull terrier, but her legs were long and whippet-like, her hips narrow and svelte. We all spent a pleasant hour circling the large park, Luna greeting her playmates, while we chatted to their companions. It was a lovely location.

"Park life in Perth. This is so not going to feel like work," I said, soaking in the sun's rays as we sat on a bench, watching Luna play tag with her friends.

"Mmm. Good choice."

Over a meal of pasta, pesto, bacon, broccoli and tomatoes, Paul explained some of the jobs he needed doing.

"Oh, and there's the windows to botch and paint."

Unlike Mark, Paul had no timetable to work to, no set working hours, and no pre-arranged jobs to complete. He just mentioned things as he thought of them, showing us around the house and garden as he did so.

I, though, had been taking notes. That evening, I wrote them up and presented the list back to our surprised host.

"There's lots of jobs here, Paul. Can you number them in order of importance for me? We'll not get everything done, but we can crack on in the morning."

Once he'd recovered, Paul numbered my list as requested before going to bed. It was 9.30pm.

One of the things we notice as we travel around the world are the different bed times (and consequently rising times) in each country.

In Galicia, the day starts late; shops open at ten, lunch is at two. But people are still '*paseo*'ing until after midnight. Dinner in Galicia begins at nine or later, and kids stay up until the early hours.

In Japan the day began much earlier, with lunch at exactly noon according to the daily siren we heard; whilst Singapore was alive 24/7, the warmth and noise constant. Here in Western Australia, we found the day began and ended much earlier than we were used to. Lunch would be at 11.30am and dinner at 6pm. Surprisingly, it wasn't a problem. We awoke as soon as the sun poured through the curtains at six, and sat up chatting or reading until we were tired at ten or eleven in the evening.

Do they have the money?

Our first working day in Perth began with me cleaning, filling, and painting some trellis for the garden wall. S had the fun job of digging out the bottom of that same wall for repainting with a waterproof paint. The sun was already hot by the time we stopped for lunch.

"I'm glad we started early," I said, wiping my brow, which was damp under my baseball cap.

"Me too. I suggest we look at what tools Paul has after lunch. We'll need screws and pliers and other stuff for the jobs he's listed."

"You're right. He said there were lots of tools in the garage. Let's go ask him."

This was when we noticed another, huge, difference from our previous host.

Mark's tool shed had been immaculate. Every tool had its own hook, gloves and other items were in labelled drawers, nails and screws in separate, neatly categorised tins.

Paul's garage was a vast, untidy muddle of a room. Just inside the door were two roller trays caked in goo. A large roller brush was cemented to one tray by dried-on paint. Screwdrivers, used to stir paint, were left, sticky with white. Trowels, used to lever off lids, sat chipped and useless. Rusty saws and pieces of sandpaper littered the floor amidst dust covered chairs, broken tables and other unloved junk.

"Okaaay, so we're going to need some supplies," I squeaked.

Every part of me was itching to tidy up this disaster area but it wasn't one of our 'jobs'.

"Why don't people clean things up?" asked S, handling a ruined paint brush.

"Oh, that's other Workawayers. I ask them to clean up but they often don't bother. We can go to Bunnings after lunch," said Paul, oblivious to our joint distress at the chaotic mess.

"He obviously doesn't make sure the Workawayers clean-up properly," muttered S, as we got changed.

"True, but you know how hard it is sometimes. You often end up re-cleaning brushes and stuff after our helpers have finished. Remember DeAnna?"

DeAnna and Maria had been two young American women who'd 'helped' us with the *Casita*, the house we renovated for my mum. They had been a delight and a disaster all in one.

"How could I forget?" said S. "I'm sure I'm still finding splotches of paint even now."

"You do exaggerate," I laughed.

Our trip to Bunnings was quite the excitement of the day. For those who don't know, Bunnings is a huge construction and DIY materials warehouse chain – the Australian equivalent to B&Q or Wickes in the UK. It was S' idea of heaven.

We pulled up in front, Paul grabbed a trolley, and we entered a wonderland.

Paul said later; "I thought we'd have to wander round for ages, you know, looking for things? But you went one way, Stewart the other, and I was left in the middle with the trolley."

For us, it was just a normal well-planned attack. I split off to find sandpaper and glue, S to collect wood and fixings, leaving our genial host to guard an empty trolley.

At one point I lost sight of the two men.

"Are you right?" asked a good-looking young male assistant, as I stood pondering which way to go.

"Yeah, thanks. I've lost the men I came in with."

Quick as a flash came the reply; "Do they have the money?"

"Um, yes. I guess so."

Do they have the money?

"Then we've no time to lose," he shouted, darting off.

I spluttered with laughter, delighted with the Aussie sense of humour.

After another lovely walk with Luna, and Paul's home-cooked cod and chips for dinner, we sat and planned our upcoming trip. No, scrub that; I sat and planned while S read his book.

Did I mention that I like to make lists, and lists of lists? I often simply relist things in a different order – just because. My lists for this round-the-world trip already covered three notebooks. Now, I was planning our drive across the Nullarbor Plain.

Nullarbor is one of those lovely names which conjures up all sorts of imaginative wanderings, especially when you discover that the name is taken from the Latin for 'no trees', *null arbor.*

I'd read some interesting internet posts about crossing the Nullarbor Plain, the arid region which encompasses some 200,000 square kilometres (77,220 square miles) across the south of Western Australia (WA) and South Australia (SA), bordering the Great Australian Bight. It was said to be desolate, dangerous and spooky.

The section of the Eyre Highway which crosses the Nullarbor Plain is a full 1,000 kilometres (621 miles) long, beginning in Norseman, WA and ending at Ceduna, SA. There are few settlements along this isolated stretch, which was only sealed in 1974.

"Did you know that the Nullarbor has the longest section of straight road in the world? 147K between Balladonnia and Caiguna. Dead straight with no bends."

"Hmm."

"Guess what it's called?"

"What what's called?"

"The straight stretch of road, I've just told you about."

"Straight road?"

"Close. It's called Ninety Mile Straight."

"'Cos it's ninety miles long, and straight."

"Exactly."

I loved the straightforwardness of Australia, where a spade is definitely a spade not a digging implement; a big arid sand-covered area is called the Great Sandy Desert, and a 90-mile arrow-straight stretch of road is known as Ninety Mile Straight.

Once we left Norseman, there would be no towns and no supermarkets, only roadhouses – the ubiquitous motel come truck stop, come shop and fuel station. Food was said to be expensive in these roadhouses, as was fuel. There was little we could do about fuel, but we could stock up on food for the journey.

Meal planning is one of my favourite evening activities at home in Galicia. Here, in Western Australia, I made a list of what we needed to take – for breakfasts, lunches, and dinners – along the way. We'd already been shopping with Paul following our Bunnings trip, at a large supermarket, called, confusingly for Brits, Woolworths. Paul had told us to buy whatever we liked for our sandwich lunches as he was paying. I think we disappointed him with our cheap choices of sandwich tuna and cheese, but the trip meant we knew Woolworths had a good range of produce.

"I think if we get one of those ready-roasted chickens, that'll do us a couple of dinners and maybe sandwiches too."

S nodded and 'hmmed', basically ignoring me and reading his book. To be fair, my musings were just that and didn't need his input.

"Then I'll get tins of stuff that won't go off. Beans, tinned spuds. Noodles are always good 'cos they're quick to cook, and cheap. Muesli for breakfast, and fruit. Oh, and orange juice. Mmm, milk. We can get long life stuff, it's what we have at home anyway. Bread for lunchtime butties. What else?"

"Chocolate."

Do they have the money?

My hubby was listening after all.
"It might melt."
"Won't last that long. Come on, it's bedtime."

The bells of St. Martin's

Tuesday morning, we were up with the sun and ready to start work by 7.30am. Our first job was removing a shower rail which Paul wanted fixing. It looked as if someone had hung off the rail and pulled it out of the wall, breaking some of the tiles in the process. I didn't like to ask the circumstances.

It took us the best part of an hour to get the rusting screws loosened and the rail off so I could clean and retile the damaged part. I carried on with this while S finished painting the base of the garden wall.

By the time the sun was getting unbearably hot, at just 10am, S had finished outside and moved onto our next job.

The kitchen units at Paul's house were pine-panelled Shaker style, but every single door had some of the slats missing. Some doors were empty frames, others had just one loose panel. Paul had all the missing panels stored, and wanted us to fit them back onto the doors. His tools for the job had been six-inch screws and 'no nails' glue. It was one of the reasons for our Bunnings trip the previous day – S wanted small tacks to refix the panels properly. I took the existing pins out of the stored panels and organised the pieces of wood whilst S nailed and glued them in place.

"You'd think they'd all be the same size, wouldn't you?" I said, sorting through the panels for a small angled piece to fit in a corner.

"It would help," replied S, rejecting a panel which was a fraction too big for the space he had left.

Somehow, we got all the doors re-panelled and back on in time for lunch. The kitchen was transformed, and I wondered again why Paul hadn't done the job himself.

"He's a businessman, not a DIYer," replied S, to my musings.

"I'm so lucky to have you, *dar-link*."

In the afternoon we caught the train into Perth city and walked towards Elizabeth Quay. I was looking forward to seeing my first Australian city, but was astonished and disappointed at the number of, frankly ugly, new builds dotted about.

"What on earth is that one supposed to be?" I asked, pointing at a beautiful red-brick building with white colonnades and black, wrought iron balcony railings. The building was colonial in style, but multiple floors of square, blue-green glass tower block seemed to be growing out of its top. It was totally incongruous, and made the whole thing look disconnected and ugly.

At Elizabeth Quay, my moans got louder.

"Oh no, that is horrible."

"Why? You liked Singapore."

"I know. But that works somehow. I don't know. It's the clashing styles. Look at that one."

The still to be completed Ritz Carlton Hotel rose in a shimmering oval of deep blue glass above the quay. In itself that was fine, but the first three or four storeys were of boxy rosewood-coloured squares which, to my mind, jarred horribly. I began to think that the city architects were just seeing how much disharmony they could create. The architecture was a mish-mash of unconnected styles and designs, as a child let loose with building blocks might achieve.

The deafening thrum of construction work, the dust, and the heat, probably also affected my early perceptions of the city.

I have no objection to modern architecture. So long as a building is in keeping with its surrounds, it can be old and elegant or modern and shocking. Singapore had some of the most innovative new builds I've seen. From the ship-like Marina Bay Sands Hotel, floating above its three skyscraper towers, to the Gardens on the Bay with their incredible 'flower trees', which we could see from the quays, the buildings were mesmerizing and beautiful.

In amongst the tall, shiny, and mismatched new tower blocks on Elizabeth Quay was one of Perth's most controversial sculptures, the Bell Tower.

Built for the millennium, and no longer visible from the quay itself, the Bell Tower is the world's largest musical instrument. It is 82m (271ft) tall and houses the Swan Bells, a range of eighteen bells originally from St. Martin-in-the-Fields church in England. In 1870, the bells of St. Martin's, which once rang to farewell James Cook on his journey to Australia, were donated to Western Australia and eventually incorporated into the five-and-a-half-million Australian dollar build.

Paul had told us that many people were very happy when the new skyscrapers enclosed the tower, though to my mind the Bell Tower was far less a monstrosity than the newer builds.

"Look at this picture," I said to S, pointing at a large laminated photograph of the quays area as it was when Queen Elizabeth II visited in 2011. The Bell Tower was clearly visible from the water front, rising proudly above the other, lesser buildings, and all around was parkland. It was lovely.

The parkland, a heritage listed public space called Esplanade Reserve, was established in 1880 on reclaimed land along the Swan River. It included a large space for events, recreation and commemorations. Work began to reconstruct the newly renamed Elizabeth Quay in 2012. In February of that year there was a protest rally, highlighting the destruction of the heritage area and concerns over water quality around the new inlet. Local newspaper, Perth Now, called the debacle; 'debate, drama, dredging and dollars'.

Since we visited Perth in 2019, the reconstruction of the area has been completed, the diggers and jack hammers moved on, and the inlet cleaned up. I look forward to revisiting one day in a more peaceful time.

Battling the undertow

"I'm going for a swim before work, grab your gear."

It was 7.30am and we were just about to start on our day's tasks, but Paul had other ideas.

"It'll only be a quick one but you'll get to see one of the best Perth beaches. You can start work later."

We didn't need any more encouragement to grab our swimming costumes and towels and jump in the car.

Scarborough beach was all dazzling pale sand against a cobalt blue sea and azure sky. The Indian Ocean waves were pounding the beach vigorously. We paddled then sat and watched Paul swim out to sea and back, enjoying the sunshine, the cries of the ubiquitous terns, the surfers, and the few swimmers battling the undertow.

"Isn't it weird to think it's still February and we're sunbathing?" I asked.

"Nice," replied S.

"I was definitely born in the wrong hemisphere, you know. I mean, I'm a sun worshipper who has a winter birthday. If I lived here, I'd have a summer birthday and could have a picnic every year."

My very favourite birthday treat is a picnic. The weather at home, in a Northern December, is suitable only on rare occasions. Here, on the opposite side of the world, the weather would always be perfect.

Back at the house we cracked on with our respective jobs. Once he'd finished the final coat of waterproof paint on the garden wall and I'd grouted and cleaned my new tiles in the bathroom, S helped me refix the shower rail. It looked as good as new, and I was pleased to see that my repairs were invisible.

"Steve's here."

"Coming," replied S, as I opened the door to a tall, dark-haired man wearing the Aussie kit of long shorts, T-shirt and sunglasses.

"Hiya, we're just set," I said, shaking his hand.

"No worries."

I was to hear that phrase often over the next four weeks but this was the first time, and I smiled.

"So Australian!"

"Hey, I'm no Australian," Steve replied, indignant.

Steve, or Stevo as he seemed to prefer, was the brother of our friend and New Zealand Workawayer, Jenny. He lived in Perth and drove the huge road trains up the coast to Broome and back for a living. When Jenny had told him of our trip, he'd kindly volunteered his afternoon off to show us around.

"So, you ready?"

"Yup, all set. Where we off to?"

"Mundara."

I was no further forward. Instead, I sat back and chatted to Stevo, enjoying the views.

Mundara, it turned out, was a huge dam out in the Perth hills. There was a lovely walk through woodland, and a pub at the end.

"Great planning, Stevo."

In the woodland we saw our first mob of kangaroos.

"Aw, they're just teeny ones," said Stevo, as I gaped at the two-metre-tall male standing on his hind legs, balanced perfectly on his huge muscular tail. Two of the females had bulging pouches and I was delighted to see a tiny head emerge from one of them.

"Oh, look! Baby joeys."

Stevo laughed at me, but I'm pretty sure he'd have been the same if he'd seen a roe deer fawn or a badger. He laughed at us ordering half pints at the pub too, as did the friendly landlady.

"Have you seen King's Park yet?" asked Stevo, downing his second pint.

Battling the undertow

"No, not yet. The botanic gardens are up there, aren't they?"

"Yep. Let's go."

King's Park sits high on Mount Eliza, a limestone bluff looking down on the curve of the Swan River and Elizabeth Quay, where we'd walked the previous day. Two-thirds of the extensive 400-hectare (990-acre) gardens are naturalised bushland of native trees and shrubs. Amongst the flora, myriads of birds pecked and fluttered as we walked a bush trail along the ridge.

"Those look like magpies!" I exclaimed.

Stevo looked askance. "They are magpies."

"Ah, yes, but Aussie magpies. Ours are smaller and have different markings. And the beaks on these are far stouter."

"Really?"

"Yeah, I think the first white settlers named the native birds after the ones they knew from home."

A sudden cawing had me jumping backwards. "What the hell is that?"

Dusk was falling and the cacophony was all around us.

"There," said S. "They're roosting in the trees."

Because we were on a bluff, the tops of the trees below were almost on a level with us. In each wide canopy were hundreds of cockatoos, their grey white beaks standing out in the dusk as they cawed and claimed their roosting spot.

"God, I couldn't live near that lot."

"D'you fancy a steak?" asked Stevo on the way home. "I can get the barbie going, or we can find a pub."

"Let's find a pub, then we can buy you dinner as a thank you."

The Oxford Hotel was as similar to an English pub as one could imagine on the opposite side of the world. In fact, we felt quite at home in Australian pubs with their pint measures and real ales.

"We start our trip across the Nullarbor tomorrow."

"Yeah, what you driving?"

"I think it's a six-berth RV."

"Bit of advice?"

"Yeah, sure."

"Let the road trains overtake if they come up behind you. They have a schedule to keep and bloody tourists get in the way."

"Sure. No problem." I'd read that these huge multi-trailered trucks were up to fifty metres long, and really didn't want to get on the wrong side of one.

"And don't drive at dawn or dusk 'cos of the roos. They can make a mess of the van. But if you do need to be out at night, always follow one of those trucks."

"Why?"

"They'll clear the road for ya."

I didn't understand at the time.

"Thanks, Stevo. And for a great day out."

"No worries."

A boomerang

"Howard says we can pick the camper up today, after all."

It was 8am and I'd broken off from working at an incoming email beep.

When we'd first agreed the RV relocation from Perth to Melbourne, we had eight days to cross Australia. We were to collect the van on Thursday morning, the 21st February, arriving at Melbourne on the 28th. There we would spend a few days with Stewart's cousin before our next Workaway, in the Blue Mountains.

My plans had been thrown into turmoil when we were advised that the camper now needed to be at the depot in Melbourne by 8am on the 28th, and wouldn't be ready to collect until late afternoon on the 22nd, leaving us just five days to reach our destination.

I'd emailed our contact, Howard, and asked him to let us know if the van might be ready earlier. I had few expectations, but now he'd come up trumps.

"That's good. We can leave after lunch."

At 12.30pm, after finishing our last job for Paul, then stripping our bed, cleaning the bedroom and bathroom, and saying goodbye to our host, we grabbed an Uber ride to collect our new home.

Mark and Paul might have been polar opposites, one organised and efficient, the other laid back to the point of horizontality, but they were perfect hosts and we'd enjoyed our time spent with them both.

§

"A boomerang. That's the first one I've seen," I joked, as we came to the gates of Boomerang Campers. "I wonder what our ride looks like."

"I bet it's that one." S pointed to a Luton van sized camper with an over cab area and bulging bodywork. The monster was three times the size of the more modest car-derived models which littered the forecourt.

"Hiya, I'm Dan. This is you." A stocky chap with a wide smile, pointed at the big RV. "Have you driven one of these before?"

"Nope. I did drive a three and a half tonner once though."

I'd been a sales rep for a hoist company, many moons ago. Our boss was always looking for ways to cut costs. His idea one year had been to hire a cheap truck and for me and my colleague, Jim, to drive it to an exhibition in Glasgow instead of hiring a specialist truck and driver. That wagon had a broken tail light, a non-functioning tachograph, and I had to stand up to reach the pedals. It had been a fun weekend.

"Okay. Well, I'm sure you'll get the hang of it. There's just some paperwork while the girls finish cleaning her then you're good to go."

That was our lesson in driving an RV over.

The paperwork took an age, mainly because Dan talked constantly. He rang Howard to check on a couple of things and I chatted to our contact for the first time.

"Oh, you're not an Aussie."

Howard laughed. "South African, born and bred."

A boomerang

"Is there a satnav included?" I remembered to ask.

"There is." Howard paused. "But – give you some advice?"

"Yeah, sure."

"Drive toward the sun in the morning, and away from it in the evening. You can't go wrong."

I laughed. Howard sounded like an Aussie after all.

Our home for the next week had a spacious front cab with plenty of room for us to spread out our maps. On the dash was a large tome listing free overnight parking spots. This book was to become our bible over the next few days as we found beautiful and remote places to 'camp'.

Above the cab, reached by a ladder, was a low-ceilinged space complete with double mattress. A second double bed took up the rear of the main cabin, with a large picture window behind.

"Can we sleep on that one?" I asked. "It feels a bit claustrophobic up top."

"And probably hotter near the ceiling too," replied S.

Between the two 'bedrooms' was a small kitchen with fridge, sink and hob; a tiny bathroom, and a four-seater table and chairs which converted into a third, miniature, double bed.

"It'd be a bit cramped for six, wouldn't it?" I said.

"And no space for luggage, either."

There was a narrow wardrobe and cleverly designed overhead lockers for storing food and clothes, but for more than two people it would have been a real squash.

I took the wheel first, struggling with the automatic gearbox.

"Oh crikey, you have to be careful not to rev it too much or it drops a gear," I groaned, trying and failing to get the thing to accelerate out of a junction. The engine screeched and I swear there was blue smoke coming from behind as the van jerked away. "I'll get the hang of it in a min."

Our first port of call was Woolworths for supplies.

"Look out!" yelled S, as I turned into the car park.

I braked. "What?"

"We can't go in that way; the overhead clearance is too low."

"Oops!"

I'd been busy watching the sides of the camper and not thinking about our height, which was printed in large letters above the front windscreen. Avoiding an early crash, I parked on the roadside and we raced off to stock up. By 2.45pm we were on the road – traversing the largest island in the world.

We arrived at Kellerberrin, a small town which said it welcomed RVers, at 5.30pm. As we'd been warned not to drive after dark, and as we were still getting used to the vehicle, it seemed as good a place as any to stop for the night.

Along a dirt track, we came to a quiet turnoff where I made our first meal on the road – Woolworths' ready-roast chicken with a hot Russian salad. And fresh plums, bought from a roadside shop on the way, for dessert.

"You know this looks rather well-manicured for a park," I mused, as we sat at our dining table, watching the lights come on in a farmhouse down the hill.

"I think it's a golf course," replied S, pointing to a short-turfed area with, now I looked, an obvious flag sticking out of the ground.

"Ah. Well, we'll probably be gone in the morning before anyone wants to play."

At that moment, a stout lady walking three dogs appeared along the track. I decided to check if we were trespassing.

"Naw, no worries. But if you go a bit further up the hill there's a bonzer parking spot. Be more comfortable. Good views too."

The very top of Kellerberrin Hill ended in a large gravelled turnaround. There were wooden seats and

A boomerang

bins dotted about, and overlooking the town below was a small viewpoint with an interpretation board.

And we had it all to ourselves.

That evening we sat on the viewpoint watching the twinkling lights below and the even more phenomenal twinkling lights above us, sipping good old Yorkshire tea, brought all the way from northern Spain (and therefore probably illegally imported). I tried to identify some of the constellations of the southern hemisphere.

"That's the Southern Cross." S pointed to an indistinct shape above us.

"Not as clear as The Plough and The North Star, is it? Oh look, Orion's on his head." Sure enough, the hunter was doing a headstand. It all looked most peculiar.

Crossing the Nullarbor, day one: Thursday 21st Feb. Perth to Kellerberrin 209km, 2.5 hours. Bed 9.30pm

Great balls of fire

"We need to drive a bit further today," I announced over breakfast. "To get to Melbourne in time we need to average 800 kilometres a day."

"Let's go then."

It was 6am on another sunny Australian morning. I planned to make it to a roadhouse at Balladonnia, some 802km along the road and the beginning of that 90-mile straight, before nightfall.

When I'd first investigated driving across the Nullarbor Plain, most of the Facebook sites I'd gone on had pooh-poohed the idea in favour of flying to Melbourne. Where's the romance in that? I wanted an adventure!

And I certainly got one.

Our early morning start meant that we arrived at Coolgardie, one of the gold prospector towns from the turn of the last century, well before noon. After a look at the railway station, which was closed, and a sandwich, we still had time for a wander. After all, this was not just a dash across country but part of our holiday, and part of our Australia experience.

"We've made good time. Let's have a look round and stretch our legs."

The Coolgardie Visitor's Centre and Museum was overseen by a lovely lady who urged us to visit the museum exhibits. There were the sort of outback pioneer items one might expect, such as leather cases, tools and drugs, an array of items doctors might use, and old beer bottles.

The most interesting and moving part of the exhibition for me was an account of the miraculous rescue of a miner in Bonnievale Mine, near Coolgardie.

Great balls of fire

When heavy storms caused the twelve-level gold mine to flood in March 1907, all the miners were safely evacuated, bar one. Modesto Varischetti was trapped in an air pocket with over fifty feet of water above him. Everyone assumed the 32-year-old miner had perished until they heard tapping from below. Divers carrying supplies eventually reached Varischetti after six days, but it was another three days before enough water had been pumped out of the mine to allow the Italian to escape his almost tomb.

A display showing the old-fashioned diving suits and the accompanying soundtrack recreating the noise of the storm and water pouring into the mine shaft, were surprisingly powerful. I was enthralled – imagining the poor man alone in the darkness, so far from rescue. As an interesting postscript, Varischetti apparently returned to mining just a few weeks later.

"Oops. It's after one. We'd better hit the road."

"Can't mess up your plans."

"Haha. Oh, look, a cloud."

I may have sounded ridiculously excited by something so simple, but it was the first cloud we'd seen since arriving in Australia. It was mushroom shaped, sitting incongruously in a bright blue sky.

"Maybe it's going to rain."

We set off from Coolgardie on the road east towards Kalgoorlie at 1.30pm precisely. At 1.45pm we came to an unexpected halt.

"What's going on?" I asked the uniformed man who approached us.

"Bushfire, ma'am," he said, shaking his head. "Where you heading?"

"Balladonnia."

"Not today. Road's closed to Norseman."

Norseman was the junction where our road joined the Eyre Highway and entered the Nullarbor Plain. From there, we would travel eastwards across Australia, hugging the coastline and the Great Australian Bight. This was *not* good news.

"That's what the cloud was. It was smoke. Is there another route?" I asked naively.

Uniform laughed. He actually laughed! I was most put out.

"You could go cross country, but not in that. And I wouldn't recommend it anyways. It's dirt all the way. Plus, we don't know which way the bush fire'll go yet."

I couldn't conceive of an area so huge which had only a single tarmacked road. It was mind boggling, but I was to get used to the vastness of the Australian bush over the next few days.

"You could carry on as far as Kambalda. It's a bit further south. Save you a few K when the road reopens."

Anything was better than retracing our steps to Coolgardie. I hate to go backwards; Kambalda it was.

We arrived in a pleasant looking village, three-quarters of an hour later. Tarmacked streets, at least wide enough for four lanes of traffic, were bordered by paved footpaths and bush – that very Australian landscape of short scrub, taller eucalyptus trees and red, red earth. Of the potential four lanes of traffic there was no sign, but an arrow pointed to 24-hour RV parking.

One thing I'd already discovered was that Australia was a very welcoming country to RVers. Every town seemed to have a parking area, and many had washing and dump facilities.

"Sounds like us."

We drove along one wide, empty boulevard after another. All perfect, all silent.

"Is it siesta time?"

"I don't think Aussies have a siesta. Looks like they have big plans for this place, though," replied S.

"There! RV parking."

We pulled on to a red earth plaza under the shade of a large tree. A lone camper, similar to our own, was

Great balls of fire

already parked a little way away. Opposite the parking area was a large building which looked like a sports hall, and beyond I could see a rose garden, incongruously English in this setting.

"Let's go explore our new home."

The large building turned out to be a modern community centre with sports facilities and brand-new showers. The lady at the desk was fascinated to talk with two English folk.

"You staying long?" she asked.

"Well, that depends on the bushfire," I said, honestly.

"Oh. Okay, well, the showers are just two dollars fifty. Long as you want. There's free wifi in the café here. And we stay open 'til four."

"Great. We'll grab towels and be back for a shower. Did I see a swimming pool too?"

Across the street from the Community Centre, I'd spotted a walled expanse. Through the metal gate, sat a gleaming, large pool. That was where I wanted to spend my afternoon. The temperature by now was in the low 40s centigrade. I was melting.

Our friendly receptionist went quiet. It was the first time she'd stopped speaking, in fact. I looked up from fiddling with my phone.

"It's closed." She sighed.

"Oh?"

"It was supposed to be refurbished last winter but it's not finished. There's a lot of bad feeling about it, to be honest."

"I can imagine. You need a pool in this heat."

"We really do."

"I think we might be spending a fair bit of time in your nice air-conditioned café, in that case." I smiled, hoping the compliment would cheer her up; she didn't suit a glum face.

"Oh, I do hope so. The cakes and shakes are great and Kambalda's a lovely town. I'm sure you'll enjoy it here."

We plodded back to the camper. It felt like walking through hot treacle; any exertion caused me to drip. The temperature in the van was unbearable.

"That soon heated up."

There was no hook-up at the RV park so we couldn't turn the air-conditioning on. Even beneath the shade of the trees, our home was turning into a large metal oven. The fridge was already struggling in the heat and we found our tub of ice-cream dripping down the shelves from the freezer box.

"Ice-cream shake?"

"Mmm, nice. Shower?"

"Sounds better," I agreed, grabbing my towel and shampoo.

Half an hour later, refreshed and clean, we sat in the little café attached to the community centre eating cookies and supping shakes. It was cool and relaxing.

Unfortunately, all good things come to an end and we were politely shown the door at 4pm.

While we were there, I'd used their wifi connection to message Howard and explain we were going nowhere further today.

"No worries," had come the inevitable reply.

The van was even hotter. The outside temperature was already 42°C, inside was much, much more.

"Let's see if we can find somewhere else with aircon," I gasped, closing the door again.

"I think I saw a Woolworths on the way in."

"Plan. Shopping it is."

On the way we saw a hotel and a tiny parade of shops. It was too hot to explore further but the hotel appeared to have a bar attached.

Woolworths was, as expected, air-conditioned. I've never spent so long debating the merits of various foodstuffs without buying anything. Eventually we left, having exhausted every corner and in danger of being ejected as vagrants, which, in a way, we were.

Great balls of fire

It was still hot in the van but I managed a meal of noodles, tinned fish, broccoli and leeks, washed down with rapidly melting ice-cream.

"Fancy a beer?" asked S, after we'd washed up.

"Thought you'd spot the pub," I laughed. "I hope it has aircon."

I got changed and put on my only dress. We were going out after all.

That, was possibly a mistake.

The hotel not only housed the town's bar, but its only restaurant. The pub was busy, the carpet sticky below my sandals, the pool table in the middle of the floor noisy with shouted instructions and revellers.

Every head turned to us as we entered.

"I think I'm overdressed," I muttered, looking around.

Both sexes wore the same uniform: vest top, shorts and flipflops (or as the Aussies called them, to our amusement, thongs).

Definitely overdressed, Lisa.

In the corner, a DJ was setting up. A board over the bar read; 'Karaoke nite, every Friday'.

"Tell me it's not Friday."

"It is Friday. Why?" asked S.

I pointed at the board.

"Ah. Let's get a beer."

The bar was polished wood with a brass rail along the front, and stretched the whole way across the large room.

"Longest bar in the world," said the barman, seeing me staring.

"Riiight." What a claim to fame this little town had.

"Are you here for the karaoke?" he continued, pulling our pint and a half.

"Erm, well, not really," I admitted. "It's good beer," I added, desperately diverting the conversation.

Luckily, or unluckily, the DJ decided to warm up at that moment with his Elvis impersonation. It was as dire as I'd expected.

"I could do a Meatloaf turn," I suggested to S.

"He's not *that* bad."

"Huh. He's not good. At least I know all the words."

Thankfully, a young woman came up to the mike and did a pretty good rendition of a couple of Dolly Parton songs before handing it to an older chap.

"That's appropriate," said S, as the new singer warmed up.

"Goodness, Gracious, Great Balls of Fire? Very."

By the time the DJ came back, we'd supped our pints.

"Can we go, pretty please. Or I'll have to join in," I added for effect.

Outside it was still tropical. A warm breeze blew in with a distinctive, acrid scent on it.

"Smoke!"

To the south there was a fierce red glow in the sky. Traces of black billowed above it. I swear I could hear crackling over the wind.

"I'm sort of glad we got stuck here now," I said, as we walked back to the van.

Day two: Friday 22nd Feb. Kellerberrin to Kambalda 463km, 4.5 hours. Bed 10pm

He fried, right there on the road

We were up at 6am the next morning, washed and dressed and on the road - briefly.

We drove confidently out of the RV park, past the hotel and Woolworths, along the beautifully built boulevards and out to the main road. It was a lovely cool morning before the heat of the day made it unbearable, and I was in a good mood.

"Today we can get to Caiguna, I reckon. There's a whale watching station there, though it's the wrong time of year of course. Even so it'll be interesting..." I paused as S stopped the van. "What's... oh!"

The road ahead had a blockade across it. A well-built, uniformed woman came across to us.

"Road's closed to Norseman. Bush fire."

"Still? Do you know how long for?" I asked. Surely a fire couldn't take this long to put out? I knew nothing of bush fires.

"Could be days. The wind changed direction last night and they're worried about the road. Dangerous if the wind changes. We don't know where it'll go next, see. Bloke died in his lorry last year. Tyres burnt out. He fried, right there on the road."

This pleasant looking woman was in full flow with her terrifying tale, oblivious to my horrified stares.

"Best thing if you get stuck, is to drive into the fire. Sounds wrong, eh? Well, you can't outrun it but if you're lucky, you can break through and come out on the clear side. Fire can't go back over what's burnt, see. 'Course that doesn't work if your tyres melt. Tricky one that."

"Erm, yes, thanks. I think we'll go back to Kambalda. Thank you."

"Oh, okay, sure. If you listen to the local radio, they'll let you know when it's clear."

"Thanks," I yelled out of the window, as S swung us round in an arc and drove back to the RV park.

"Home, sweet home," I sighed as we parked up in the exact same spot.

The park had filled up since we left, no doubt other motorists in the same boat as us. Opposite was an older couple swigging beer out of cans and listening to a transistor radio.

"Morning," said the man as we drew level. "Any luck?"

"Nope, road's closed still."

"Yup. Radio says it might be another two days. Wind's changing direction. Want a tinny?"

"Er, no, thanks. See you later."

We walked to our new favourite café for shakes and cakes. The local radio station had a Facebook page, but nothing seemed to be happening so we wandered into the rose garden I'd seen the day before. It was surprisingly cool beneath the arbour of climbing roses.

Built as a memorial garden, there were statues and engraved stones amongst the roses. One tiny memorial was to a baby of eighteen months. It all seemed rather poignant, and put our travails into perspective.

After thrashing S at scrabble under the arbour we walked back to the van. The elderly couple were still there, and still supping 'tinnies'. A large rubbish bag held their empties.

"Looks like the road might open this arvo," shouted the man as we passed. "We're going fishing."

"Fishing?"

"Yeah, for yabbies. In the lake."

I wondered how much he'd had to drink, and why none of what he'd said made sense.

"A yabby is a big prawn, like a crayfish," explained S, seeing my confusion. "And arvo is afternoon."

"Oh, right. And the lake? It's pretty dry round here."

"I don't know about that. There're a few salt lakes about."

He fried, right there on the road

"I'm going to check the website again," I announced after our lunchtime cheese and tomato omelette. S was reading beneath the integral awning, sitting in one of the two folding chairs we'd found stored below the van.

"Okay."

It looked like the road was indeed open. I walked as fast as the intense heat would allow, back to the camper.

"It's open, let's pack up."

This time I drove; out of the RV park, past the hotel and Woolworths, along the beautifully built boulevards and out to the main road. There, a blockade sat across the road. The same uniformed lady came towards us.

"Road's closed to Norseman. Bush fire."

"I thought it had reopened."

"Naw, 'fraid not. Could be days. Wind changed direction, see, and they're worried about the road. Dangerous if the wind changes. We don't know where it'll go next. Bloke died in his lorry last year. Tyres burnt out. He fried, right there on the road."

It was déjà vu, all over again. With a swift wave, I turned the van around and drove back along the wide boulevards, past Woolworths and the hotel, and into the RV park. Locals waved to us cheerily as we drove past.

"That was fun," said S, as I parked up in the exact same spot beneath the trees.

The community centre closed early on Saturdays, so we had a shower in our tiny bathroom in the RV, then sat outside reading and trying to find a breeze until an hour we considered reasonable to go to the bar.

"At least it's not karaoke tonight."

"No, it's a, erm, poker jackpot."

"What on earth is that?"

"No idea."

"What's the jackpot thingy?" I asked the barman, pointing at the board.

"Oh, right. Yeah, it's great. You get a tab with each beer and then the winner gets the whole pot at the end of the night. Cool, eh?"

"Erm, yeah, cool," I replied, hoping against hope we didn't win the jackpot. We might get run out of town.

This evening I'd gone dressed to blend in. Off-white shorts, off-white vest top, scruffy cream baseball cap, and unfastened sandals. No one blinked an eye. And the barman had our order off pat by the second round. I was seriously pleased, and decided I rather liked Kambalda.

Day three: Saturday 23rd Feb. Kambalda 4km (there and back again), 1 hour. Bed 10.30pm

Sounds of silence

There was a thunderstorm that evening. The sky, already lit up by the flames from the bush fire, sparkled as lightning flashed all around. Thunder rocked the van, but by morning the red dust was still just that – dust. It was as if the storm had never been.

We were up at 6am again for a walk in the relative cool of the early morning. I could say that Kambalda was quiet at that time, but, to be honest, Kambalda was always quiet; its wide streets devoid of traffic, its bush empty of people. Even the community centre with its free wifi and lovely café was quiet – only the hotel bar seemed busy and gregarious.

We wandered back for breakfast and sat outside the van, watching the ants crawl in an orderly line along the red dust and listening for the sounds of silence – any sound, in fact. It was windy that morning, probably a left over from the storm earlier, and the red dust was swirling around, getting into my tea.

At 10.15am it was time to make our way to the air-conditioned cool of the café.

As we entered, the girl on reception looked up. "Hi, how you doing? Road's open."

"Really? Wow."

"Yeah, they just announced it."

"Great, thanks." I turned to leave, then turned back. "And thank you for everything. You've all made it a lovely break."

"You're welcome. Do come back."

On our way to the van, I pondered on this friendly little town. A town where a 'usual' was the third drink you'd ever ordered at a place and where people waved and smiled like long-lost relatives after one day. At the tiny book and second-hand shop, the lady had already asked if we were buying a house here. Looking at the prices in the estate agent window next door, it held a certain appeal.

"Look," I said, as we passed, "forty thousand Aussie dollars for a detached four bed on its own large plot. That is so cheap."

"But we are two hundred kilometres from the nearest proper town."

"True. I bet you could rent it out to the workers, though. The lady next door said they were mining lithium nearby. One of the biggest mines in Australia, she said."

"And Stevo said that most workers are now helicoptered in for their fortnight's work then helicoptered back home. No one lives near the mines anymore."

"Maybe that's why they have all these lovely wide streets here. They must've been expecting a boom. It is rather a friendly town, isn't it?"

"It is. And the karaoke's not bad either."

I punched my husband on the arm. "Let's get out of here before they close that road again."

As we drove away, S asked; "Did you mean what you said at the community centre?"

"About them making it a lovely break? Yeah. I've enjoyed it. It's been... different."

"It's certainly been that."

"Anyway, it's got me thinking about being less organised maybe, and going with the flow more."

S just stared at me.

"Anyway, we should get to the observatory at Eyre today if we don't hang about too long. It's only about six hundred K, though we're a bit late starting out. Norseman's a big town, for round here anyway, and we should be able to find a supermarket there to buy enough to last us across the Nullarbor. We don't want to have to buy anything at the roadhouses if we can help

Sounds of silence

it, they're supposed to be really expensive. Do you think we should have shopped at the Woolworths before we left? But it didn't open 'til eleven and then we'd have been even later setting off. No, I think Norseman'll be fine, it's not far now…"

I prattled on, planning the next stage of our trip, oblivious to my husband's wry smile and the fact that I'd contradicted my earlier statement within a few seconds of uttering it. We were on the road again, and life was good.

When we drive long distances, S and I have a routine. We drive one hour on, one hour off, spelling each other at the wheel. Every second hour we stop for a brief wander, a cup of tea, or lunch, depending on the time of day. This not only adds interest to a lengthy journey, but keeps us fresh and alert.

We arrived at Norseman, just two hundred kilometres down the road, at exactly noon.

Norseman was closed.

Every shop was shuttered, only the service station was open and the fuel price was outrageous compared to our last top up.

"Is there a supermarket in Norseman. A Woolworths?" I asked the service station attendant.

"Yeah, just down that road," he replied, pointing towards what looked like an empty street.

"Great, thanks."

As I turned to leave, he piped up; "But it closed at midday. Opens again on Monday."

I spun round. "What? Is it the only one?"

"In Norseman, yeah. Probably one open in Kalgoorlie."

"But we're going the other way. Across the Nullarbor."

"Ah, right. No, no supermarkets that way 'til you reach Ceduna, I reckon."

Ceduna was 1,200 kilometres away. Just perfect.

"We should have waited for the Woolworths to open," I said, dejectedly, getting back into the cab. "Everywhere's shut 'til Monday."

"We'll manage. I'm sure you over-provisioned anyway."

I was about to snap that I never over-provision and had actually worked it all out so very carefully, when I realised how ridiculous I sounded. I shut my mouth and started the engine. "Nullarbor, here we come."

Towards the sun in the morning

"I see a tree," I said. "And another one. And a…"

"I don't think scrub counts as trees. The bigger ones are probably planted."

"Huh. Just 'cos I spotted one first. There's a car!"

"That *is* a first," replied S. "At least in the last four hours."

Although we had seen plenty of the huge multi-trailered road trains on the highway, and the odd RV like ours, ordinary cars had been singularly lacking. A combination of wilderness all around, few motels, and even fewer towns, meant that like a snail, one needed to bring one's own house along to cross this desert-like land.

This was to be our world for the next few days; barren, stark, hot, and incredibly beautiful. I loved it already.

Our first stop after Norseman had been at a rest area for lunch. There are rest stops at regular intervals along the Eyre Highway; overnight parking is allowed at some, usually with the proviso that the vehicle is displaying its self-contained vehicle certification badge, and most have picnic benches dotted about. All are little oases of peace away from the road.

Fraser Range Rest Stop was on the edge of a large salt pan called, bizarrely, a lake. Green plastic picnic benches perched beneath tall blue gums which almost, but not quite, gave shade. We'd eaten our cheese sandwiches and crisps, one hand wafting away the hordes of flies which were trying to share our picnic lunch, beneath the trees' canopy, whilst gazing at the empty landscape. The virtually treeless plain stretched out on either side of us, red and vast except where the low scrubland, or occasional eucalyptus, had managed to grab a toehold.

We drove slowly, stopping frequently, and it was dusk as we pulled in below the trees at Eyre Observatory Rest Stop near Caiguna. A kangaroo bounced across our bows.
There were two other RVs parked up, but the space was large and the trees hid us from each other's view. I stir fried our ubiquitous noodles (two dollars for a pack of twenty) with left over chicken breasts. Dessert was some refreshing, nicely melted and refrozen, ice cream. As soon as we'd started driving once more, our overworked fridge had begun to cool itself down and the air-conditioning kicked in, keeping the van wonderfully cool, even after we'd parked up for the night.
I lay in our double bed at the back of the van, gazing through the large rear window at a mob of kangaroos grazing just outside and thinking how lucky I was to be able to do this.
"Do you feel a draught," asked S, intruding on my thoughts.
"No. Why would I feel draught with the windows closed?"
"I don't know. Never mind."
I drifted to sleep counting kangaroos.

Day four: Sunday 24th Feb. Kambalda to Eyre Observatory, Caiguna 598km, 6.5 hours. Bed 9pm

§

"It's a bit windy out," I said.
We were driving along another stretch of empty road, the twin of the previous day. The landscape was the same red earth and grey-green scrub. The sky, the same sapphire blue. The road, the same shade of empty.

162

"Mmm, it's blowing the van around," said S, from the driver's seat.

"What's that flapping noise?"

"Dunno. Something loose?"

We'd left our overnight rest stop at 6am. By eight we were parked up and breakfasting at the delightfully named Cocklebiddy.

The low, red roofed, motel-come-restaurant-come-shop sat in splendid isolation amongst the ankle high dusty scrub and dry terracotta soil. A sign, incongruously told me there was no parking across the golf course. Of any obvious golf course, there was no indication.

It's a long way to come to play golf," I said, before returning to my earlier concern. "There was definitely something flapping," I repeated.

S looked down the length of the van. "I can't see anything."

"It only does it when we're moving. It seems to be that window thing above the bed. I think something's loose."

"The canopy?"

"Possibly. I don't know."

S clambered out of the cab and tried to peer along the roof of the van. "I can't reach to see properly, but I think the canopy's missing."

"Is this bad?"

"The roof lights have a perspex canopy over them that can be opened for ventilation. It should be closed while we're moving for safety. If it's missing then we have no protection against bad weather."

"Ah. Not good. I wonder where it went?"

"No idea. I don't remember hitting anything, do you?"

"Nope. After that first supermarket stop, I've been very careful about heights. Do you think it was missing when we picked the van up?"

"I'd have thought we'd have noticed."

"Not until it got windy."

"Mmm. Not that it matters. We'd just better hope it doesn't rain."

"Don't worry, the Nullarbor gets less than 225 mil of rain a year."

"Good to know," replied hubby, grinning.

"Humph. We need some more bread, and our drinking water's getting low. I was going to top up at Norseman," I said. "We may as well look here."

It's not like there was an alternative. One of the things all the websites warned of was running out of water. There's no fresh water to be found along this desolate plain. Running out of bread for our lunchtime butties would be almost as disastrous.

The prices in the small shop were as outrageous as I'd expected; the water in the ten-litre container we bought was foul stuff, which tasted of battery acid and deep-sea gunge.

"Five quid for a sliced loaf!"

"And the chocolate was even more."

I looked at my chocolate-loving hubby. "Only you would think of chocolate at a time like this, and in this heat."

"There's never a bad time for chocolate."

Not long after our breakfast stop, I spotted the sea.

"I see the sea, I see the sea," I chanted, pointing over my right shoulder at the vivid duck egg blue of the Great Australian Bight, blending into the sapphire sky.

"There's a viewpoint coming up, shall we stop?"

"Why not."

It was another beautiful sunny Australian day. We parked in a gravelled parking area at Great Bight View Point and walked the few hundred metres to a walkway which stretched along the cliff edge. All around were mounds of low-growing, aromatic shrubs – silver and bronze and dull grey-green against the red earth. The sea was dazzlingly blue with only the tiniest trace of breakers where it collided against the base of the cliffs.

Towards the sun in the morning

The wind howled around us, but otherwise everything was still and quiet.

When we arrived there had been a group of motorcyclists just loading up. We'd crossed paths with these intrepid souls a number of times already and were destined to continue to do so. After all, there was only one way to go…

"Towards the sun in the morning and away from it in the afternoon," I mumbled to myself, quoting Howard's words from that first day.

By the time we'd explored the cliff top path and been thoroughly wind-blown, our RV was the only vehicle left in the car park; the only man-made thing in sight. I took a photograph of it, looking like a white Tonka toy against the low scrub. On the picture, the gravel path leading to the car park blends into the background, and just on the horizon there is the outline of a building, possibly a farmhouse, possibly a shack.

It was so quiet, despite the main Eyre Highway running only a few hundred metres away, so intensely empty. No telegraph poles spoilt the view, no buildings. It was incredible. I was happy we'd decided to motor across the Nullarbor Plain instead of flying. After all, what could possibly go wrong?

Manic Monday

When we'd first told S' cousin, Gerry, that we were driving to Melbourne from Perth, his wife Jeanette's comment had been; "You're driving across the Nullarbor? What could possibly go wrong?"

When we'd collected the van, the service warning light had been lit. 'Service overdue', it had said. 'Service 3,000km overdue', it had actually said. I'd mentioned this to Dan, but he said it wasn't a problem as the vans were checked before each outing. After we left the Great Bight View Point, more warning lights appeared, including the battery warning light and the ABS light.

Despite these additional problems it was a lovely drive that day. We passed Eucla with its abandoned telegraph office; the Big Kangaroo, Rooey II, at Border Village, where we crossed into South Australia; and Ambrosia Rest Area which made me pine for rice pudding in a tin.

At Nundaroo we filled up with fuel for the cheapest price along the Nullarbor Plain.

"I'm new," the Indian man serving us told me. "There is a consortium here along the highway. It keeps prices up. I hope to be different."

I thought he already was, and not just because of his turban. He was going up against the big boys, and I wished him luck.

Along kilometres of empty roads, we drove. The only wildlife were the too frequent carcasses of kangaroos which had come off worse against the massive road trucks. I finally understood Stevo's cryptic comment about the trucks clearing the road. The only signs of life were those trucks themselves, racing up behind our meandering RV before passing in a blast of air and air horn. The scenery was never changing; short scrub, red earth and scrawny trees bent sideways by the winds

Manic Monday

whipping across this vast emptiness. Occasionally, a low house would break up the view, its red roof blending into the landscape.

Trying to make up time we pushed on to Ceduna, a seaside town towards the far end of the Nullarbor Plain.

The Big 4 Caravan Park at Ceduna welcomed us, and the cheerful receptionist directed us to a huge corner plot complete with hook up. It would be the first time we'd had the luxury of aircon overnight, and electricity we hadn't had to generate ourselves.

It was dark by the time we were set up so we walked to the pier, looking along the way for a likely pub for an evening drink – now we were back in civilisation. What we found were gangs of indigenous peoples, lying or squatting on street corners or queuing at huge liquor warehouses. White people moved around them and stepped over them, avoiding eye contact. It was a complete contrast to Kambalda, where white, aboriginal, and mixed-race individuals all drank together, chatted together, played pool together, and seemed to get on together without rancour.

The long wooden pier at Ceduna stretched out into the sea. The streets were paved, neat and tidy, and for the most part silent. The rocky beach was empty, except for seaweed and the odd seagull which tiptoed amongst the detritus. The wind was fresh, and triangular topped pine trees stood sentinel on each street corner.

But all I could think of were the lost folk lying on the street corners or queuing at the liquor stores.

I know the 'problem' of indigenous peoples is a long and convoluted one for many Australians, and one which still causes all sorts of arguments. I don't pretend to understand the question, never mind the answer. (The obvious one, which is that we should never have invaded their country, is too late to do anything about.) But it seemed to me something was broken here, where huge warehouses competed to sell cheap booze to a population which had no hope and no capacity for liquor. On one desolate corner, a modern building announced it housed 'lawyers for indigenous peoples' above the door; it seemed to compound the doom I felt in Ceduna town centre.

The holiday park, by contrast, was clean and cheerful. The showers were hot and powerful and the outdoor camp kitchen tidy, and a joy to use after our cramped kitchen on board the van.

"Just another manic Monday, wasn't it?" joked S, later that evening.

"Ha. I hope the van sorts itself tomorrow. I'd better contact Howard. What are your memories of the Nullarbor?" I asked sleepily.

"Emptiness?" said S. "And trees."

"Yes. There were trees, weren't there?" I agreed. "Not so 'null' after all."

"For me it was the primary colours, all reds and blues, and the lack of people. No telegraph poles or electricity pylons."

"The dead straight roads. And no traffic."

"Yeah, we've hardly passed a soul, have we?"

Day five: Monday 25th Feb. Caiguna to Ceduna 765km, 7 hours. Bed 10pm

§

I messaged Howard first thing next morning using the site wifi, to explain about our warning lights. He suggested we ask at a garage.

We did, I replied. *They're all busy and can't fit us in. The earliest anyone could see us is next Wednesday.*

I went back to our plot, noticing as I did so that the camper next to ours was the exact same model. Two guys were standing outside, hanging out their washing.

"Hiya. I notice we have the same model van," I said, approaching them.

"Yeah. Do you want a look round?"

Manic Monday

"Oh, well, yeah. Okay, thanks."

Whilst our camper had been set up as a cramped, six-berth holiday home, our new friends' RV was a roomy, four berth. Where our rear bed was, they had a U-shaped seating area with a central table, TV, plenty of storage and comfortable sofas.

"I like it," I said, admiringly.

"How long you had yours?" asked the taller of the two men.

"Oh, it's not ours. We're doing a campervan relocation back to Melbourne from Perth. Actually, I wondered if you knew anything about these models as we have a problem…"

Give a man a suggestion they may be useful and they swing into action. These two were no different. They followed me to the van and after a quick tour (it doesn't take long to poke one's head around a door and examine a twenty-five-foot (8m) RV after all), they popped the bonnet.

"John, go get the leads, eh?" said the shorter man.

He turned to me as his mate trotted off. "We're electrical engineers. The van's mine, but John keeps me company on long trips. We go fishing."

Seems I'd struck the maintenance jackpot. Within seconds John, and the van owner, Simon, had hooked up their diagnostic equipment and were humming and haaing like proper mechanics.

"Your battery isn't charging. Look, this indicator should be up here…" Simon was telling me something important about the battery but my brain had switched off, so I can't explain what it was. Suffice to say there was a problem.

"It's most probably the alternator. If that isn't working the battery won't charge up as you're driving, so it'll drain over time. That'd explain your warning lights too. Did you notice it getting warm in the cab?"

"Yeah, actually. The aircon didn't seem to be working as well as before, now I think about it."

"Mmm. You need a new alternator, I reckon," said Simon.

This time I rang Howard. "But there's still no garage available to do the work," I ended miserably.

"Is there a spares' shop nearby?" he asked.

"Yeah, just down the road. Why?"

"I'm thinking, buy a new battery. It may just be not charging properly 'cos it's old. A new one'll solve the problem. If you keep the receipt, I'll pay you back."

"But what about the alternator?"

"You don't know for sure that's the problem, right? The guys just said the battery wasn't charging. So, try the new battery and let's see. She'll be right," he added in a mock Australian accent.

"Cheers, Howard," I said, laughing along.

Jeanette's words played over in my head. At the time I'd thought she was being sarcastic, but this isn't the Australian way. The further into our adventure we went, the more I realised she was simply being realistic. After all, what *could* go wrong driving across a thousand kilometres of wilderness in a hired RV, with no experience behind us?

We were about to find out.

Stuck in the middle with you

The spares' shop, conveniently next door to the caravan park, agreed to replace the battery and fit the new one for us.

"Two hundred and ninety-nine dollars," said the assistant.

If it seemed expensive, I knew Howard was paying. We were done and on the move by 10.30am.

"Great, we can still make up the time. I reckon we'll be there by Thursday afternoon, latest. Howard'll be pleased."

I was confident and content. We were back on the road and had made a couple more friends on our trip.

My contentment didn't last long.

I drove first shift then S took over for an hour. At the beginning of my second shift, fifty kilometres beyond the small town of Wudinna, disaster struck.

"It's getting warm in here again," I said.

"It is. The aircon's on full." S twiddled the controls.

"Mmm. I suppose the sun *is* shining directly in the front windscreen."

Suddenly, warning lights started to light up the dashboard in vivid reds. First the battery light, then the aircon light, then the ABS braking system. The dash was lit up like a Christmas tree – until it wasn't.

"Oh, that's better, all the warning lights have gone out..." I started. "Oh, shit."

I'd lost all power in a microsecond. The power steering and ABS were unresponsive. The vehicle was as heavy as a large dead lump of metal could be, and just as I thought I'd be able to limp a little further, the engine cut out.

"What happened?" asked S.

"Haven't a bloody clue. It just stopped on me. Battery must be dead. Or it's some stupid safety thing or...I don't know. Now what?"

We were stopped on a narrow, single lane main road, unable to pull in, unable to put on the hazard warning lights without power. I'd not seen another vehicle all morning and it was quickly heating up to unbearable temperatures inside the box which had been our home and transport.

I stepped onto the scrubby verge and looked around. The landscape was as barren and unforgiving as it had been for the last five days. Sweat instantly coated my body.

"God, it's hot out here," I said, fiddling with my phone. "Idiot. There's no wifi in the middle of nowhere, is there?" I threw the phone on the verge in disgust.

"I don't mind being stuck in the middle with you, *darlink*," said S, grinning.

For once, I wasn't really paying attention to our song lyric game. I was staring round at the harsh landscape, wondering how much water we had left and how we could stop ourselves from frying. Could we walk to Kimba, another fifty K ahead? No chance. What if we stayed here? We had no cooking or cooling facilities and the van would be a tin tomb in no time.

Then, I saw a mirage.

Ahead of us, maybe fifty yards away, was a small side road which I'd been hoping to limp to before the engine cut out. At that junction, a van rolled into view followed by the largest combine harvester I'd ever seen. Curtis New Holland, it said on the side in three-foot-high letters.

No sooner had I seen this shimmering green steed than I was down the road, waving my arms.

"Hiya, we've broken down and have no phone signal," I gasped.

I must have looked a sight – red-faced, hair sticking to my neck, drenched in sweat (whatever they may say, this lady does not 'glow'. I must be a horse.).

Stuck in the middle with you

The wiry, dark-haired man leapt out of the van's cab, thankfully ignoring my appearance, and ambled back to the combine harvester. After presumably explaining our problem, the combine driver clambered down to join him. Both then ambled ever so slowly over to the RV.

"Sounds like the alternator's broke," said van man, after I'd explained what had happened.

"Shit. Should have listened to Si and John." I sighed. "Could you call the breakdown for me? My phone doesn't work."

"Naw, signal's crap here. I use the radio to talk to the office."

We stood briefly in silence, then van man brightened. "I've got a spare battery in the van. I reckon we could hook her up and you could limp to the nearest garage."

He thought a bit longer. "Here's the thing, though. It's fifty K on to Kimba, where there might be a garage open, or its fifty K back to Wudinna where our office is. We could probably fix you up there. What do you reckon?"

It wasn't a difficult decision. Fifty kilometres forward with no guarantee of finding somewhere open, or fifty kilometres back with a probable solution.

"Okay," said van man, coming off the radio. "We can order you a new alternator and fit it in the morning if it gets couriered here in time. Just needs authorising before we order it. I've told 'em you're coming. You can't miss the place. Big yellow and blue sign as you come into Wudinna, on the left. We'll be following on, but much slower. The big fella can't get above thirty kph."

The 'big fella' grinned.

"I'm sure we passed the New Holland place on the way out." I said, once our saviours had jerry-rigged the spare battery to the van. My legs dangled above barely concealed wires.

"It'll be easy to find then."

It was, thankfully. After a long fifty-kilometre journey (it always seems much longer when retracing one's steps,

I find), we saw two huge tractors in a field at the side of the road, and the welcoming yellow and blue sign of New Holland on a pale green building.

The young man behind the counter gave a beaming smile as we entered.

"You made it then?"

"Yes, thanks to your colleagues. We'd have been stuck or else."

"Yeah. You don't want to be stuck out there," the young man said, nodding wisely. "Can get pretty warm on the road. So, I can get your alternator for ya. Thing is I need to know if you want the original parts or the generic ones. Those are cheaper, obviously. Then we just need the money."

"Okay. I'll have to ring the company and get their approval."

"Sure, go 'head." He pushed the phone across the desk at me.

"Howard? Hi, it's me again. Yeah, great. Well, not great really. I don't think we're going to get to Melbourne on time, mate."

Howard was surprisingly laid-back about the whole thing.

"No worries. This is Australia," he said. "Something always goes wrong. Get it back whenever you can. Now, let me talk to this Curtis guy before I authorise anything."

Job done we stood about wondering what to do next. The smiling young man came to our rescue.

"Okay, that's on order for ya. But look, it'll be morning by the time they courier it over. There's a caravan park next door. Why not book in there then bring the van back first thing? Nine o'clock will do ya," he said, looking at the clock behind him.

That clock read one thirty. It had read one thirty when we'd arrived and I was thinking that it always read one thirty. I looked at my phone, which said it was one fifteen. The smiling man glanced at my frown, then at the clock.

"Ah. That don't work."

"Oh, okay. So what time is it now?" I asked.

"Well, it's three forty-five, Australian Central Standard Time," he said. "That's South Australia, where we are now. But you're probably still on WA time." He paused. "Or Australian Central Western Standard Time, since you've come across the Nullarbor from Eucla. Eucla's three quarters of an hour ahead of WA and three quarters of an hour behind SA, in winter."

"Three quarters of an hour? Seriously?"

"Yup. It'll change again when you get to Melbourne," he announced, cheerfully. "They're on Australian Eastern Standard Time. That's another half hour ahead of us."

"Great."

"'Course WA and Eucla don't use daylight saving, so we're currently another hour ahead of Eucla." He stopped speaking momentarily. "That's an hour and forty-five minutes in total. So, it's just about two o'clock in Eucla right now."

My head was spinning so I excused myself.

I'd never heard of a three-quarter hour time zone before, nor a half hour one.

Australia is full of time anomalies, but the Central Western, or Eucla, time zone is the oddest of the odd. It spans just 350 kilometres of the Eyre Highway between Cocklebiddy, where we'd stopped for breakfast the previous day, and Border Village where we'd entered South Australia that same evening.

The old telegraph office at Eucla, which we'd also passed the previous day, used to employ people from both Western and South Australia. The one and a half hour time difference (two and a half in summer) between the two states caused problems, with WA employees working on Western Standard Time and SA employees on Central Standard Time. To relieve the confusion caused, the two state governments agreed a local 'Eucla' time zone, half way between the two. Unbeknownst to me, we had travelled through the Australian Central Western Standard Time zone for a whole day.

My phone hadn't known, and of course it mattered little to me, but as this whole trip had been like something out of the twilight zone, a three-quarter hour time zone was not so weird really.

The caravan park next door had plenty of space for us to park, and provided hook up so we didn't need to deplete the loaned battery which was, by the way, still sitting in the passenger side footwell, making getting one's feet arranged around it rather tricky. Although it was the same type of battery as ours, the loaned one was much bigger and didn't fit in the space below, instead hulking like some monster on the floor.

This caravan park was more basic than the one in Ceduna, but the showers were hot and the small indoor pool icy cold. I enjoyed splashing around and chatting with a couple of other ladies, whilst our respective husbands drank beer or read, lounging in deckchairs along the edge of the pool.

We hooked up the van and left the aircon on all night long for the first time. It was still sweltering, not helped by the fact that since we'd discovered the missing canopy, we'd moved our sleeping quarters to the space up front. It meant we wouldn't get rained on by bugs in the night, but the low, claustrophobic space above the cab was hotter than a sauna.

Day six: Tuesday 26th Feb. Ceduna to Wudinna 318km (100 of those repeated), 3 hours (possibly, depending on what time zone I'm in). Bed 11pm South Australia time – maybe.

A thirty-foot-high parrot

"Well, I thrashed you at pool," gloated S, the following morning. "I thought you were an expert?"

"In my youth. In my youth. I haven't played for years, and I swear that cue was bent. Come on, let's go see if this alternator's arrived."

The previous evening, we'd gone looking for a pub. The tiny bar attached to the camp site was empty and the beers were all bottled lagers, so we set off walking along the highway towards the main town of Wudinna. I'd promised our rescuers a beer that evening, not thinking to specify a venue. Luckily there was only one option.

Like most of the remote settlements we'd seen on our travels, Wudinna struggled to fit into the category of 'town'. There were a couple of shops and there was a large pub-hotel.

That bar had been empty, too, but we'd got a couple of decent beers and sat on stools near to a pool table. It was then that I foolishly challenged S to a game.

When I lived in London in my twenties, I was a pretty decent pool player – a result of many evenings drinking and playing pool in the local Irish pub. It had, as I admitted to S, been many years though and my eyesight is not what it was. I'm running out of excuses now so I'll just drop the subject, I think. Better part of valour and all that.

By 10.30am (SA time) we were on our way with a brand-new alternator, heading towards Kimba once more.

"Oh, look at that one!" I shouted, as we passed a thirty-foot-high parrot, sitting, pink-breasted and white crested, on the forecourt of a bakery.

Australia is full of these sculptures. Mainly made of something like papier-mâché over a wire frame, they vary from lobsters to kangaroos, parrots to koalas. Bill Bryson mentions a few in his brilliant *Down Under* travelogue.

The 'Big Parrot', and Kimba itself, is said to sit at the centre of Australia (presumably east to west rather than north to south). It was certainly an arresting sight for a Wednesday morning.

Beyond Kimba, the place names began to get embarrassing. Iron Knob got a snigger from both of us and I insisted on taking lunch a little later that day.

"I cannot eat my lunch at a place called Iron Knob. I'll choke."

"You probably would," agreed S, with an admirably straight face.

I'll just add that I'm one hundred percent sure Iron Knob is a lovely place, just, you know…

Our late lunch meant we hit Adelaide, the first city we'd encountered since leaving Perth six days and over 3,000 kilometres ago, at rush hour. For the first time, I programmed the satnav. Up until that point, we'd just followed Howard's sage advice.

We'd been seeing signs of civilisation for a while; cars, electricity poles, houses, dual carriageways, sheep grazing in a field, and in the distance, the Adelaide hills.

The satnav worked perfectly in the city – until we came to some roadworks. I turned left, following the diversion, but the satnav kept trying to get me to 'turn around' or 'take the next right' in order to return to the place where we'd deviated from its instructions. In the end we turned the thing off, navigating by luck and a raised damp finger into the breeze.

S took the wheel for our last stint for the day, and we arrived at Murray Bridge campsite just before dusk.

Our first job, after parking up on the gravelly carpark-like plot, in a neat line with all the other campervans, was to check out the pool. It was empty and deliciously cool, and the hot water in the attached shower block washed away the sweat and tears of a dangerous city

A thirty-foot-high parrot

drive. I decided I much preferred the emptiness of the Nullarbor Plain to the busyness of Adelaide, though I would like to return and visit the city properly – when we have more time.

I used the campsite wifi to contact Howard and give him the latest on our journey while S did the washing up from our tuna and noodles dinner.

"No worries. Bring it in Saturday if you like," he said in his laid-back drawl.

"But…you said you needed it for Thursday evening, then Friday morning…" I was lost for words.

"Don't worry so much. She'll be right."

Day seven: Wednesday 27th Feb. Wudinna to Murray Bridge 651km, 8 hours. Bed 11pm

West world

"I know why the pool was empty now," I said, as I met S on the way back from the shower block the following morning. "It closes at seven and we went in at…"

"Seven thirty," finished S.

"It's written on the gate. I didn't notice yesterday."

"No worries. We can say we're still on Eucla time."

I grinned at my hubby. "*You* are turning native, my dear."

On the way out of Murray Bridge, we paused for a photo opportunity in front of the town's namesake, the 1889 bridge over the Murray River. The narrow metal bridge was long, spanning a large meadow before reaching the river itself, and was held up on numerous tall columns. Cows grazed at its base and the scene was quite bucolic. The river seemed, to my European eyes, a mere trickle and hardly needful of a bridge at all.

We pulled in at Old Tailem Town Pioneer Village for breakfast in their car park. Time no longer meant anything, and our trip across Australia was coming to an end. The car park was full of ancient bulbous-nosed trucks in reds, blues, greens and, predominantly, rust. Beyond was a low wooden building; on its roof was painted, 'pioneer village'. I was intrigued.

"Shall we go and look round?"

The lady running the open-air museum was friendly, but the 50A$ entrance fee for the two of us was a bit steep for our purses.

"Come and have a quick look anyway. The boss isn't here at the minute and it's really interesting."

She led us through a back door into another world; a Wild West world.

West world

"He collected all the buildings himself over the years, there are over a hundred now, from the 1860s to the 1960s. And the vehicles too."

"Wow. It's like something out of the movies."

The dirt street in front of us was lined with wooden buildings which wouldn't have looked out of place in a John Wayne western. There was a church and a general store. A low-roofed shed housed a medley of ancient bicycles rather than horses, though I could see hitching posts in front of the store. A green pick-up truck sat further along the dusty street.

"The village was started in 1982 and opened to the public five years later," our unofficial guide told us.

I'd love to have explored more, but we still had a long way to go.

A little further on, we began to see the painted silos. The Silo Art Movement began in Northam, WA, in 2015. Artists were contracted to paint the sides of the huge grain silos, and on occasions water towers. The Silo Art Trail now boasts over fifty pieces of artwork across the country. My favourite was the first one completed in SA, in 2017. On a series of thirty-metre-high working grain silos at the side of the Dukes Highway, along which we were now travelling, artist Guido Van Helten painted five primary school children. The black and white images show incredible movement and fluidity.

"What a lovely way to make an ugly necessity beautiful," I mused, looking at a thirty-metre-tall child reaching up the side of one silo, his hair seeming to move in the breeze.

My 'unusual place names' game continued with Keith, where I insisted on taking a photograph for my nephew (whose name is, fairly obviously I guess, Keith). S vetoed me 'borrowing' the actual sign post as a gift which was, I felt, a shame.

"We have to have a pie, at least. We haven't had a proper Aussie meat pie yet and Keith is famous for them – according to that signpost we passed anyway."

Bordertown, a little further on, was also famous – for their albino kangaroos. That was our lunch stop sorted.

Sadly, the kangaroos had not been well-trained. They hid in their shelters away from the blazing sunshine while we sat at a picnic bench munching the famous, and delicious, Keith meat pies, and supping orange juice. As I slowly fried under the Aussie sun, I did think the kangaroos were the sensible ones and that, had I been albino, I'd probably be hiding too.

"Pink lake. We have to stop there," I announced, as we came to Kiata. We'd already stopped at a green lake and a blue lake (neither of which were particularly colourful) and I needed a pink one to complete the set.

Pink Lake, which gets its name and colour from the mineral salts which make it up, is not overly pink; neither is it a lake, but once more a huge salt pan.

Close up, the colour was on the dusky pink side of white. But more than anything, it looked like a vast ice rink. The effect of the sunshine on the salt crystals was blinding, the thrill of walking on the surface of an actual lake (even one totally devoid of water) incredible. It was another Australian wonder I'd not forget.

Beyond Kiata was an exciting find.

"It's the Big Koala!"

We'd seen the Big Parrot and had passed by the Big Scotsman, a five-metre-tall kilted bagpipe-playing Scot, just before Murray Bridge. A Big Koala made the perfect hat-trick.

Actually, this one was called Giant Koala. He was fourteen metres high, grey and benign looking, with a Mona Lisa smile and brown button eyes. I cleverly parked the van so it looked as if the giant mammal was growing out of our canopyless roof light.

West world

"Maybe we could tour Australia looking at 'big' sculptures," I mused, eating ice cream from the shop in Giant Koala's belly.

"Why?"

"Why not?"

S had no answer to that.

A little while later, we entered our third Australian state, Victoria. At the border, an official looking guard asked if we had any fruit on board. As we'd eaten the last of our Nullarbor peaches that morning, I said no.

"But why?" I had to ask.

"Fruit flies," the guard replied. "This area is a pest free zone, so no fruit."

I couldn't help but wonder who told a flying insect it wasn't allowed to cross the border.

The large red signs along the right-hand side of the busy dual carriageway amused me. 'Wrong way, go back' they screamed.

"They must have lots of country folk like us coming in from the Nullarbor," said S, grinning.

"Or too many confused Europeans. It says the turnoff for the RV parking is just down on the right," I said.

Our 'Map of Rest Stops in Australia', which had been left in the van, was on my knee. We had used this book to choose virtually every campsite or rest stop we'd found, and it hadn't let us down – yet.

"It says it's a few K on unmade tracks then there's a large parking area for self-contained vehicles only. It's a national park. Erm, Lederberg National Park. And the camping's off O'Brien's Road."

We turned and bumped along a road which had obviously been graded with a giant comb. It was corrugated in undulating ridges and extremely uncomfortable. I thought back to one of the 'do not do' rules for the camper. In addition to not driving at night, we were not supposed to off-road.

We were still bumping along at less than ten kilometres an hour as dusk fell. Now we were breaking two rules. Kangaroos appeared at the edges of the track and bounced in front of us.

"How much further," asked S, plaintively.

"I don't know. The map entry says its only five K altogether from the main road. We must have done that on this bouncy stuff. D'you want to turn round?"

"No. We'll go a bit further."

The decision was made for us beyond the next bend. A large sign was planted at the side of the road. 'No parking for 6 km beyond this sign', it read.

"Right, we'll stop here then," said S.

"What at the side of the road?"

"Well, it's not exactly a road, is it? And there's no one around."

"But it's not the camping area," I said, my unreasonable fear of breaking rules coming to the fore. I don't know why this happens sometimes – I blame my mother.

"Look. It says no camping beyond the sign. It doesn't say no camping this side of the sign," explained S, calmly.

Alone beneath the tall eucalypt trees, the kangaroos came out to play for us as we ate our Big Soup (from a tin) sitting at the back of the van watching their antics from our picture window. It was the perfect last night in our van.

Except that I didn't sleep a wink for worrying a ranger would come and arrest us.

Day eight: Thursday 28th Feb. Murray Bridge to Ararat 620km, 9 hours. Bed 10.30pm

Culture shock

We'd parked up in the last wilderness before the sprawl of Melbourne, and emerged the next morning unmolested by rangers or kangaroos. The idea was to get the van to its destination early that morning before making our way into the city to stay with cousin Gerry and his wife Jeanette for a few days. We were looking forward to some R&R after our long drive, but I was surprisingly sad to be leaving our travelling home of the last nine days and 3,626 kilometres.

"You know I could happily live like this," I said, as we drove into the beautiful gold and red of the rising sun for the last time.

"Like what?"

"On the road. In a camper. Travelling around Australia. There's so much to see, and I've been looking at relocations. I reckon if you planned it right you could get the whole way round doing campervan returns. There's even one down from Darwin to Adelaide. That'd be fun."

S, sensibly, didn't reply. He thought I was joking.

I wasn't.

Bento Boxes, Boomerangs & Red Foxes

By now we were entering the suburbs. We'd stopped for breakfast at a rest stop and cleaned the van thoroughly from top to bottom. I couldn't believe how much of the Nullarbor Plain we seemed to have brought with us; there was red dust in everything and on everything. We cleaned melted ice-cream from the freezer compartment and laid the remains of our packets of noodles in a cupboard, along with a lonely tin of tuna, for the campervan office staff. The end of a block of cheese and a single banana went into my bag. My quartermaster skills had been meticulous. There was very little waste.

The disgusting ten litre container of water we'd bought along the Nullarbor, we left next to a bin at the rest stop – it wasn't fit for consumption by anyone.

We arrived at the campervan office at 10.40am; just a day behind our original schedule. Given the adventures we'd had, I was pretty chuffed.

I showed the camper guys the leftover food and they thanked us for cleaning the vehicle. "You wouldn't believe the state some people leave it in."

"Must be a lot of work for you," I replied.

"It is. Disgusting some people. Here's your paperwork. Howard'll sort out refunding you for the battery and stuff. Okay?"

"Okay, thanks. How do we get into Melbourne City?"

I was sort of hoping for a lift; Ringwood, where the camper office was situated, was way out of town. No such luck.

"Walk that way and you'll see the train station. You can get into the city from there."

It was a long, hot walk that morning, pulling our two wheelie cases and carrying our rucksacks. Rosie's wheels were slowly wearing away, and she'd not really recovered from her Japanese ordeal. It seemed hotter still in amongst the buildings and the hustle and bustle

Culture shock

of a busy suburb. I was suffering from culture shock. I longed for the quiet of the Nullarbor again.

"Hi, two tickets to Southern Cross, please."

"You need a Myki card," the scowling woman at the train station said. "That's six dollars each."

"But we're only making one train journey. Can we share the card?"

"No. You need one each. You can use it in the city too."

"I don't think we'll need it again. It says here the fare into the city is only a dollar."

"Yes, but you need the card first. That's fourteen dollars total."

"That's outrageous."

The woman shrugged, in a bored manner.

We bought our Myki cards, the first of a veritable selection of travel cards that we eventually collected, but I couldn't help thinking the Japanese railcard was so much simpler, if considerably more expensive.

Thankfully, the train was quiet and fast. From Southern Cross, we were able to catch a free city tram to Docklands where Gerry and Jeanette had their apartment.

Cousin Gerry is twelve years older than S. He moved to Australia in his twenties so the cousins were never close, but S had been close to Gerry's mother and had visited his cousin in Queensland at the turn of the century for the millennium celebrations. We'd met Gerry and Jeanette again in 2014 for a fun, long weekend in Barcelona and they'd visited our house in Galicia the following summer, spending an enjoyable week partying with us all at our local fiestas. We were looking forward to seeing them on their home turf.

When we finally found the apartment, after seemingly scouring the whole of the harbour area, Gerry came down in person to let us in.

"Couldn't get the door unlock to work," he grumbled, opening an inner door into a plush lobby, complete with comfy chairs, walnut veneer, and a quiet air of exclusivity.

Their apartment on the 23rd floor had incredible views over the harbour to the Etihad Stadium (which was actually now the Marvel Stadium, the sponsorship having changed though the city maps had not), and the huge Melbourne Star Observation Wheel opposite. As night fell, we sipped a very decent wine (Gerry and Jeanette only had decent wine) and watched the lights come on over the city. The 120-metre-high Ferris wheel gleamed in an ever-changing light display. It was beautiful in a different way.

"You know, I think you jinxed us," I said to Jeanette, after we'd finished telling them the tale of our extraordinary journey.

"Why?"

"Saying 'What could go wrong?'."

"But I was just thinking of all the things that *could* go wrong crossing the Nullarbor," she replied.

"Quite. We survived to tell the tale at least. Cheers!"

Day nine: Friday 1st March. Ararat to Melbourne (Ringwood) 120km, 2.5 hours. Bed 10.30pm, Victoria time. Total distance 3,626km, 40 hours driving, 842A$ in fuel.

No worries, sport

Without a doubt we were staying in a most privileged position in Melbourne. Gerry and Jeanette's apartment (not flat, as I'd erred in saying on more than one occasion) had outstanding views of Docklands from every single, large picture window in the place. It was also an ideal spot from which to explore the city.

That first evening, Gerry had taken us on a walk around the harbour area and an early evening pint. It was an enjoyable wander round a lively area, and a perfect way to get our bearings. Early evening is when many of the bars have a two for one offer on beers. With the usual price of over ten dollars a pint, this was a great way to stretch our budget.

The bars were full of commuters that sunny evening, enjoying a beer before heading home to the suburbs. I perched on a tall stool, contentedly watching the bustle all around.

I nodded to the sun, reflecting on the calm water a few metres away. "This is the life, Gerry."

Gerry lifted his pint in reply.

The following morning, we woke in time to see a spectacular sunrise from our bedroom window. After breakfast, Jeanette gave us a pile of walking route leaflets.

"You can go off and explore for the morning."

Aussies, I've found, are nothing if not direct. And we were more than happy to comply and get out from under our hosts' feet. I was looking forward to exploring the streets of this city.

Melbourne centre is a compact area full of tiny lanes and grand shopping malls but its best feature for me was the free city tram, which we caught from just outside the apartment. One of the trams running on the circle line was a beautiful ancient creature, all polished wood and brass. Even the commentary was free as we passed landmark after landmark.

"Oh, we had an email from Howard this morning. They discovered the canopy was missing."

"What? Didn't you tell them when we dropped the van off?"

"No. Forgot all about it. Anyway, I apologised and told him to take it out of our deposit."

"It wasn't our fault."

"I know. Listen. This was his response; 'No worries. You were both good sports about the alternator. This new family are right whingers. She was screaming at me down the phone. Honestly. Can you imagine? I had to tell her to shut up in the end. Anyways, have a safe rest of your trip. Your deposit and the money for the battery should be in your account this week. Howard'."

"Yes, that wouldn't have gone down well. Aussies are laid back 'til someone shouts."

"Same with South African Aussies, I reckon. No worries, sport!"

Our first morning in Melbourne was spent exploring the lanes and the riverside. We meandered aimless, but happy. Later, we bought a couple of chocolate muffins and a soft drink from a Woolworths and sat next to the Yarra river to eat and people watch.

"How do you get this cap off?" I grunted, trying to unscrew the soda bottle.

I passed it to my hero and was astounded to find he couldn't open it either.

"I know. Watch this."

I stood up as two young men came towards us. They'd both been working out by the looks of them, and smiled as I approached.

"You two look like the saviours I need," I said, holding up the drinks bottle. "Screw cap's stuck."

No worries, sport

Both men guffawed, before bickering over who was going to sort the recalcitrant cap for me. Within seconds the deed was done.

"I knew you wouldn't let me down," I said with a grin, as they sauntered on looking proud and beefy.

"Flirt!" said S.

"Shut up and drink your drink."

By lunchtime we were hot, sticky, and walked off our feet.

"Would you like a swim in the pool?" asked Gerry, when we returned to the apartment.

"Oh yes, please. That would be great."

"I'll just put my shoes on."

"It's okay. Just tell us where it is, I'm sure we'll be fine," I replied, hating to be a nuisance.

"No, I have to come to let you in. I can sit and read while you're swimming."

"Oh."

My guilt at putting Gerry out didn't last long once I saw the pool room. A few floors below the apartment, it had views over the city and a 25-metre black-tiled pool. Beyond was a gymnasium, and through another door I could see what looked like a massage table. This place really did have everything.

We swam up and down for a while in the cool water while Gerry sat and read his paper, and I day dreamed about owning an apartment like this.

"We thought we'd eat out tonight," said Jeanette, later that day. "There's an Asian fusion restaurant nearby. Charlie is a dear. I'm sure you'll love it."

The food was, without a doubt, delicious; rich beef rendang, crisp twice-cooked pork, and tangy chicken stirfry. Everything was cooked and seasoned to perfection; it was a far cry from our campervan meals. The bill, too, was a far cry from our noodle meals in the

RV, and I realised those day dreams would stay just that.

§

"Shall we try one of those walking routes?" I asked, early the next morning.

"Looks like being another hot one. Is there somewhere cool we could walk?"

"What about this?" I said, sorting through Jeanette's leaflets. "It's a walk through Fitzroy Gardens and into East Melbourne. Should be shady with a bit of luck. We can get the free tram to Treasury Gardens, I think."

I was right. Fitzroy Gardens was delightfully cool amongst the trees.

"That looks rather English," said S, pointing at a red-brick, steeply roofed house amongst the trees. It had a brick chimney and was surrounded by a proper English cottage garden.

Cook's Cottage, the 1755 home in Great Ayrton, North Yorkshire of Captain Cook's parents (though Cook himself never lived there), was taken down, shipped from England in 253 cases and 40 barrels and rebuilt brick by brick in these Australian gardens. It certainly looked quintessentially English with its clay chimney pots, red tile roof, and English flowers - though I couldn't help marvelling at the cost and reasoning behind shipping such a thing across the world.

"Oh, I love this one." I ran up to a gnarled, dead tree stump, intricately carved with birds, elves and lizards.

The Fairies Tree, carved in the 1930s by author and artist Ola Cohn, 'for the fairies and those who believe in them', was fascinating to my inner child. I loved following the intricate designs and discovering the many different creatures carved into the old stump. We sat a while, on a convenient shady bench, just…doing

No worries, sport

nothing. It was incredibly relaxing after our busy few weeks.

An avenue of English elm trees was a poignant sight. They're just trees, you might say – but English elms were decimated in Britain after the small, but deadly, elm beetle rampaged through the country in the 1970s. Imported into Australia by immigrants in the 1800s, English elms thrive in south east Australia, and in Victoria in particular.

Since our trip, Melbourne has ripped out many of these elms in favour of native species. Whilst I understand the desire to plant natives, those magnificent specimens were some of the last of their kind, and I feel saddened by their destruction.

From Fitzroy Gardens, we made our way into the beautiful East Melbourne area with its early Victorian and Edwardian homes rubbing shoulders with Art Deco designs and newer builds. It felt as if we had transported the Melbourne sunshine back to 'good old England'. As I love nothing better than looking at houses and pottering in beautiful gardens, it was a delightful morning.

§

Thursday the 7th March was our last morning in Melbourne. It was a city I'd taken to heart: from the waterfront to the lanes, the bustle of the city CBD area to the peace of the Victorian houses, and from the beautiful botanical gardens to the stunning modern architecture, I'd enjoyed it all.

Unlike Perth, I'd not found Melbourne's architecture grating. Here, as in Singapore, glass blocks rose above the water and intricate designs acted as a foil for the sculptures all around. I definitely wanted to return.

In a fun-filled week, we'd caught a ferry to Port Arlington with amazing views back to the city from the boat, and viewed Melbourne centre from an ancient tram. We'd followed the well-designed tourist leaflets to discover a new area each day, wandering the streets, parks and riverbanks. We'd eaten Italian, Asian fusion, and Chinese (including our now ubiquitous noodle lunch at a tiny Chinatown restaurant). We'd drunk Australian beers and partaken of 'proper' wine tastings. And we'd enjoyed chatting to our cousins.

That last morning was spent wandering the city to Federation Square. A market was on in the area below the museum. We ate chicken wraps from a pop-up café and watched a display of dancing by a group of t'ai chi aficionados.

Back at the apartment, we repacked our bags, shared a last tea and slice of cake with our hosts and said our farewells.

The airport bus only left from the esplanade just below us but we still had to run to make it. Rosie was joggling along behind as I dashed across the boardwalk towards the waiting, bright red bus. Gerry and Jeanette stood near their apartment block, waving, and laughing as hard as they could.

We'd had a lovely time, but had blown our budget in Melbourne with fine dining and wining. It was time to get back to Workawaying.

The journey to the airport for the next leg of our adventure, was quick and easy. The short Virgin Australia flight left on time, and even landed early in Sydney.

Then things began to go awry.

Blue Mountains this way

Actually, I lie.

Things began to go awry at the customs check at Melbourne airport, before we'd even got on the flight.

My hand luggage had been sitting inside the x-ray machine for an inordinately long time. The operator, staring intently at his screen, was soon joined by two *compadres*.

I tried to angle my neck so I could see what they were looking at. Sweat was beginning to roll down my back as I tried to visualise everything in the bag. What illegal substance could I have inadvertently packed?

"There's a knife in here," said the first customs officer, eventually.

I opened my mouth to say 'no, of course not' then stopped as I remembered – my hand luggage contained my working clothes, ready for our next Workaway. The zip-off trousers had lots of useful pockets for balls of string, pencils, ...and penknives.

"It's in the zip pocket of the trousers," I said, sadly.

It was a brand new penknife. S had bought it for me from our local DIY store a few weeks before we left.

Bright shiny red with a nice sharp blade and no unnecessary gadgets, I'd loved it.

I watched as my new toy was tossed into the trash bin alongside the bench.

"Never mind," said S, giving me a hug. "I'll get you another one."

"I was looking forward to showing it to Jenny."

One of the things we planned to do on this trip was to meet up with Jenny and Dakota, our lovely New Zealand Workawayers. New Zealand hadn't been feasible on this occasion but when Jenny suggested Workawaying together in Australia, we'd jumped at the chance.

I'd found a perfect Workaway on a farm on Tasmania, but sadly the flight times from New Zealand meant we would see our friends for less than a day. I think it was then that it hit me just how far apart Australia and New Zealand really are. I'd been thinking in terms of popping across to Europe from Britain, but the flights were four hours, more like Brits visiting the Canary Islands or Africa.

It hadn't been easy to find a Workaway host who would take three adults and one pre-teen for a long weekend. The ones with more capacity were looking for long-term commitments, whilst the ones who would accept a few days' work only needed one person or a couple.

I did find a whole raft of possibilities for another lifetime of Workawaying though: from a yoga retreat to a working farm in the Adelaide hills, fruit picking to construction work, and, my favourite, a couple who wanted a house sitter for their property on a tiny island near to Melbourne. That position was for three months, involved watering the plants during the week and being abandoned on a semi-tropical island for days on end. It sounded idyllic.

I'd finally found a friendly sounding couple in the Blue Mountains, inland from Sydney, who were happy to

Blue Mountains this way

take our ragtag group. I'd booked the Workaway, Jenny had booked us a hire car, and we were all meeting at Sydney airport that evening.

Being a domestic flight, our Virgin Australia plane landed at a different terminal to the New Zealand Airways flight, so our first job was to make our way to the international terminal to see if our friends had arrived.

"Oh, no! The Wellington flight's two hours late," I exclaimed, looking at the arrivals board. "That's going to put us back a bit. I'll see if I can get the shuttle to the car village. Maybe we can get the paperwork sorted, then come back and collect them."

"Sounds a plan."

Unfortunately, I couldn't log onto the airport wifi. Instead, I rang the car hire firm from a pay phone.

"Aargh!" I yelled, banging down the handset. "I hate talking to machines."

S looked at me, no doubt waiting for me to elaborate.

"The stupid bot won't accept Jenny's code, and there's no option to talk to a real person."

"What about having a look outside, see if we can spot the right shuttle bus?" suggested S.

"Good idea, Batman."

Having nothing better to do, we wandered the shuttle bus area but failed to find any transport with the name of the car hire firm Jenny had booked. Defeated, we returned to our long vigil.

By the time the New Zealand flight finally landed at 8pm, I'd recalculated our journey time over and over.

"We'll be lucky to get there tonight, I reckon," I said, gloomily, after welcoming our friends.

"Don't worry, I'll ring the company now."

The telephone problem turned out not to be me; Jenny couldn't get through either.

"We'll have to get a taxi to the car rental office."

By now, it was completely dark outside and the taxi driver seemed to know even less than us about the whereabouts of the elusive rental place. His driving in circles cost our friend 41A$ and took us almost three quarters of an hour. So much for a cheap car rental.

"There!" shouted eagle eyes, S. Across the road was a lighted hut, on an empty lot in the middle of nothingness.

Thankfully, the guys were friendly and the car didn't look as if anything would drop off over the next few days. We collected our paperwork and hit the road. It was 9pm.

Our next problem was getting out of the city. We were disorientated after circling the airport for so long and there were no helpful signs saying; 'Blue Mountains this way'. I've often thought city planners miss a trick not having signs pointing simply east, west, north or south, rather than to some unknown suburb.

Having escaped the city, the M4 had heavy roadworks.

"I'm hungry," said Koty, as we finally exited the slow-moving traffic jam.

"There's a McDonald's," said S, to Koty's delight.

"Yay!"

I pulled onto the forecourt and we piled inside.

"It's still another hour or more to the Workaway. We're going to be too late to just turn up tonight. They'll be in bed. What do you think to stopping somewhere and arriving first thing?" I asked the group.

"I'm game."

"Okay."

"Sounds a plan."

I rang our hosts, who were more concerned about our wellbeing than our lateness, but who agreed an early morning arrival would be best.

Now we just needed a bed for the night.

That was easier said than done. The few hotels we passed along the road had already closed their check-in for the evening. It was like wandering through an accommodation desert. Then a bar owner suggested we try a motel, a little way up the road.

"It's 24-hour," he said.

Wary as I was about motels – after an interesting experience in Galicia involving strangely shaped shower caps and things that went bump, bump in the night, and where they are certainly not 'Motoring Hotels' – I was tired and would have slept under a hedge, had there been one.

By the time we saw the flashing motel sign it was 11pm and we'd all, one way and another, been travelling most of the day.

"Where's the desk?" I asked in alarm, as we all piled out of the car once more.

"I think it's self-service," replied Jenny. She pointed at a large keypad and box on the wall.

"O-kay. This is a first." I read the instructions, then read them again. I looked at Jenny. "Ready?"

"Sure, go for it."

"Right. Single, double, triple or quadruple? Quadruple's cheapest."

"We're happy to share with you guys."

"Okay, quadruple. One night. 135 dollars. Credit card, there. Key should be…"

There was a click and a thud from a nearby slot, and Dakota reached in and removed a key.

"Amazing."

Our room was clean, and downright bizarre. There was a double bed in the centre of one wall with a single one squashed in the corner next to it. A further single bed lay along the foot of the others, leaving just enough space to manoeuvre around.

To the right of the entrance door was a tiny kitchenette and, we discovered, the only sink in the place. The bathroom had a huge, incongruously sited bath, a toilet, and acres of empty space, but no washbasin. It was very strange, but it was also very late and we were soon all sound asleep.

§

"Come on, wakey wakey."

The hump in the bed groaned and rolled over, taking most of the covers with her. I laughed. "Come on sleepy head, we need to get on the road."

"I'll get her up," said Jenny, coming to my side.

"Nooo, Mum. It's too early," groaned Dakota, as the covers were unceremoniously ripped off her.

"Ten minutes, or we leave you behind."

We were on the road by 7am and arrived at our new Workaway by eight.

"I am so glad we didn't try to find this place in the dark," I said, as Jenny swung in the gates. "It's a busy road, and such an odd turn."

"The instructions are good, but I don't think we would've seen the gateway in the dark," agreed Jenny.

Jack, our host, met us in the large gravelled yard.

"You found us then?"

"Thank you, yes."

Jack led the way into a modest bungalow. It had two bedrooms and a bathroom to one side and a large crumpled living room to the other. At the back, beyond the open plan kitchen was a dining room with a second bathroom off one side and a third bedroom off the other. Behind was a sunny deck with a large wooden table and chairs.

"Right. Breakfast. You must all be hungry with that early start?" said Jack, plonking a large jar of jam and a butter pat on the table.

"We are!" we chorused, pulling up chairs.

Jack chatted to us about his home and life whilst we ate.

"Do you have animals?" was Koty's first question.

"We have a dog." Jack pointed below the decking where a scruffy looking mongrel lay. "And we have goats."

"Aw. Can I stroke him?" asked Koty, inevitably. She had been desperate for me to find a Workaway placement on a farm, but sadly it wasn't to be.

Jack harrumphed. "He's a working dog, not a pet."

He still let Koty say hello to the animal though. For his part, the dog thumped his tail madly at the unexpected attention.

Our job that day, Jack explained, was to build a shelter for his caravan down in the woods. It was to be made from galvanised steel posts and all the equipment was already on site. Jack himself would show us what to do.

"I can't do so much myself now, so it's good to have young people around to help out."

I looked around our group. Whilst Jenny couldn't be considered old at forty, only Dakota was genuinely 'young', and S was considerably older than Jack himself. It struck me, not for the first time, that age is about far more than the number of years you've been on the planet.

"Right, let's get stuck in."

That was one of the hardest day's work I've ever done.

From nine o'clock until lunch at one, we lifted huge galvanised steel 'I' beams into place to create a framework. Then we learnt how to drill into them for the huge bolts.

At first our drills sheared off the smooth metal and went whizzing into space.

"No, gently. On, off, like this," Jack said, demonstrating with utmost patience until finally we were getting the hang of it.

We took it in turns to use the drill and to bolt the framework together like a giant Meccano set, but even so my hands were cramping by the time we broke for lunch.

"We should get it finished this arvo," Jack said, over bowls of homemade soup and bread. "We've broken its back now."

Jenny looked at me in shock, and I shrugged. Workawayers usually work four to five hours a day, but we were only here three days and I was happy to get the work done for this welcoming man.

In the afternoon, Dakota amused herself with the goats while we continued sweating over the huge framework.

"Watch out for those," said Jack, pointing to where a couple of young billy goats were edging closer. "They can be a bit playful."

One of the goats suddenly ran towards Dakota, who jumped onto the truck bed, laughing.

By 5pm we were finished, both physically and literally. Our bodies were exhausted, but the new framework looked like it would withstand a hurricane. Jack was pleased, and I was proud of our hard work.

We'd spent the day clambering up and down like monkeys – swinging on rails and hanging off ladders on the flat bed of Jack's truck to reach the most awkward of drilling holes. It had been fun.

Whilst Dakota went off to church with Jack's wife, Shirley, the three of us hiked to an old tunnel Jack had pointed out.

"It's a great walk, but don't go out the other end of the tunnel. The bloke who owns that side is a nutter. He's been known to shoot at intruders."

Great! What an interesting place this was turning out to be.

The hike was the perfect antidote to tiredness. It was hot in the gulley – carved out of the hillside for who knows what purpose. The sheer rock sides were striped in golds and greys, whilst sherds of pottery and larger boulders were plastered into the rock face. I would love to have spent time fossil hunting there.

Nearer the tunnel, shrubs grew; brambles thick with fat juicy blackberries which we gathered and ate greedily. Inside the arched brick tunnel, it was dark and damp. The cool, after the heat of the sun, was a welcome relief. Bats flew overhead, water trickled down the curved walls, and the silence was complete.

We all slept well that night.

Sisters

The next morning, our hosts declared we were to have the day off as we'd all worked so hard. My protest was, admittedly, half-hearted, but we only had today left with Jenny and Dakota who had to fly home that evening for work and school. The prospect of a full day enjoying the area with our friends was too good to miss.

Many years earlier, S had been to Katoomba, in the Blue Mountains. He'd described the place so many times, I was anxious to see it for myself.

"It's not far," said Jenny, taking the wheel of the hire car.

She drove us first to the well-known tourist attraction called the three sisters. Three Triassic red rock towers, called Meehne, Wimlah and Gunnedoo, protrude above the deep Jamison valley. At the base of the rocks the landscape is thickly wooded, green and vibrant.

"Somewhere down there is the oldest known forest in existence," said S, pointing out into the wilderness.

I looked at him. "Explain."

"Botanists discovered some ancient, prehistoric trees, older than the dinosaurs. It's only a small area and the exact spot is kept secret."

"Wow!"

According to Wikipedia, the dwarf mountain pine (*Pherosphaera fitzgeraldii*) grows near to waterfalls where it benefits from the continuous spray. It is found only in the Blue Mountains, and only in a nine-kilometre (five-mile) stretch between Katoomba and Wentworth Falls. It's one of the oldest living trees in existence, being around in the Jurassic period along with the dinosaurs which would have towered over its stunted, slow-growing form.

I could easily imagine dinosaurs still living down there as we peered over Echo Point lookout to the valley below and the thin mist which swirled around us. The rock pillars floated above the trees as we stood with dozens of other tourists, photographing the forest below.

As it was a cool morning, we decided to descend the 300 metres (1,000 feet) to the bottom of the Jamison valley. The 998 steps of the Giant Stairway were too tall for my short legs. In steel and stone, some of the steps were definitely built for giants and I felt quite wobbly by the time we reached the valley floor amongst the eucalyptus trees, huge ferns, and the sounds of running water.

I gulped from my water bottle. "Wow, that was hard on the legs! I'll be getting fit if I'm not careful."

"It was fun telling the people going up how much further they had to climb, though," replied S, straight-faced.

"Do *we* have to walk back up?"

"No, we can get the incline railway from the other end of the trail."

"Phew."

The four-kilometre-long Federal Pass Trail was not arduous, being for the most part level along narrow earthen pathways and across metal bridges above gentle waterfalls. It was pleasantly cool, wandering along, peering at rotting trees and photographing each other in silly poses.

"The railway runs up to the visitor centre at the top of the hill," said S. "There are great views of the three sisters from its waiting platform."

Scenic World, who run the railway and the nearby cable car, also know they have a ready-made customer base willing to pay for a comfortable ride back up the cliff. The short journey was not cheap. It was worth it, though, for the look on Dakota's face as our train seats, facing back down the steep 52-degree slope, began to tilt alarmingly downhill as the carriage was winched up the steep incline. We were almost doing a headstand as we passed through a tunnel, cut into the hillside for the original coal and oil shale mining operation back in the 1880s, before emerging into the lights of the visitor centre. It was over far too quickly.

At Evan's Look Out, a short drive away, the mist had obscured the whole valley. The view beyond the trees of the park was a blank whiteness, unrelieved by any shape or form. Instead, we sat and ate our cheesy rolls looking at photographs of the spectacular view on a fellow tourist's camera. Their party had arrived just moments before the mist rolled in.

Sulphur crested cockatoos wandered the park as sparrows might in England, though much larger and more colourful to our European eyes. And to her delight, Dakota made friends with a rather tame crimson rosella which was soon, literally, eating out of her hands.

Our friends were leaving that afternoon, taking the hire car with them. S and I were staying a further day, before catching the train to Sydney and our fourth Workaway.

I was looking forward to the rail journey through the mountains, but first we needed another travel card to add to our collection.

The Sydney Opal card was similar to the Melbourne Myki but with different rules and regulations (of course), and bizarrely could not be purchased from the railway station itself.

"Hi, we need to get an Opal card for the train to Sydney."

"Not here. Newsagents sell them."

"But I'm here at the station."

"I can see that. But I can't sell you one. You can top up here if you have a card already." The assistant pointed at a machine on the wall.

"I haven't. I just got here. There's no newsagents anywhere near and I don't have transport."

Sisters

The latter was admittedly untrue, but could well have been. It took the four of us half an hour of searching to find a newsagent that was: a) open on a Saturday evening and b) had any Opal cards in stock. It was as well we'd been good girl and boy scouts – prepared!

A foot-operated handbrake

Back at our hosts' bungalow, the tiny living room was strewn with toys and balls of wool, and there was the lively chatter of happy voices. Shirley and Jack's kids were visiting. This was one big happy family and I was so pleased to have been a part of it, if for only a brief time.

"I'm sorry it was so short, but we'll definitely be over to New Zealand next time. I promise," I said to Jenny and Dakota, as they prepared to leave.

"Next year," replied Jenny.

"Maybe." I glanced at S as I replied, but he just smiled. Result!

After our friends had left, I turned to my hubby. "D'you fancy a pint?"

"Yes."

We decided to take a walk to the nearest pub, leaving our hosts to enjoy their weekend family time.

"You can't walk. It's too far," said Shirley, as soon as I mentioned our plan.

"It's okay, we like walking."

"No, that road isn't safe and it's almost four kilometres. Take the car." Shirley fiddled in her bag and threw a set of keys at us.

"Are you sure? We don't mind walking, honest."

"It's only an old banger. Go on and enjoy yourselves."

Outside, an elderly Toyota Corolla sat on the gravel. I volunteered to drive there and turned the key. The engine fired up and I popped the automatic gear lever into drive. We crawled out of the yard more slowly than I expected, even for first gear.

On the main road I tried to accelerate, but the car was holding back.

"It doesn't have any oomph," I said to S.

A foot-operated handbrake

"Well, it is old."

"Mmm. Feels more like the brakes are on."

We crawled along at 30kph. Cars and trucks whizzed past us in an alarming manner.

"Is the handbrake on?" asked S.

"There isn't one."

I parked outside a short parade of shops in the nearby village, and S bent to the wheel rim. "It's red hot!" he exclaimed.

"Oh bugger!"

We both spent some time looking in vain for a handbrake. I mean, how many hiding places are there for a handbrake in a car?

"I'll google it in the pub. Come on."

Over a pint I typed, 'handbrake on a Toyota Corolla', into the search engine and was surprised to get a raft of hits.

"I'd never have found that," I said, showing S the diagram of a foot-operated handbrake. At least it seemed I wasn't the only one to be fooled.

We wandered back outside to find the offending item – which was well hidden beneath the edge of a mat in the footwell.

"Well, that's that sorted. I just hope I haven't wrecked the brakes." I grimaced.

"I'm sure it'll be fine. The wheels have cooled down now anyway. Let's see if the other pub is doing food."

The second of the two, side by side, pubs had an extensive menu outside, written on a board. The battered fish and chips called to us both. I got a pint for S and an orange juice for me and ordered our meals.

"No worries, be with you in a bit," assured the barman.

The bar was lively. There were a number of tables occupied by diners and a further long table was laid in a back room. A large group of people were filing in and chatting loudly as they took their seats. It was a multigenerational gathering, with lots of balloons and glitter. I decided it was a family birthday.

To the side of our small table were a couple of the betting machines which seemed so popular in Australia. A huge green façade with a bank of buttons and gizmos topped by a TV screen, listed all the horse and dog races plus football and other sporting events. Its popularity had me thinking about the differences in gambling between countries.

In Spain, the favourite gambling options are the 'one-arm bandits' found in most bars, where drums spin and line up and winnings drop into a tray at the bottom in a fountain of tinkling coins; and the national lottery, where for a tiny outlay one could become a multi-millionaire overnight. In Japan, S had shown me the crowded pachinko halls; casino-like arcade game malls and gambling dens where bleary-eyed Japanese play for hours trying to beat the system.

Me, I never got beyond spending 2p on the original one-arm bandit at the fairground. I remember being disgusted that it ate my pocket money, and have never really gambled since.

We had long since finished our drinks, and there was still no sign of our meal. Waitresses were dashing about delivering food but we seemed to be sitting in a desert of desserts. Or main courses. I was getting hungry by now so I approached the bar once more.

"Hiya, do you know how long it'll be for our meals? Only we've been waiting an hour now and I'm hungry."

"Oh sorry, we had a rush on. It won't be long."

At 9.30pm, after many more meals had bypassed our table, and after I'd seriously considered tripping one of the waitresses just to grab the food she was carrying, one finally came over.

"Hi there, can you tell me what you ordered?"

"Fish and Chips. But wait a minute, are you telling me you don't even have our order cooking yet?"

A foot-operated handbrake

"Sorry, we've been busy," the waitress said, nipping off smartly.

"This is ridiculous. I'm going to complain."

As I stood up to go back to the bar, an older man came to our table.

"I'm sorry for the delay, can I get you another drink while you wait? On the house."

"No thanks, I don't want another drink. I do want my dinner though," I said, grumpily.

"A couple of pints, is it?" said the man, who I presumed to be the owner and who quite clearly wasn't getting the message.

"No thanks," repeated S. "I've had enough now. We'd like our meal please."

"Just a pint then?"

"How long will the food be?" I asked, ignoring his efforts to force-drink us.

"Erm, an hour? We're a bit busy you see. I'll get you that pint, eh?"

"An hour? We've been sitting almost two hours now."

"Yes, you see we have a party in."

"And I presume they'd pre-booked?"

The owner nodded, then made to leave. "I'll bring your pints."

"We don't want another pint, thank you. But I do want my money back," I said, through gritted teeth.

"Oh, well, yes, of course. But you can still have a pint on the house, eh?"

As we walked back to the car, me still grumpy and hungry, S said, "He wasn't for giving up, was he?"

"Probably never had a free pint turned down before. I hope Shirley won't mind us making a butty for supper, I'm starved."

S drove back with none of the problems I'd had. I guess not having the handbrake on (or footbrake maybe), helped.

Glowing in the darkness

I hadn't mentioned our little footbrake/handbrake issue to Shirley. It wasn't that I was hiding it, there seemed to be no problems with the brakes on the way back, but I was too embarrassed to admit I'd had no idea where it was.

Our hosts had been indignant on our behalf over our disastrous non-meal. Luckily there was plenty of bolognese left from our dinner the previous night. We'd tucked in, sitting on the squashy sofa and chatting with our hosts – righting the world in politics and discussing travelling. It was a most pleasant evening.

"So, what do you want us to do today, Jack?" I asked the following morning. It was hot and sunny, and we were raring to go.

"Oh, right." Jack seemed at a loss. "We've done the job I needed doing so you don't need to do anything, really."

"Thanks, but we're here three days and we've only worked one so far. I'd be happier if we did something for the food and board."

I like Workaway because you know where you stand, both as a worker and a host. Four to five hours work a day equals food and board. Not all hosts were as generous as the ones we had encountered so far and we'd heard horror stories from some of our Workawayers, who had seemingly worked endlessly for a scrap of food like modern day Cinderellas.

Eventually, Jack agreed we could stack some firewood for him. They were huge tree trunks, left to dry out in the sun. The logs were awkward, but we soon had a neat pile stacked. It was still only 9am.

Next, Jack asked me to clean a new pane of glass to one of the workshops. The stickers which had covered the new glass had left smeary, gummy marks. A bit of

Glowing in the darkness

solvent and a clean rag soon sorted that problem. In the meantime, S had sawn off the top of a waste pipe for a new disabled-friendly toilet the firm was installing. It was still only 10am.

"Okay, that's it. I'll take you up to the glow worm caves. Go make yourselves a picnic and get changed," announced Jack, when we found him at the front of the house.

"But..."

"No, you've done enough. I'm more than happy we got that framework built."

The glow worm tunnels in Wollemi National Park were a short drive away along flat, winding roads.

"It's an eight K walk there and back. You'll love it. I'll meet you here, at say, three thirty," said Jack, pulling up in a car park.

Opposite, a walkway led over a small bridge. In the distance I could see a few people hiking, rucksacks on their backs, walking boots on their feet.

"It's an old railway line for most of the way. Flat once you get up the hill there." Jack pointed at the line of red-coloured cliffs in front of us, before turning back to the car. S hoicked the rucksack of food and water onto his shoulders and we set off.

At first the path was gravelly and steep, through saplings and the heat of another lovely New South Wales autumn day. As we reached the line of cliffs, the path turned along the ridge. We climbed slowly and steadily before levelling out. To our left, the cliffs loomed, to our right, the path disappeared over the edge of the world.

We were now high above the road; the few cars down there looked like the matchbox toys I played with as a tomboy child. The path was sandy dirt and easy to walk on. Occasionally we'd spot a piece of railway equipment; a short section of line, a bent cart decorated with huge bolts, some welded piece of unidentifiable metal.

"I wonder what happened?" I asked.

"Guess they stopped digging for whatever it was."

Further on, large boulders had partially blocked the path. Above us, the cliffs rose in red, gold and pink stripes. Where a lump of rock had come loose and crashed to the ground below, the stripes became whorls and splashes of colour as if someone had finger-painted the rock wall. Against these, the grey-green eucalypts stood out, the sky so bright it was white hot. The gum trees hung at precarious angles over the sheer drop to our right, and a large lizard sunned itself on a flat rock ahead.

We shared that huge flat rock, eating our butties in the shade of a blue gum and gazing at the cliffs on the opposite side of the valley. Those cliffs had loomed over the car as we'd approached the car park; now they were level with our picnic spot.

"We've hardly seen anyone else. It's so beautiful. I'm surprised there aren't more people spending their Sunday enjoying the countryside here," I mused.

"Probably busy in the garden or buying up Bunnings."

As we neared the glow worm tunnels, the vegetation began to change. Tree ferns littered the pathway and the air felt cooler. The tunnels themselves were dark, the glow worms literally that; tiny worm-like creatures which were glowing in the darkness, calling to their mates.

"Oh, I thought they'd be like our glow worms," I said, after we'd got close enough to peer at the tiny creatures.

In Spain, what we call glow worms are actually a type of beetle. Related to tropical fireflies, the female has no wings but sits, bum in the air, on the edge of the roadside on a warm summer evening, glowing with an intense yellow light. The males, flying around looking for this light are, sadly, more often than not fooled by the brighter lights of homes and gardens, street lights and solar lights. It's said that in past times there were so many glow worms in England that one could read by their light. Now they are extremely rare.

These Australian glow worms were definitely more worm-like. They shone with a pale blue light and seemed to have the 400-metre-long tunnel to themselves. I hoped they were happy there.

Jack was waiting for us when we got back to the car park on Wolgan Valley Road.

"Thank you, Jack, that was fantastic."

"You're welcome. Now, if you tell me what time you need to leave, I'll give you a lift to the station."

And he did. It was a typically generous offer from this lovely couple who had welcomed us into their home. That home was comfortable and lived-in, full of love and life. Our hosts had been welcoming and laid-back. We couldn't have asked for more.

Introduction to Sydney

The previous day I'd booked a room in a Sydney hostel, online. It looked basic, but was cheap, an important consideration on a budget, and central. I was looking forward to a day exploring Australia's most populated city (Pop. 4.96 million) before moving on to our next Workaway in one of its suburbs.

The hostel, when we found it, was in a rather run-down area of the city. Outside, a group of drunks were begging for money. It felt a bit threatening, but our second-floor private room, though basic, had clean sheets and a large floor fan. We dumped our bags before hitting the streets with our new Opal cards.

At Circular Quay we finally got the fish and chips I'd longed for the previous night, with a pint included in the price. Nice. It was then that I discovered something about the Opal cards I really liked. At weekends, there was a travel cap. Once we'd spent 2.80A$, any further travel was free.

"We've already hit the upper limit with our train in," I said.

"Let's go on the ferry round the harbour then," suggested S.

We got our free tickets and sat back to enjoy the experience. By now it was dark and the harbour area was lit up brightly. The Opera House's huge 'sails' glowed white while Sydney Harbour Bridge competed with its own twinkling lights. Ferries, plying up and down the river, were illuminated around their hulls, and of course the city itself blazed with light. It was cool and peaceful on the river, a rather special introduction to Sydney.

Despite the stifling heat in the room, we slept like logs to the rhythm of the fan. I wanted a shower the next

Introduction to Sydney

morning but there was just the one cubicle for some twenty souls on our floor. The door was closed each time I checked back, so I had to make do with a wash in the tiniest sink in the world in the separate toilet 'cupboard'. Unlike our room, the hostel bathrooms left much to be desired; toilet paper littered the floor, which was itself awash with water. I was pleased we were only staying the one night.

Over breakfast baps, bought at a bakery next door and eaten in the hostel kitchen, washed down with our own (illegally imported) tea, we chatted to a young Glaswegian man who looked like he'd been hit by a train.

"Ach, I don't rightly know," he replied to my query about what had happened.

After a convoluted, and not altogether coherent, story, I gathered he'd been out with his mates and fell somehow, breaking a number of bones and smashing up his face. Where and how, neither he nor I had any idea. Tom was stuck in the hostel until he was fit to travel. He seemed happy and content, and the smouldering, sweetly pungent nub end next to him probably accounted for at least some of that contentment.

We weren't meeting our new host until 7.30 that evening so had the day to ourselves. Leaving our bags at reception, we set off to explore Sydney.

Our first port of call was the Royal Observatory. Built between 1857 and 1859, the building houses the metrological station, observatory, and museum. I enjoyed looking at the brass horological devices, and the views from the top floor across the river were stunning.

On our way back, a large heron-like bird flew in low and settled on the path in front of us. Oblivious of humans, and traffic, it sauntered across the road, dipping its beak every now and again to savour some taste or other. I later discovered this bird was an Australian white ibis, also known as a 'bin chicken' from its penchant for scavenging for discarded food in city bins.

Bangaroo Park was created from an old industrial site, the six-hectare headland space was filled with greenery, joggers, and high-speed walkers. I felt totally unfit in this city of beautiful people.

"They're tiring me out, lapping us," I muttered to S. "Is it lunchtime yet?"

We found ourselves at one of the many reimagined wharfs, full of workers enjoying their lunch break in one of the riverside cafes or sitting on the wooden steps. A Greek café beckoned us with its grilled octopus salad. Living in the land of octopus, Galicia, I was interested in how another culture treated this delicacy. Smoky and tender, paired with a crisp salad and balsamic dressing, it was just right for a hot day in the city.

"I want to see the botanic gardens," I announced after lunch. "It's interesting comparing the different ones around the world."

So far, we'd been to botanic gardens in Tokyo, Kyoto, Singapore, Perth, and Melbourne. They were, without exception, an escape from the bustle of the cities and I'd enjoyed gazing at the different exotic and native plants.

"I've been before. I have to show you the fruit bats. They're huge. You'll love them."

I do love bats. They are such clever, interesting, and maligned, creatures. Mum is still convinced they'll get tangled in her hair, and is terrified of them.

We have many tiny pipistrelles in our village, and the occasional larger horseshoe bat. These aerial mammals were living inside *A Casa do Campo* when we first moved in, to Mum's horror. We even found them sharing our bedroom on occasions. Over the years, as we improved the house for ourselves, the bats moved into the barns instead, to feed on the hibernating peacock butterflies. It was the ideal solution for us all.

Introduction to Sydney

But the fruit bats S wanted to show me, which had once hung from the branches of trees in Sydney's botanic gardens, had been ousted; a new road system had driven a swathe through the centre of the park, making it noisy, and a constant hammering from the myriad works in progress across the city started to thrum inside my head.

Maybe I'd walked too much that day, but I was pleased to grab our bags and head out of town to our next Workaway adventure. Carly had been friendly and chatty in our email conversations, and wanted us to do some painting. The 'A' team could do that no problem.

The 'A' team

We first got our 'A' team nickname from Jen, a friend in Galicia for whom we did odd jobs in the early days in exchange for a hot shower and the occasional Sunday lunch. We would arrive in matching blue overalls, wellies and baseball caps, ready to tackle any job.

"It's the 'A' team," she'd said.

"I don't think Stewart is much of a Mr T look-a-like," I'd replied.

Our train arrived on time in the Sydney suburbs, but there was no sign of our lift. I wandered back and forth over the bridge by the station, peering at cars and pedestrians until, with a squeal of brakes, a small car shot into the car park.

A window opened, and a voice called, "Sorry I'm late get in quick I can't park here it's not far to the house I've been busy hurry up hurry up."

The small, neatly dressed, grey haired woman spoke in a rush, her words falling over each other in her haste to get the next one out.

"What did she say?" whispered S. He was totally lost with his deafness.

Carly was an erratic driver; luckily the house was only five minutes away. She parked up on a gravel driveway next to a pretty bungalow set in its own neatly manicured gardens, we got the bags out of the car, and I wheeled Rosie to the front door. As I went to lift my case over the threshold, a screech had me almost dropping it in shock.

"Don't wheel it inside you'll scratch the floors take your shoes off no shoes inside carry the case don't wheel it..."

The 'A' team

"I wasn't..." I began, but Carly had gone, leaving me to tiptoe carefully into the hallway, carrying Rosie high above the gleaming floor.

Inside, the floors were all polished wood. Our large bedroom was showroom perfect, with white counterpaned double bed and polished surfaces – I was terrified of touching anything. The attached bathroom came with its own set of cleaning cloths and a long list of instructions.

"This is your bathroom keep it clean and remember to clean the shower after you have used it so the water doesn't stain the cloths are there the window is locked the key is here but put it back so it doesn't get lost and don't leave the window open if you go out remember to clean the shower every time you use it or the water will stain..."

Carly was in full flight again, and I could see S looking bewildered at the single sentence, rapid-fire instructions.

She led us into the kitchen. "Here are the cereals you can have those or those but not the other ones as they are mine you can help yourself to fruit I will make lunch and dinner for you is there anything you don't eat no good dinner will be ready in half an hour go and sit in the living room if you want or you can use the pool don't touch anything in the kitchen though because I know where everything is."

"Does the woman ever pause for breath?" asked S, as we escaped to the cool of the lawn out the back. "I can't get half of what she's saying."

"Don't worry, it's mainly don'ts. I'll fill you in later. She repeats a lot too. Dinner smells good, though."

Dinner was good. Carly turned out to be an ace cook. The salmon and potatoes with stir fried vegetables, was fresh and delicious. Throughout the meal, Carly kept up a mumbling monologue. Poor S couldn't hear her and I wasn't sure if her burbling was directed at us or not. The odd time I tried to respond she'd looked at me in surprise, so I concluded it was an inner monologue verbalised for herself alone.

§

We were up at seven the following morning to start work. Unfortunately, Carly's long rambling introduction to our task – which was a simple painting job we could have done blindfolded – took another hour, by which time I was flagging.

Eventually, she decided we knew what we were doing and wandered off. Another screech echoed around the bungalow.

"Now what?"

"My keys my car keys have gone where are my keys?" Carly was frantically sorting through a teetering pile of magazines on a hall table. I rushed over to staunch the inevitable avalanche.

"Maybe they're in your handbag," I suggested.

"No I never put them in there they are always on this table that's where I always leave them nowhere else where are my keys?"

"Are these them?" S asked, picking up a set of keys from the kitchen worktop.

When she finally left the house, we both sighed with relief.

"I think I've gone deaf," I said. "It's okay for you, you don't have to listen to her mumblings all the time."

"But I never know if she's talking to me or not. She complained this morning because I used a J-cloth to wipe the top. Apparently, *that* cloth was a special one which she dries in the microwave each time it's used. And it's only for wiping one counter, never the other one."

"Oh dear. The house is beautiful, though. And she's a good cook."

"And it's peaceful while she's out."

The 'A' team

We happily spent the morning cleaning and painting wardrobe doors. A friend of Carly's joined us for lunch so we were spared some of her monologue whilst we ate delicious three-storey sandwiches. It was just as well; the sandwiches needed all my attention.

In the afternoon Carly encouraged us to make use of her pool. Of course, this came with a long set of instructions.

"Clean the cover first or there'll be leaves in the water roll back the cover like this no not like that it will crease get the leaves out of the pool first there's a net there remember to re-cover the pool after you have finished…"

The water was cool, and the lawn a pleasant place to soak up a little sunshine. Carly produced another tasty evening meal, this time of seafood and noodles, then went off to watch her 'series' on TV.

As we weren't invited, and had no idea what she was watching anyway, we got out our travel scrabble and sat at the dining table.

"Yes! MOLESTED at seven down. Thirteen, plus fifty for using all the letters."

I couldn't believe I'd got all my letters out on only the second turn and was metaphorically polishing my nails. Then S started laying down his tiles. "CROATIAN. I don't believe it. That's another seven letters out. What's the chance of that?"

I heard Carly grumbling from the living room and winced. We must have been too loud in our excitement.

Kookaburra sits, (not) in an old gum tree

Wednesday the 13th March dawned drizzly. A fine mist coated the pavement and the pool cover. It was the first day since we'd arrived in Australia that real rain had fallen, and the coolness was welcome as we continued painting in the bedrooms.

After another lunch of towering sandwiches, we walked the short distance to the train station and rode back into Sydney. I wanted to explore the botanic gardens further.

We walked across Sydney Harbour Bridge in a steady drizzle. The river was slate grey and the Opera House, no longer white, reflected the louring clouds.

"The weather changes the whole feel of the place, doesn't it?" I said, shivering.

The first thing we saw as we entered the park was a kookaburra, not sitting in an old gum tree as I'd expected, but on an old wooden post, surveying his kingdom. At least that's what it looked like; he certainly had no fear of the tourists, taking his photograph from all angles.

"This is my best side," I imagined him saying.

A little farther on was another giant koala. This one, though, was a framework through which grew green leafy plants. He had pendulous lime-green lichens growing for his ears and his shiny black nose was a painted rugby ball.

By now the rain was really pelting down. My toes were cold and wet in my cheap sandals. Defeated, we sheltered in the gift shop before walking back to Circular Quay to warm up with a hot chocolate.

Now, I'm going to go on here but this is my pet subject so bear with me – or feel free to skip forward.

Spain, I am absolutely certain, makes the very best hot chocolate in the world. Spanish *chocolate caliente* is thick enough to stand a spoon up in, needs that spoon to eat it, and is rich and dark. I've tried hot chocolate in many countries across the world and have not yet found one as good. Most are watery sweet stuff which we call Cola Cao, or sweetened drinking chocolate. They are not for me.

In Sydney we chose an expensive chocolatier for our hot chocolate. The waitress asked us to choose a flavour from an extensive list then bustled away. It was warm in the café and my toes were melting as they defrosted, creating puddles on the tiled floor. Our chocolate muffins were delicious and I looked forward to the hot chocolate with relish.

Along came a white china cup. In the bottom of the cup sat a solitary chocolate. Mine was, I think, orange flavoured. A small china jug was placed next to the cup and we were wished a merry, 'enjoy', by our charming waitress. The china jug contained hot milk. Our 12$ hot chocolates, then, were a single, solitary, flavoured chocolate each topped up with hot milk. Oh well, better luck next time.

Okay, those who skipped ahead - rant over, let's carry on exploring Sydney.

Stormy weather

After a further wander round the Quays area in a steady drizzle, we topped up our Opal cards at the station ready for the next day, and set off back to our chatty, slightly batty, host.

The rain intensified overnight into a full-blown storm. S' first job the following day was to clear out all the gutters, which were cascading gallons of dirty water down the windows.

The rest of our working day was a repeat of the others, painting yet more wardrobe doors. Carly was planning to move house and wanted the place tidied up first. It was a pretty immaculate bungalow, to my mind, bar the incredible amount of 'stuff' everywhere. The spare bedroom, which we were painting that day, was filled almost to the ceiling with gym equipment, old furniture, and suitcases. Clothes spilled from every surface and what space was left was occupied by paper; newspaper, cartridge paper, coloured paper, and cards.

"I wouldn't like to be the one to pack up all this," I remarked to S, once our host had gone out.

It was another peaceful morning, alone in the house. Carly had left us the remains of the previous evening's cheesy pasta for lunch, which we enjoyed whilst watching the rain pattering on the swimming pool cover below us.

The stormy weather had reverted to drizzle by the time we arrived in Sydney that afternoon.

"Oh, look. There's an exhibition of carnivorous plants in the botanic gardens. Can we go?"

I've been fascinated by carnivorous plants since Dad showed me how a sundew plant trapped and dissolved

Stormy weather

a fly. I loathe flies – anything which eats them is a good guy in my book.

The Sydney exhibition was in a glasshouse with an interesting information display as well as many carnivorous species. Pitcher plants grew from straw bales over steaming pools of water to keep the humidity and heat high, whilst sundews draped themselves over tree branches. I had a great time.

"Rain's cleared, shall we go for a walk along the harbour?" asked S, after we came out of the steamy 'jungle'.

"Good idea."

From the botanic gardens, we took a pathway to Mrs Macquarie's Chair and along the harbour to one of those delightful Australian place names, Woolloomooloo. I loved the way some of the indigenous place names roll off the tongue in such rounded beauty. Their counterpoint with the English, Scottish and Irish place names dotted around the country is intriguing. It makes one feel simultaneously at home and yet in that most foreign of environments.

Two beers in a pub in Woolloomooloo cost us twenty Australian dollars.

"I think we'll stick to happy hour prices," said a shocked hubby, counting out his money.

A bag of crisps (or chips as the Aussies called them) caused an argument with a shop keeper. He refused to honour the discounted price, which he said was incorrectly labelled on the shelf. After his other customers joined in, enjoying, it seemed, being a part of a revolution, the shopkeeper gave me the crisps for the labelled price.

I'd once asked our Aussie Workawayer, Jarrad, if using the same term for crisps and fries wasn't confusing. "Ah, you can call 'em cold chips if you like," he'd replied. Clear as mud then.

"That was a success," I said, crunching on a cold chip/crisp. "Better not go back there though, eh?"

Bento Boxes, Boomerangs & Red Foxes

Once more we topped up our Opal cards at the station, ready for our trip to the airport in the morning and the next leg of our round-the-world trip. It had been an enjoyable few days with Carly and, we realised, the wettest since our holiday began, six weeks earlier.

Groundhog Day

Our flight to Santiago de Chile was not until 1pm but we left the house early that morning, after tidying our room and scrubbing the bathroom to within an inch of its life. Carly was meeting a friend in the city and we walked together to the station. She caught the 8.15 train, but we waited for the cheap rate, post 8.30am, train to Sydney, bidding her a fond farewell on the platform.

Although totally batty, and more than a little uptight, Carly had been a lovely host and we'd enjoyed our towering sandwiches, delicious dinners, and painting her beautiful home.

Despite waiting for the later train, we were still at the airport for our Qantas flight by 10.15am.

"I think I'm getting the hang of this self-service check-in," I said, as two tickets emerged from the machine, along with a roll of sticky-back label.

S laughed as I tried to peel back the sticky part of the luggage label to affix it to my bag. It twisted like a live snake and stuck everywhere it wasn't supposed to. An airline assistant came racing over. She snatched the offending tape out of my hand and wrapped it neatly around the handle.

"Humph. There used to be staff to do this, once upon a time."

Our last ten dollars were spent on two delicious Vietnamese rolls, and I pocketed the remaining eighty cents as a memento of our month in this varied and incredible land.

Australia had carved itself on my heart during this trip. We'd passed through four of its states, explored three of its great cities and a good swathe of the wonderfully deserted Nullarbor Plain. We'd seen blue mountains and dried pink lakes, intense sapphire skies, and more ruby red earth than I believed possible. We'd swum in pools across the country and dipped our toes in the sea. We'd visited giant koalas, giant kangaroos and a giant Scotsman, and had seen myriads of birds, insects, and plant species new to me. I wondered why it had taken me so long to visit.

"It's a long flight, plenty of time to relax," I said, as we boarded the Qantas 747 jumbo jet – the first one I'd been on in years.

"Oh look, we have a row of two, to ourselves," said S.

"Yup. I chose these specially. The only row of two seats on the plane. No one to push past when we want to go for a walk, and plenty of space to spread out."

This was our sixth flight of the trip, and it stood head and shoulders above the rest. There was so much space in the jumbo compared to the newer streamlined aircraft; wandering about during the twelve-hour flight was a joy, rather than an obstacle course of tripping over passengers' feet and avoiding oncoming trolleys.

The food was pretty excellent too, and Qantas made my sweet-toothed hubby's day when he discovered shelves full of Tim Tams in the galley at the back of the plane. He even woke me up to tell me of this wondrous discovery. (For anyone who doesn't know, Tim Tams are a chocolate covered biscuit similar to a British Penguin biscuit with various fillings, such as toffee, and are well worth being woken up for.)

Our flight left Sydney at 12.50pm on Friday the 15th March and landed at Santiago de Chile, almost half-way around the world, at 11am on Friday the 15th March. We'd crossed the International Dateline and gained a day. This is quite an amazing feat, and did my head in for the rest of that Groundhog Day.

"It messes up my diary, too," I griped. "There's no space for two 15ths of March."

Groundhog Day

Customs at Santiago was slow, and exceedingly thorough; Chile is almost as careful as Australia about what foodstuffs are admitted into their country. I watched a handsome Labrador on a lead sniff a young backpacker's rucksack. The girl turned to pat the dog, seconds before being led away to a holding room. The sniffer dog may have looked friendly, but it had a job to do.

S had collected some seed cases in Australia and, despite my objections, declared them to the customs officer who was responsible for sorting out the incoming visitors. This meant that he was shunted into the red queue and I emerged the other side without him.

This is where my careful plans began to unravel once more. I couldn't see S, or the line he had been pushed into, and we had no way to communicate. I held our only phone, which in any case was still not roaming anywhere.

I stood just the other side of the customs x-ray machines for a while, then went out of the door to see if he had exited from a different direction. I went back inside the customs hall and back out again like some kind of crazed jack-in-the-box.

I accosted a young officer and asked in Spanish if there was a different exit. I explained I'd lost my husband, and must have looked so pathetic that he immediately went over to his colleagues to ask if S had been detained. Thankfully the answer came back, no.

I collected our bus tickets, but was reluctant to leave the airside lobby in case I couldn't get back in. Eventually, worry won out over indecision and I walked through the sliding doors into the warm Chilean afternoon. Just outside, a huge crowd of men were holding up banners and yelling at departing passengers; "Taxi, taxi, madam, sir, taxi. Very cheap, very good."

And there, pushing his way through the hordes, yelling back; "No. No. NO!" was my S. I've never been so relieved in my life.

Of course, what came out was; "Where the hell have you been? I've been waiting hours."

"I came out of a different door and have mainly been trying to fend these guys off."

I hugged him, hard. "I've got our bus tickets, anyway. Let's go."

We pushed through the crowds towards the bus stop. A particularly persistent chap followed us.

"Taxi. Much cheaper. Much better service."

"How much?" I asked, feeling devilish.

"10,000 pesos."

"The *autobus* was 3,800 my friend, but thanks anyway."

With that we climbed aboard the coach for our journey to the city centre.

I love bus journeys. You get to see so much as they wind their way around, picking up and dropping off passengers. You see residential areas well away from the tourist trail – some interesting, some less than salubrious.

The greater conurbation of Santiago de Chile was busy and smelly. We passed through areas of dereliction and poverty, and other areas bustling with stalls – the smell of freshly frying *empanadas* filling the air. At each stop, people pushed onto the already overcrowded coach. They stood in the aisle and squatted on the edges of occupied seats. At one stop, a lady climbed aboard carrying a large wicker basket of fresh *empanadas* and fruits for sale. Somehow, she managed to push her way along the length of the coach selling her pies, before alighting at the next stop, no doubt for a ride back to the start.

It was like watching a movie. I felt like an observer to a different world. We had just travelled 11,340 kilometres (7,055 miles), to relive the 15th March 2019 in a totally alien city.

30,000 miles, I've roamed

Chile was the fifth country we'd arrived in since leaving our home six weeks earlier. We'd already travelled more than 30,000 miles on our journey around the world, and had many thousands more to go. I was looking forward to exploring yet another different culture.

"That'd make a good song, you know." I grinned at S.
"Go on." He sighed, waiting.
"30,000 miles, I've roamed, just to call this place my home."
"Ugh!"

Chile is a ridiculously elongated country, 4,270km (2,653 miles) long yet barely fifteen and a half kilometres (9.6 miles) wide at its narrowest point. Superimposed on a map of Europe, Chile would reach from the Arctic circle to the Straits of Gibraltar. From the Atacama Desert in the north to the glacier bound Magellan Straits in the south, and the long Andes Mountain chain which forms much of its eastern border, Chile has variety galore.

From the beginning, I knew we had no hope of exploring this vast country in the two short weeks we had there. I'd initially set about looking for Workaway placements which would at least give us a taste of different areas.

I'd found an interesting Workaway with a bee keeper in Valdivia that I really fancied. The town, around two hours flight south of Santiago, seemed ideal. We were off on our cruise through the Magellan Straits afterwards and would be half way to Punta Arenas, our boarding point. Unfortunately, all transport seemed to pass through Santiago de Chile. To go south from the Workaway was a mess of difficult links, so I had a rethink.

"Was it Valparaíso, you visited with the Merchant Navy?" I asked S one evening at home.

"Yes. We docked there six times in all."

"Do you think you'd recognise it?"

"Who knows? Why?"

"I've found a Workaway placement there. It's a lovely looking old house. I thought it'd be fun to visit more of your old haunts."

The accommodation I'd booked in Santiago was only a short walk from Los Héroes, one of the many bus and metro stops in the city. It was a hot and dusty trek pulling our wheelie cases and carrying heavy rucksacks. On the way, I was drawn to the street stalls whose goods spilled on to the pavement at our feet and made the whole experience one of dodgems as we weaved and jinxed amongst the crowds. The wide two-laned road was split down the middle by a long park, shaded by trees. The Chilean flag waved at one end, welcoming us to the country. I longed to dash across the traffic into the coolness of the trees.

"I think it's this road," I said, turning into a street filled with vendors selling fresh fruits. "Oo those avocados look good. And the grapes."

I handed over a few paltry Chilean pesos for a large bag of juicy grapes, then juggled them whilst dragging

30,000 miles, I've roamed

Rosie over the bumpy paving slabs towards an impressive, colonial style building.

Rodolfo, with whom I'd been emailing for a while, was a charming host. The Plaza Paris Amistar was a series of studio and one bedroomed apartments in an historic building. At ground floor level there was a concierge behind a polished desk, and all the rooms had a keypad entry system.

"You said we could leave some of our luggage here?" I confirmed, as we entered the lift. This was one of the reasons I'd chosen this hotel; I'd booked four separate nights here, spaced between our various trips around Chile, and it would be useful not to have to lug all our baggage up and down the country.

"Of course, you are welcome to leave the luggage here!" Rodolfo exclaimed. "Here is your *apartmento*. It is one bedroom. We upgrade you." He smiled, delighted with my surprised reaction.

Another reason for booking the Plaza Paris Amistar was its proximity to the centre of Santiago and the Plaza de Armas.

"Right, shower then explore?" said S, as we dumped our bags on the sofa in the small living room/kitchen area.

"I'm going to change into something cooler too," I replied, sorting through my rucksack for shorts and a vest top. "It's hot out there."

First stop was lunch at a nearby café. The *menú* was cheap, but I was strangely disappointed. I'm not sure what I expected, but the meal was both tasteless and lifeless. The salad was limp and the lasagne stodgy, sitting heavily in my stomach. At a nearby supermarket, I found that one of the notes we'd been handed in our change was a counterfeit.

"This is very common, sorry," said the shopkeeper, handing me back my illegal note.

I swapped it for an authentic Chilean ten-thousand-peso bill, and disposed of the counterfeit note back to the same café later that evening in exchange for two beers.

"It's pleasant just sitting, people watching, isn't it?" S said, as we sat in the Plaza de Armas, watching children running about, parents chatting, and old men playing chess at stone tables.

"Perfect."

We'd exited our hotel that afternoon, straight into a huge procession. In a foreign country, any large demonstration is a little disconcerting but luckily on this occasion it was a peaceful protest.

Friday the 15th March 2019 was one of the first worldwide climate strike days. Students from over a hundred countries took part in marches and demonstrations, demanding governments take serious action to halt climate change and protect our planet.

In Santiago de Chile, the marchers took up the entire roadway outside our apartment block, carrying homemade banners and chanting happily. The armed *carabineros* who escorted them that sunny autumn day seemed cheerful and relaxed.

Just six months later, those same students would bring about the fall of the billionaire president, Sebastián Piñera, and begin a coup which would see 29 dead, 2,500 injured and over 3,000 arrested in the *estallido social* (social outburst) which rocked Chile for over a year. Protests over increasing metro fares, inequality, and the cost of living, began as a fare evasion campaign in Santiago but rapidly escalated to the wholesale destruction of the metro system, demonstrations, and riots throughout the country.

It just shows that, as tourists, we know little to nothing of the underlying tensions in an area. Santiago seemed, to us, to be a happy city. It was as well I didn't know the future as we walked its streets that balmy evening.

We were late up the following day. Music had been blaring out from a nearby apartment block until after four in the morning, the noise of the huge aircon unit at the foot of our bed not enough to drown it out. After six weeks of early nights in countries which went to bed well before midnight, I'd forgotten how different Latinos are. We would have to readjust our body clocks to Spanish time.

By 10am we were washed, dressed and breakfasted, and had left our bags with Patrice, Rodolfo's colleague at the hotel. It was time to explore Santiago.

"Google says the Cerro Santa Lucia is a good place to explore early in the day. There're supposed to be market stalls all the way up the hill."

"Sounds good."

The seventy-metre high (230 foot) green hill, one of many dotted about the city, was a pleasant walk in the relative cool of the morning and the views from the top were outstanding. On the apex of the hill were the short octagonal, red brick towers of Castillo Hidalgo, a fortification built in 1816 during the *Reconquista* (Spanish reconquest) of Chile. There were cannons, turrets, and arched doorways as short as us. Across the city we could see the larger hill, or *cerro*, of San Cristobal. That one was on my to-do list for our return visit.

Of the anticipated stalls, I saw not one.

"It's getting hotter, fancy a sit down?" I asked, after we'd returned to city level.

"Yes."

"The Parque Forestal is supposed to have a market on," I said, weaving through the increasingly busy streets.

The park was a narrow triangular strip of greenery between two main roads, a popular picnic spot for the city dwellers. Couples sat on the grass, old men on benches, and a group of women did their morning yoga, legs in the air like a land-based synchronised swimming team. There was, however, no market, which I discovered is only on a Sunday.

Santiago was determined to prevent me spending any money.

We bought the third of our collection of travel cards at the metro station. The Bip (from the sound it makes when one tags on and off) was a cheap way to travel the city, though the ticket clerk tried to get me to part with double the amount of pesos.

"This is the wrong change," I said in Spanish, holding my hand out to the fat woman behind the perspex screen. Her eyes were too close together, her mouth set in a permanent snarl, and her blouse, which tugged at her ample bosom, had large damp patches below the armpits.

"Humph," she muttered, giving me a different, and still incorrect, pile of notes.

It took three attempts to get the right change, and I pondered on the various railway station employees we'd met on this trip. With the exception of Japan, where courtesy and helpfulness seemed to be innate, our experiences were not, on the whole, positive ones.

With our bright red Bips in our pockets, we made our way back to the aparthotel and collected our rucksacks from Patrice, leaving Rosie, and S' blue wheelie case, in store there until our return in one week's time.

We were off to Valparaíso to do some renovation work.

This old house

I'd first contacted José and Juanita back in summer 2018. Their Workaway profile showed a beautiful colonial, gable-roofed building set on a hillside behind a stone wall. The text said they were restoring their historic home. José was interested in furniture restoration so I immediately offered our experiences renovating the old sweet chestnut furniture, doors, and floors in our Galician houses, together with my special wax polish recipe. Alongside our other building experiences, it got a 'yes please' from our hosts.

It was a lovely bus ride through the suburbs of Santiago, the countryside between, and then the bohemian city of Valparaíso, or Valpo as locals called it. At the bus station, my phone was, of course, still not roaming anywhere. I had to resort to a pay phone to contact our host.
"This is hopeless, I can't hear a thing in here," I moaned. Amongst the barking dogs, shouting children and loudly conversing Chileans, I struggled to understand our host's Spanish.
"I think he said the car was broken down but he was on his way," I said, replacing the receiver. "Let's wait outside."
As we exited the station, a *carabinero* approached. Even after so many years in Spain, gun-toting policeman make me nervous. I tried not to look guilty as he walked towards us. Thankfully, he just wanted to warn us to keep an eye on our bags.
"*Muchos ladrones,*" he said, pointing around the busy concourse.
"*Gracias,*" I replied, sighing in relief.
José finally arrived by taxi, explaining that his car was in the garage awaiting repair. We jumped in and made

our way to the house where we would be spending the next seven days.

This old house looked exactly as it had on José's Workaway profile. Set on a hill, it gazed down from its lofty height onto the road where we stood. At road level there was a stone wall which rose some three metres above the pavement. Into this was set a wrought iron gate. José unlocked the gate and ushered us through.

Beyond, a stone path zigzagged its way up the slope. Parts of the path were cracked and damaged, and some slabs were missing entirely, but I could see it would look beautiful restored to its former glory. As we turned the second bend, I dodged to one side to avoid a rather large pile of dog poo. S managed to do the same and we continued on. To either side of the path were once glorious flower beds edged in stone and set within terrazzo stone terraces. A few magnificent palms survived, but in the main these beds seemed to be giant litter trays for the animals of the household. The terrace nearest the house had a pond set in it. There were lilies floating on the top of the scummy water, fighting the pile of leaves and debris which threatened to overwhelm them.

At the very top, we came out onto a narrow stone-flagged terrace enclosed by a stone balustrade. From here, to our left, we could see the whole of Valparaíso set out below us. To the right, along a sweep of sandy bay, was Viña del Mar, the next town over.

As I was admiring the view and getting my breath back, a bouncy black Labrador came hurtling towards us. He was just a puppy and desperate to attract our attention. I gave him a pat, and S rubbed his belly before José opened the door to the house.

"No, he stays outside," he said, as the dog tried to follow us indoors. "The other dog, he does not like him."

The puppy whined softly as we closed the door behind us.

This old house

Inside, the hallway was laid with dark, mahogany-coloured, polished wood flooring. There was a bedroom off to the left and a large high-ceilinged living space to the right. The living room walls were papered in a vintage, possibly original, forest green wallpaper embossed with a geometric pattern rendered by silver fleurs-de-lys. Two large shuttered windows let in the evening sunshine on one side, whilst double doors opposite led to the kitchen.

The kitchen itself was dominated by a large scrubbed table in the centre. There was a fridge to one side with wooden shelving units around and to the other a dark wood, almost black, unit, inset with a marble sink. It looked Victorian-era, and could have been magnificent. Another large window looked out on to more terracing at the rear of the house.

"It's a beautiful house," I said, gazing around appreciatively, and already planning in my head what I would do with the place – were it mine.

"Come. I show you the rest."

José led us out of the back door where we were assaulted by a large, friendly Alsatian-cross who jumped up, trying to offer me a slobbery ball to throw. A handsome black and white cat prowled along the balustrade, eyeing us warily.

It was clear that the house itself was not, as I'd thought, on the top of the hill. Beyond the terrace I could see through the kitchen window, the garden climbed another twenty metres to a final stone terrace. Off the lower terrace were three rooms, used for storage. Up half a dozen steps was a second terrace, with a washing line, and another room off to the right. This was to be our 'home' for the week.

More steps climbed to the top terrace with views over the rooftops towards the coast and more stone-edged flower beds. These beds held a magnificent fig tree, heavy with fruit, a couple of lemon trees, ancient roses, and more dog poo than I wanted to imagine. On the roof of one of the buildings, a grey Siamese cat stretched out, content and relaxed.

"We will have dinner when Juanita returns from work. I leave you now to relax." With that José disappeared into the house, leaving us alone.

"It's a gorgeous house but it'll be so much work to bring it back to what it deserves," I breathed, pushing open the door to our room.

The room was dominated by a double bed with a colourful quilt on it. On the black and white tiled floor there was a small sofa, a night stand, and a wooden shelf. A wide, dark mahogany doorway led to a bathroom with an old cast iron bath and Victorian style toilet.

"Well, looks okay to me," said S, sitting on the bed.

A cloud of animal hair rose from the quilt as he plonked himself down.

"Oops!"

I sneezed in response. "We'd better go down."

José and Juanita were vegetarians. Dinner was a tasty lentil stew accompanied by a thick grained bread.

"Delicious Juanita, thank you," I said, after we'd washed up and made tea for everyone. "So, what is the plan for tomorrow?"

"Tomorrow is Sunday, there is no work," replied José.

"Oh, I thought as we'd just arrived..."

"We work only the days of the week. You can visit Valparaíso. I have a map for you."

"Oh, great. Thank you."

We got up to return to our room when a thought struck me. "Is there a key for our room, José? Only the door doesn't close well and I think the cats sleep in there."

"Ah. No, no key."

"Okay. Goodnight."

This old house

I love all animals but am allergic to their dander so prefer to keep my bedroom an animal-free zone. We already knew the animals visited the room from the quantity of fur lying around on the floor and the bed. As I pushed open the door, which was ajar, my fears were confirmed. In the centre of our bed was the Siamese cat I'd seen sunning itself earlier.

"Hello, beautiful. You can't sleep in here I'm afraid," I said, going over to stroke her. (I know, I'm allergic, but what can you do when a friend wants to be made?) "Oh. She's only got one eye."

Indeed, the cat's left eye shone brightly but where her right one should have been, there was a sewn-up slit. She seemed not inconvenienced by her disability and stalked out of the open door as the Alsatian dog bounded in.

"Oh no. We're going to have to do something or we'll be sleeping with the whole menagerie."

S stuck one of the chairs under the doorknob and we settled down to a symphony of scratching and a low whining from outside.

Streets broad and narrow

José had told us they had a lie in on a Sunday after a busy working week. We waited until 9am to go down for breakfast, but the house was deserted and the bedroom door firmly closed. There was bread, soft cheese and avocados set out on the kitchen table. We helped ourselves and made a welcome cuppa as we revised our plans for the day.

"José's map looks a good start," I said. "You've been to Valpo before, you can be our guide."

"Very funny. It was a long time ago; 1968 the last time, I think. We docked right in the harbour."

"Did you explore much?"

"Erm, not really. We only went in one bar. It was right opposite the docks."

"And?"

"There were ladies."

"Ladies?"

"Well, one lady."

"Oh, yes?"

I was intrigued. S rarely talked about his personal past and I enjoyed his stories when he did. On this occasion he remained silent, though. I guessed this was not the day for big revelations.

"I wonder if you'll recognise anything?"

"I didn't do so well in Japan."

"That's true. Ready to go?"

José had told us that the *microbús* into Valpo stopped at the bottom of the road and cost just 400clp (Chilean pesos), around forty cents. He also warned us to beware of drivers charging foreigners extra, and of not giving out tickets.

"That way they keep the fare for themselves," he'd said.

Streets broad and narrow

Forewarned, we arrived in Valparaíso with no problems. The little bus amused me. It was full to bursting with elderly ladies carrying baskets and youngsters dressed in the latest fashions. At regular intervals, someone would climb on board to sell chocolate bars, drinks, and other goods. It was a novel way of shopping, and very handy if one was in need of sustenance on the fifteen-minute hop to the city.

"So, the port. You must recognise this," I said.

We were standing in a large open plaza where a market was in full swing. In front of us two tall white towers framed a view of the sea. The other three sides of the square were bounded by magnificent old colonial style buildings and newer, clunky office blocks. A glass tower block glowed deep blue reflecting the bright sky. Older buildings were classical style; painted render with high, evenly spaced windows set into stone lintels. One was pink and red candy striped, another vanilla ice-cream white. A recently renovated historic building was pale blue, the stone features picked out in cream.

Between the plaza and the road was a large, white stone monument. On its plinth were ten-foot-tall figures depicted in black.

"It looks like a mausoleum. You must remember that."

"I think I do but..."

"But what?"

"The harbour seems further away. I'm sure when we got off the ship, we could see that statue closer up."

"I don't think the sea can move." I laughed. "Or this monument. It's huge. Maybe there're just more buildings than before. I'm sure these office blocks are younger than the sixties." I pointed at the blue glass building.

S didn't seem convinced.

"Or your eyesight was better," I joked.

"Let's head uphill," replied S.

Valparaíso is basically a series of hills rising out of the sea, its housing and infrastructure adapted to the terrain. UNESCO calls the World Heritage Site of the Historic Quarter; 'An excellent example of late 19th century urban and architectural development in Latin America,' with; 'A well-preserved industrial infrastructure such as the numerous 'elevators' on steep hillsides.' The square where the market was taking place, Plaza Sotomayor, was the last flat area we saw that day.

José had said to look for the funicular railway to take us to the top of the hill. "It's cheap," he'd said. "And better than walking."

We walked.

Not because we wanted to get fit. Nor to prove anything. Not even because we were too mean to buy a ticket. No, we walked because we totally failed to spot the entrance to the funicular railway which was housed in one of the old classical buildings off the plaza.

Still, it was an interesting walk, winding through streets broad and narrow, cobbled and tarmacked. We passed shops and cafes, dogs sunning themselves on warm paving slabs and cats sitting in shop doorways as if they owned the place (which they probably did). And throughout the various streets were paintings – graffiti if you like, but what magnificent graffiti: colourful flowers rising up the side of a house, cartoon cats, elderly ladies with their hair tied in a bun, and a plethora of weird and wonderful faces. There were golden angels melting like spilled honey, intricate drawings of Valpo itself and a huge green and blue chameleon staring out from a wooden shed. It made the place seem alive and vibrant.

From the balconied street at the top of the hill, there was another magnificent view down to the harbour and the colourful town of Valparaíso rising up all around us. Buildings glowed blue, pink, and yellow, hundreds of

Streets broad and narrow

them, climbing the hillsides to the very top of the highest pinnacle.

We found the entrance to Ascensor El Peral at the top and jumped on for the two-minute, forty-metre, ride back down to the plaza.

There were thirty or more (no one seems to know for sure) funicular railways built in Valparaíso in the late 1800s and early 1900s to transport residents up to the higher *barrios* of the city. Of those, sixteen are still in use. Concepción is the oldest, built in 1883, whilst El Peral, built in 1902, was the first to use steam traction.

"They're beautiful, aren't they?" I said, wistfully. "I love well-preserved old things – just like you, *dar-link*."

S ignored me.

Back at harbour level we found a place for lunch.

"That's not a *churrasco* as we know it!" I exclaimed.

The plate in front of me was filled with a large, soft bread bun dripping with guacamole, topped with a thick meat patty and smeared with mayonnaise. The guacamole had soaked into the bread making it impossible to pick up.

I was forced to remember that much as England and the USA are two countries separated by a common language, so are Spain and much of South America. In Galicia, the word *churrasco* refers to a large mixed grill of pork ribs, beef fillet and *chorizo* style sausages – nothing like this Chilean version.

Still, my odd meal tasted okay and we enjoyed watching the world go by as we ate.

"Shall we look at the harbour itself? Maybe you'll recognise that."

"Haha."

UNESCO calls Valparaíso's harbour; 'An exceptional testimony to the early phase of globalisation as a leading commercial port on the sea routes of the Pacific coast of South America.'

In the 18th century, Valparaíso was the first, and most important, seaport for the western coast of Latin America. Merchant ships would sail between the Atlantic and Pacific, through the Magellan Straits, calling at this bustling port to load and unload goods. When the Panama Canal opened in 1914, development slowed in Valparaíso, leaving the port preserved in its early 20th-century state.

That day, the harbour was full of small, brightly coloured fishing boats and tourist sightseeing ferries; a towering cruise ship rose above them looking like a giant in a Lilliputian world. Huge derricks and a dirty blue-black coloured tanker ship delineated the working area of the docks. On the harbour front, people sat on concrete seats or wandered in the sunshine. A puppet show was setting up, the man enacting all the voices for his collection of puppets, delighting children and adults alike.

Inside the harbour building was a shopping mall, and alongside the doorway was an old black and white picture blown up to over four metres square. It was a photograph of the dock area, the large monument to the heroes of Iquíque in the square clearly visible in the background.

"Hey, look at this," I shouted to S.

We both peered at the picture. "The perspective looks off," I said. "The docks look much closer to that statue, and there's no road between it and the harbour area."

"That's what I said."

"Hmm. Your memory might be right for once. Look, it says here that the wharf area was built out over previous sea land."

In fact, the first passenger wharf at Valparaíso was built over the top of a stranded frigate, which was beached in 1825. It has been adapted and changed numerous times since. Whilst researching this piece, I couldn't find any specific record of alterations since the

Streets broad and narrow

1960s. Maybe my hubby's memory was wrong after all, or maybe it wasn't. Who knows?

It was 7pm by the time we walked back up the hill that evening. The house was still deserted. A pan of soup sat warming on the stove and bread had been left out for us. We ate soup and drank our imported tea. And we played scrabble until it was too dark to see, before retiring to our room to read.

Hi ho, hi ho, it's off to work we go

"Aitishoo." I was sneezing madly and my sinuses were flowing freely by the time I woke up the next morning. "We're going to have to do something about these animals," I said miserably, through red, puffy eyes.

"Never mind, Sneezy. I'll sort out a way to bar the door from the outside. Then I'll mop the room this afternoon when we finish work, to get rid of the fur."

"First though, 'hi ho, hi ho, it's off to work we go', says Sneezy." I grinned and sneezed again. "C'mon, Happy."

We'd been here a day and a half now and I was aware that we had yet to earn our keep. In addition to reroofing an old shed, José wanted us to clean a couple of old and heavily varnished wooden doors.

"Do you have sandpaper?" I asked him.

"Yes, here. And I have this paint remover too."

I looked at the sandpaper, and read the label on the paint stripper.

"We have used this product before on old varnish and it is very bad. It makes the varnish sticky and impossible to remove. Sandpaper is better, but we will need a much rougher grade. *Más grueso*," I explained.

If there's one thing we're experienced in, it's removing old paint and varnish from wood.

Galicians seemed to delight in painting layers and layers of, usually blue, paint onto every wooden surface. Mum had stripped so many doors for her cottage, *A Casita*, that she swore she never wanted to see another 'Galician blue' door, ever.

"We should have brought Mum along," I mused.

"Ask if he has any old glass," said S, no doubt thinking of his favourite weapon in the fight against ancient paint.

Not only had poor Mum had to strip the cottage doors by hand, but S insisted that pieces of glass made the

Hi ho, hi ho, it's off to work we go

best scrapers. They did, but I had been more than a little concerned about the health and safety aspect: elderly parent + sharp glass = an accident waiting to happen. Thankfully, Mum, and the doors, survived. And they all look right at home in the renovated cottage.

José said he would buy more sandpaper on his way to work, and asked us to sweep the terraces and tidy up the leaves and rubbish littering the place in the meantime. I was happy to get stuck in to some work.

"These inset tiles are quite beautiful you know," I said, brushing leaves from the tiny Italian terrazzo floor tiles.

"It must have looked incredible during its heyday."

"Oh yuk!" My brush had swept up something soft, and a tell-tale stink rose from the tiles. "That's disgusting!"

The piles of dog poo were not confined to the flower beds, which S was diligently clearing, but hidden under the piles of leaves too.

"Some of this has been here for months. Don't they ever clean up?" I asked, through dry heaves.

I'm not good with poo, and especially not someone else's animal poo.

"Probably they're too busy," replied S.

We hosed down the terraces and watered the poor neglected palm trees. S bagged the poo and put the bags at the bottom of the steps ready for José to remove them. Those bags remained there for the rest of our stay.

I understood that these kind and friendly people were busy and worked long hours, but I couldn't understand anyone allowing their animals to foul such a beautiful spot.

"I don't think they think like that," said S, when I expressed my distaste. "They obviously don't walk the dogs, and probably don't have time to tidy up after them. You can hardly ask a dog to poo in a bag."

"I don't think clearing it is something you should ask Workawayers to do either," I responded. "I'm going to make a start on that door with what we have. I'm not shovelling any more shit."

With that, I stalked up the back stairs to ferociously attack the first door. S, more sanguine than I, finished the job we had been asked to do and diligently tidied up every piece of excrement he could find. The terraces looked something like their original selves by the time he'd finished. It was a shame that the first thing the black Labrador puppy did in his excitement at seeing S, was squat on the newly cleared path.

After a quick lunch of leftover lentil soup, we set off for the beach.

This Workaway had to be in one of the best spots ever. Just a few minutes bus ride from Valpo in one direction and Viña del Mar in the other, it was also a ten-minute walk to a long beach of golden sand and violent breakers. We spent most afternoons topping up our tans and reading, and I could almost forgive our hosts the animal shit for this magnificent location.

Once more the house was deserted when we got back. While S cleaned and mopped our room, I concocted a meal of left-over rice and vegetables from the many Tupperware containers in the fridge. It seemed that Juanita made one large meal at the weekend which was reincarnated each weekday until it ran out. It was a filling supper, and I won at scrabble so the day ended well.

§

"I slept better," I said the following morning, yawning.

"Did it do the trick?"

"Yes. Thank you, *dar-link*." I kissed my husband on the nose and jumped out of bed. "Crikey, it's cold in a morning."

"It is autumn, I suppose."

In the house there was silence again.

Hi ho, hi ho, it's off to work we go

"This is starting to feel like the Marie Celeste," I said, over avocado on toast.

"It's peaceful," replied S, always one for a quiet life.

"Hmm. True. And I could get used to this *'palta'* for breakfast."

José had left us a roll of heavy-duty sandpaper on the kitchen table and we spent the morning sanding and scraping varnish from the old doors. The intricate mouldings were especially difficult to clean, and S' pieces of broken glass, discovered whilst cleaning the terraces, were well used.

I heated soup for lunch, which we ate with left over salad. The gas popped out before the soup was quite ready so we had to forgo our cup of tea.

"Disaster. I hope José gets another gas bottle before tonight."

"Beach?"

"Definitely."

The beach was quiet. We laid out towels and read our books. I briefly pondered the damage sand could do to a Kindle as a little storm blew in and scoured our position, but it seemed to be functioning okay.

The Kindle was my present to myself before this holiday. I'd never really wanted an electronic book, loving the feel, smell, and even the sound of a paper book. There was one big drawback, though – I read quickly. When we visited Costa Rica for twelve days, I took four books; I read those, and the two S had taken, in not much more than an hour a day. Half of my luggage for this eight-week trip was going to be books. I took the plunge and bought a Kindle. It felt weird to be holding so many novels in my hands and it didn't evoke the same feeling in me as a paperback, but boy did it lighten my luggage.

After an hour reading and watching the huge rollers, we walked a little way along the road towards the fish market. The stalls were all shuttered this late in the afternoon but the odour pervaded the whole area, attracting all the cats and dogs in the neighbourhood – and more than a few seagulls.

"You know, I'm getting stodge cravings," I said on the walk back. "There's lots of lentils, but I'm missing my pies and cheese butties."

"What do you have in mind?" asked S.

I pointed.

In front of us was a tiny wooden shack. Large painted letters on its side declared '*empanadas de queso, 1000clp*'. Inside, a short round lady in an enormous apron was busily frying large pasties in a deep fat fryer. The smell of hot melting cheese and lardy pastry was going to my head.

"Chilean cheese pasty?" I asked.

We sat on a conveniently placed bench, timidly nibbling off the ends of the tea plate sized pasties to let some of the steam escape. A long string of cheese attached itself to my tongue and I screeched as it scorched its way down.

"These are so good," I mumbled, round another carefully nibbled mouthful.

"Mmm, not bad."

That was high praise indeed from my undemonstrative hubby.

"I love the crispy pastry. Feels like my arteries are hardening instantly with all that lovely cholesterol."

"They're definitely good value," commented S, wiping his greasy hands on his shorts and shaking the crumbs on to the floor for the nearest dog.

"About a euro? Rather! No waste either."

The recipient of our crumbs, a scruffy, mottled mongrel, obviously felt he needed to work for his lunch by escorting us home. He walked just in front of us all the way along the busy road to the pedestrian overpass, which would take us across five lanes of traffic back to

Hi ho, hi ho, it's off to work we go

our Workaway home. There he sat, panting and watching us as we waved goodbye.

We both had showers to wash away some of the wind-driven sand before making our way to the house. It was, once again, empty. But the gas was back on, so someone had been home. I made tea, and stir fried some of the left-over rice from the fridge. No one appeared as we played scrabble that evening.

Two pints (of beer) and a packet of crisps, please

For the first time in days, we caught up with José. He came to our workspace, on the top terrace in the shade of the newly reroofed shed, armed with various grades of sandpaper.

"Oh thanks, José. That will help."

"How is it?" he asked.

"Going slowly," I replied. "The varnish is very thick and difficult to remove."

He pointed at the half-finished door. "This is complete, no?"

I was horrified. "No, no. It's not finished. See, we have to clean the varnish from in the grooves here. And to sand it smooth. It's still very rough."

José seemed disappointed.

"I thought he did furniture restoration," I said to S, once our host had gone.

"I don't think so. Or at least he may want to, but I don't think he's ever done anything like this before."

"Hmm. I hope he's happy with the end result. I think he expected us to have done more by now."

"We can only do what we can do," replied S, philosophically. "I'd rather do a proper job slowly than a poor, rushed one."

"True."

We bent to our tasks and had the first sides cleaned and sanded to a silky smoothness by lunchtime.

For a change, both Juanita and José were home for lunch – a tasty *tortilla de patatas* (potato omelette) with TVP (textured vegetable protein) and tomatoes.

"How do you like Valpo?" asked Juanita.

Two pints (of beer) and a packet of crisps, please

"Love it!" I said, through a mouthful of omelette. "It's so colourful. I love the art work on the walls. The dogs seem to rule the streets and the cats the shops."

"Yes, this is true."

The beach was as beautiful and as peaceful as it had been the previous two days. The wind had risen, causing a light salt spray to coat our arms and backs.

"D'you fancy a pint?" asked S, as we walked back that evening.

"Yeah, sure. Where?" We hadn't seen a bar nearby.

"I thought we could get the bus into Valparaíso. We saw plenty of bars when we walked round."

"Great idea."

Valpo had a different, happening, vibe at night.

"That plaza's busy. Oh, there's a market on. Shall we have a look?"

We exited the bus into a crowd of people and stalls. The plaza was lit up brightly and people wandered around bartering, buying, and sampling. The stalls sold everything from jewellery to *empanadas*.

"Oh, look! Chicken pasties with pumpkin pastry. They sound interesting. Fancy one?"

I juggled the warm pasty whilst we continued to wander the streets.

"Okay. But not as good as the one by the beach," I announced, wiping my face with a tissue.

"Mmm, not my favourite. It wasn't hot all the way through either."

"Not good."

"Beer will kill any bugs," said S, heading for a busy, lighted bar. "Two pints?"

"And a packet of crisps, please."

"I've got the munchies," I said, on the way back to the bus stop.

"Still?"

"Oo. *Chocolate*."

A small stall was overflowing with huge bars of chocolate.

"*Cuanto es?*" I asked.

"*Mil pesos.*"

"One thousand. That's good for such a big bar."

"Dearer than the bus," said S.

"I'll share," I replied, grinning and nodding to the stallholder before pocketing the chocolate bar for later.

§

The second side of one of the wooden doors was proving to be stubborn, and our new sandpaper was becoming clogged and worn.

"This is a nightmare," I said, scraping at a recalcitrant piece of varnish in a lovely intricate piece of moulding. "José didn't seem happy this morning. I hope he doesn't think we're shirking."

"We're not. Anyway, he's never here to notice."

"True, but I feel guilty."

"Why? We're doing a good job. Stop worrying."

"I can't. It's my nature."

S threw me a new sheet of sandpaper and grinned. "Get on with it."

That afternoon we caught the little *microbús* in the opposite direction, towards Viña del Mar, in order to change some dollars. We'd found that whilst American dollars were accepted in most shops, the exchange rate was inevitably poor.

Viña was more refined than Valpo. Less chaotic, less bohemian, more of a delicate constitution. There was less street art and fewer dogs sleeping in the shade. The streets were wide and well kept. The beach, however, was littered with sun worshippers in designer bikinis, and the beachside toilets charged 500clp (50p) for a wee and a single sheet of toilet paper.

Two pints (of beer) and a packet of crisps, please

We had the same dog escort for our walk home. The road was busy and the heat rising from the tarmac, along with the stink of car fumes, overwhelming. It was an interesting walk, though.

"Look at that wooden house," I said, pointing across the road.

A four-storey house, looking like something from an ancient horror movie, sat across from us. The dilapidated façade was made entirely of wooden slats, running horizontally like a matchstick house. Eight rows of windows to a floor looked out onto the busy four-lane highway. On the second storey, half the windows protruded from the walls in tiny bays – broken panes giving them a hollow-eyed look. The roof was of rusty tin, and one end rose into a sort of tower. Behind the house, which sat isolated on the roadside, rose tall, modern office blocks. It was as if it had been lowered into position, a relic from an earlier time.

Friday was a repeat of our other working days. We finally finished sanding the second side of the doors and I offered to polish them for José.

"I can make some wax polish if you like. They will look lovely."

"No," replied José. "I think I will varnish. Or maybe to paint it."

I quickly walked away before I said something I'd regret.

That evening José's teenage daughters joined us for a loud, chaotic, and good-natured meal. They enjoyed practising their English on us and asking about our trip. It was a fitting end to our fifth and final Workaway.

Our last day in Valpo was a day off, being a Saturday, so we once more headed into Viña del Mar to explore further.

Museo Fonck kept us interested for a good couple of hours. There were displays of natural history on the first floor; thousands of insects in glass cases and stuffed mammals in large display cabinets showed the fauna of the country. The ground floor was given over to anthropology and the ancestors of the Chilean peoples. There was a whole room dedicated to the Easter Islands, a Chilean territory in the middle of the Pacific Ocean.

"I'd love to visit. There was a Workaway placement on Easter Island, you know?"

"Come on, let's climb a hill," replied S.

It was still misty and cool as we set off for Vergara Park and its view point. In hindsight, it was probably not the best day for visiting a viewpoint. We enjoyed a vista of mist, and I was pleased to have my warm Mexican agave jumper with me.

"Have you seen the kennels?" I asked S, as we entered the park gates.

Beneath a tall hedge, three kennels sat, side by side. Each was a slightly different style: one rose pink, one with a fancy gabled roof, one pale green. Each kennel had blankets piled inside, and each was occupied by at least two dogs.

"José said they're community dogs. Everyone feeds and looks after them. They sleep where they like and eat where they like."

"These guys certainly look content."

My plan to have a last cheesy *empanada* at the beach hut on the way home was thwarted when I discovered it closed and shuttered.

"Well, that's not right, is it?" I grumped, as we crossed the road using the elevated walkway.

S laughed. "I'll buy you a last night pint instead."

How could I resist?

The beer was dark and flavoursome but I still couldn't get used to the Chilean habit of adding a 'voluntary' tip to the bill.

The first time this happened had been in Santiago. I'd been surprised that my change from a 10,000clp note

Two pints (of beer) and a packet of crisps, please

had been somewhat less than expected. Below the price of the beers on the receipt was a line saying; '*propia voluntario* 10%'.

"Not very voluntary, is it?" I'd said, at the time.

Since, I'd made a point of giving the right change for anything we bought, often to a look of disgust from the waiter.

This last evening in Valpo, I'd given the waiter the exact money for the beers as usual. He walked to the till and, in a loud voice, yelled; "*¡Sin propia!*"

"That was subtle," I said to S. "Now everyone knows we don't give tips."

I must just add that I understand the tipping system in places like the US and parts of Latin America, but I don't agree with it. I sincerely believe people should get a living wage, not have to rely on tips. Tipping just props up an unequal society. Pay a living wage and make the beer dearer, but don't patronise the workers.

In Galicia hardly anyone tips. When I've tried to add something to the bill for outstanding service, it has often been handed back to me with waving of arms and shaking of heads.

S' objections are more personal. "It's all very well tipping a waiter, but those of us who are in the kitchens doing the cooking and cleaning up never get tipped. Why tip a cab driver but not a bus driver? Why a waiter but not a chef?"

I had no answer to that.

Mountains high

We stripped the bed and cleaned our room thoroughly before allowing the friendly black and white cat, Tiger, to give it a careful inspection. It was funny to watch him poke his little black nose into every corner. He even looked in the bath to make sure we hadn't missed anywhere, and finally came to rest atop the wooden shelving as I packed the last of our bits and pieces away.

"So? Do we pass?" I asked him.

He stared at me, in that way only cats can, then jumped down from the shelving and stalked out of the room, tail in the air.

"I'll take that as a yes."

Goodbyes over, we caught the little *microbús* into Valpo for the final time. At the bus station, we boarded our coach back to Santiago.

"I'm sure we didn't come this way," I said. The coach had left the main road, heading into a range of hills.

"I think there was a diversion leaving Valparaíso," replied S, who had been taking more notice than me.

"Ah, right."

The coach began to climb. We wound our way slowly around the hills, the view of the fields below expanding as we climbed higher and higher.

"Well, this is different."

The road was much more picturesque than the motorway between the two cities. It was also much, much slower. The one-hour journey evolved into two as we spun through the empty roads, higher and higher.

Back at 'our' flat, Patrice had kept Rosie and Blue safe for us. He handed them over, together with a new code for the apartment.

Mountains high

"I fancy Chinese," I said.

"Fine by me."

Other than our cheesy *empanadas*, I'd been sadly unimpressed by Chilean food so far. The Chinese was tasty enough, but I still felt there must be something more to this long narrow country's cuisine. Something we were missing.

We found it that evening.

The Plaza de Armas is the place to go for the evening *paseo*. All the Chilean families take to the streets in the cool of the evening to walk arm in arm, children running around. Elderly couples and youngsters walk together, and families sit on painted benches watching the children playing. This evening walk, or promenade, is such a traditional Spanish sight that I felt right at home.

In the plaza, a group of actors had set up, performing some kind of play. An artist was painting caricatures of willing customers, and a lithe young woman was doing impossible acrobatic stunts. At the north end of the square, I could see the beginning of a street market.

Sellers, mainly young black men, had their wares laid out on blankets. Shoes were neatly paired, one slightly overlapping the other. Belts were tightly wound and placed just so. I'd never seen such neatness, and couldn't help but compare it to the chaos of a Galician market, where the game of the day is to find the matching pair to the shoe you have fallen in love with in the muddle of leather and cheap plastic.

At the far end of the street were food stalls. Kebabs mingled with fried chicken, chips and corn cakes. People queued for the best stalls and I instantly regretted the Chinese meal we'd had earlier.

When we come back, I promised myself.

The following day, we were off to the end of the world.

§

It had been another typically noisy night. Kids screamed and music blared until around 4.30am, when the city fell into a kind of stupor.

We were some of the first people on the streets that morning as we left the apartment for the now familiar ten-minute walk to the bus stop. Our cruise began at eight in the evening and the four-hour internal flight, taking us 1,077 kilometres (670 miles) south to Punta Arenas, left at 1.30pm.

The Turbus was already waiting when we arrived at Los Héroes, bodies hanging on to every railing. We couldn't see the driver for the masses sitting and standing in the doorway.

"I'm sure that's not legal." I laughed. "Shall we wait for the next one?"

"Yes. We'll be at the front of the queue that way."

"And might get a seat," I added, looking down at Rosie.

We'd left our rucksacks with Rodolfo at the Plaza Paris Amistar that morning, packing our long list of special items for the cruise into Rosie and Blue. One of the reasons we'd needed two separate pieces of luggage was this particular trip. The packing list for the cruise had included waterproof trousers and jacket, waterproof gloves and boots, warm hats, sun lotion and sunglasses. And our cheap Latam flight charged for each piece of luggage. As I said earlier, the way to pack lightly is NOT to visit both summer and winter destinations in one trip. In the case of Chile, it was within one country.

This final adventure on our round-the-world tour was also the most extravagant, and my 70th birthday gift to my husband – a four-day cruise from Punta Arenas at the bottom of Chile, through the Magellan Straits. From the heat of Santiago in autumn, our destination was frozen Cape Horn, the end of the world.

Mountains high

The cruise docked in Ushuaia, Argentina – the sixth country we would visit on this trip (if I counted our chaotic pause in Moscow). There was to be an epic ten-hour bus ride back to Punta Arenas and a final couple of days relaxing in Santiago before we headed home to Galicia at the beginning of April, just in time for spring planting.

When the second Turbus arrived, we fought our way on board and claimed two seats. The remaining seats soon filled up, but instead of closing the doors the driver continued letting passengers on until I thought the bus would rip open like a rotten tin can.

We set off along the road, stopping, inevitably, to pick up yet more passengers. By the time we reached the airport, those nearest the door had to shuffle about in order for it to open. Having spent an hour at claustrophobic groin level to those standing, I wasn't sure having a seat was an advantage after all.

The check-in for our Latam internal flight was a joke. We were told we had to use the self-service machines but not one of them actually worked. Instead, we joined the long snaking queue for the solitary, open, check-in counter.

At the boarding gate I glugged down the bottle of water I'd forgotten I was carrying whilst one of the check-in staff looked on, amused. As we drew level, I showed her the half empty bottle.

"I'm drinking as fast as I can," I joked in Spanish, pointing to the long line in front of me.

"Is no problem," she replied in English. "You can take water on board."

Well. So much for security.

"I suppose terrorists aren't very interested in an internal flight to the end of the world," said S.

Latam internal flights may be basic, and without frills such as food, drink or entertainment, but the view from our shared window surpassed any movie I could have watched. We flew over the Andes in the clearest of clear skies, looking down on peaks which became ever more snow covered the further south we flew. Below us were wispy clouds, lakes and rivers, volcanic cones, and snow-capped mountains towering above the rest. It was the most spectacular flight I've ever taken.

The terminal at Punta Arenas was tiny in comparison with Santiago's international airport. The exit was mere steps away, and we were soon in a taxi heading downtown to the docks.

The taxi dropped us in a vast car park in front of a large, hanger-like building. We trudged across the parking area into a gale force wind.

"Cor, it's draughty."

"Not much to stop the wind, is there?" replied S, pointing at the flat landscape around us and the churning sea.

I shivered inside my winter jacket and pulled my woolly hat down over my ears. The sea was whipping its white horses into a frenzy; they looked enraged in the face of the violent wind.

Inside the hanger it was much warmer. At a counter, a lady checked in Rosie and Blue and gave us a thick folder of information.

"We sail at twenty hundred hours. Please be on board by seven."

The mix of military and informal time, puzzled me momentarily.

"Ah, right. Okay. Is it alright to go into Punta Arenas for a bit then?"

"Yes, of course. We will put your bags into your cabin for you. Do have gloves?" she asked, concerned. "It is very cold."

"We do. Thank you."

The wind followed us all the way in to the port town of Punta Arenas, Chile's second most southernly city at

Mountains high

53°10' south, and the capital of its southernmost region, Magallanes y Antárctica Chilena. Once we were in the main streets of the town, and out of the vicious wind, the sunshine felt warm and I relaxed.

We walked through a park, failing to get a map from the tourist information kiosk which, it seemed, didn't stock any. They directed us to a different council building which also had no maps. I guessed there wasn't too much call for them in this tiny Chilean outpost. Instead, we wandered aimlessly until we found a chocolate shop and café.

The hot chocolate was warming but once more I was disappointed. Even, it seemed, a Latino country couldn't produce proper Spanish hot chocolate.

I was reminded of an incident at London Stansted airport, with Mum. She asked for a hot chocolate, but only likes weak drinking chocolate. Concerned it would be too strong, I asked the vendor how much cocoa powder he put into his mugs.

"This much," he said, lifting a teaspoon into the air.

"Ah. Fine for Mum then; I'll have a tea," I'd said.

Boarding that evening was slow, but I was more than impressed with our cabin, with its large double bed, desk and armchair (singular), its picture window overlooking the grey sea, and its neat en-suite.

"Not bad," I said.

"Did you say it was an upgrade?" asked S

"That's right. When I booked, all the third-class cabins had just gone to a large party. I said the second-class ones were too expensive. They were another thousand on top. The girl then upgraded us at the same cost. A nice result I have to say."

The evening orientation meeting was interminably drawn out. I'd long since lost interest and was itching to explore our new floating home by the time the speakers finished.

"Dinner is served in half an hour in the dining room downstairs. We will hand out your table numbers at the door. You will keep the same tables throughout the cruise. Where possible we have kept people speaking the same language together. We have, let's see, Americans, Germans, Dutch, Spanish and French on board."

"No English?" I asked S, as we went back to change.

"We booked from Spain. I guess we're honorary Spaniards."

S was probably right. Our table of six seemed to be the 'leftovers' table. Two Bostonians, a French/Spanish couple and us, English emigres living in Spain. It made for a lively and confusing meal. The Bostonians, Rick and Bev, spoke only English. Manuel, from Madrid, spoke Spanish, French, and a little English. His Parisian wife, Evelyn, spoke French and Spanish. Then there was us. Our international table muddled through in Spanglish/French.

Each table had their own waiter for the duration. Hoswald was professional and attentive. If I'd been disappointed in the Chilean food we'd eaten thus far, the cruise restored my trust – and expanded my belly accordingly.

We started that first night with grilled octopus, followed by pumpkin soup. The main course was beef medallions and there was *flan de crema* for dessert. It was all washed down by copious wines.

"I'll be so fat by the time we leave this cruise."

"A cup of tea would be nice, though," replied S.

"That is true. We'll have to find the café tomorrow."

Chile
Magellan Straits

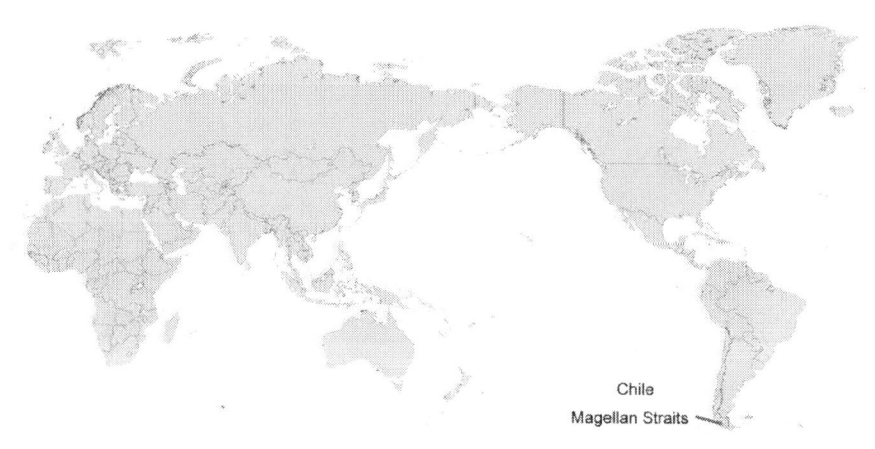

Deep forest

"Wake up! It's eight thirty already!"

"I slept well; what's the panic?" asked S.

"Breakfast started at eight and our first shore landing is at nine thirty. We'll never make it."

After quickly dressing and making our way to the deserted, and closed, dining room, I discovered that ship time was an hour behind Santiago time. It was still only 7.45am here.

"Oh well."

Breakfast was buffet style. The very worst (and best) sort of meal for someone like me. I love food and hate to miss out. I also easily get food envy – if S chooses something different to me, that immediately looks better than my choice and so on.

That first morning I managed fresh fruit and yoghurt, bacon and eggs, freshly baked rolls, muffins, pancakes with eggs and maple syrup, orange juice, tea (S was happy), various cheeses, and smoked meats. I swear I rolled back to the cabin to change for our first landing.

Our twice daily trips ashore were conducted with military-like precision using rigid, inflatable Zodiacs. Each passenger had been issued with an appropriately sized lifejacket which was kept in the cabin. I donned waterproof boots, waterproof over-trousers, a thick jumper and waterproof over-jacket, waterproof gloves and a woolly hat. By the time I'd added the bulky fluorescent-orange life jacket, I could barely move.

"If I fall in, I'll never be able to swim anywhere with this lot on. I'm sweltering."

Before setting out, we were taught the correct way to clamber into the rubber-sided Zodiac. Fifteen passengers were squashed along the two sides of the boat, clinging on to the ropes for dear life as we motored towards shore in a thick mist. The sky and the sea were the exact same shade of slate grey. The black Zodiacs were almost invisible in the water but for the vibrant orange jackets decorating their edges.

Our first landing was Ainsworth Bay. The beach was the same dark grey as the sky and the sea and seemed to be made of shale. We walked across scrubland with just a few clumps of weedy looking grass growing, towards a line of hills. As we cleared the beach, the ground became marshy. Mosses flourished in tones of rust-red and forest-green. In the distance a few taller pine trees grew.

Our leader was a Spanish botanist called Marc. He explained how life takes hold in this inhospitable land. "The forests here grow very slowly due to the temperatures. It can take many years for a tree to become established. The flora begins with these mosses and lichens, then eventually a small bush will begin to grow in the damp, warm space where the mosses are. After many, many years we get trees. This nothofagus forest is very old."

Nothofagus antarctica, or Antarctic Beech, is native to Chile and Argentina below latitude 36 degrees south, and is part of the threatened temperate rainforest ecosystem. Within the deep forest, mosses grew more

Deep forest

thickly on the bark of the trees. The air was heavy and damp, even without the steady mizzle which soaked our faces.

Interestingly, Galicia also has a number of temperate rainforests; the plant species are different, but the soft damp air is the same.

In *Voyage of the Beagle*, Charles Darwin, who had little love for this remote area (nor its native 'Fuegians'), described the forest thus; '...one's course was often arrested by sinking knee deep into rotten wood; at other times, when attempting to lean against a firm tree, one was startled by finding a mass of decayed matter ready to fall at the slightest touch.' Little had changed in this forest in the 190 years since the round-the-world voyage of *HMS Beagle*.

Although it was damp, the air temperature was much higher than I expected and Marc confirmed that it had been a mild year so far.

"That looks like a beaver dam," one of the American passengers said, as we walked through the forest.

"Yes. There is a big problem here, and Argentina is not interested in solving it."

"Why Argentina?" I asked, naively.

"The two countries jointly manage the Magellan Straits and Magellanes National Reserves. We are struggling to eliminate non-native wildlife because Argentina will not agree on a strategy," the guide replied, looking angry. "Meanwhile the beavers are destroying the nothofagus forests."

I guessed there was no love lost between skinny Chile and its much larger, more corpulent, neighbour.

On our return to the ship, we were all handed mugs of weak hot chocolate, infused with strong whisky for those who wished. It seemed churlish not to.

"That warms the cockles," I said, slurping the unfamiliar brew.

Lunches on board were themed buffets. That first day was Italian, with bean-based salads, pastas, and delicious meat and fish dishes. Desserts took over an entire display and the chef proudly explained each creation as passengers approached. I think I had five desserts that day – though I could have forgotten one or two.

After lunch, the crew announced a visit to the engine room for anyone who was interested. S told me he'd seen more than his fair share of engine rooms during his merchant navy days, so I went down with a delightful Texan lady we'd met ashore. Donna was travelling alone and had been to many places around the world. We chatted as we toured the noisy but surprisingly (to me) spotless rooms below and found we had much in common. We were also the only two people on the tour not to have to duck beneath the low metal pipework which zigzagged across the ceiling. I was rather proud of that.

Our second trip that day was around Tuckers Islet to see the cormorants, waders, vultures, crested ducks, and, hopefully, some penguins.

"This is late in the season for the Magellanic penguins," said Marc, as we cruised into position. "If we are lucky, they will be on the shore preparing to leave."

Magellanic penguins range along the southern parts of the coasts of Chile and Argentina, breeding in the frigid Antarctic waters of Patagonia but migrating as far north as Peru and Ecuador during the southern winter.

Luck was on our side.

"There they are," I whispered, frightened that somehow my voice would scare them away.

A waddle of small penguins stood on the rocky shore in front of us. They had black backs and white fronts with a black band at chest height. Their heads were black with a contrasting white band around the ears.

Deep forest

"The colouring is camouflage against predators," said Marc, in a normal voice. "The black is invisible from above in the dark water, and from below the white matches the sky."

"I don't think you needed to whisper," said S.

Indeed, the penguins were entirely oblivious of the brightly-coloured humans drifting just a few feet offshore, and the clicking cameras and smartphones focused on them.

Back on board the ship, S valiantly posed for a photo on deck in his T-shirt. "I didn't expect it to be so mild."

"I know. I brought all this snow gear and we've hardly used it. Even Japan had hardly any snow."

"Global warming," said S.

"Humph. Anyone who still doesn't believe in climate change now is an idiot," I said, succinctly.

Our lecture that evening was a well-presented explanation of glaciation in preparation for our sailing through Glacier Alley the following evening. I wish I could have taped it, or there had been a handout. My days of taking notes during lectures are behind me, and my memory doesn't retain things as it once did.

Dinner was a delicious meal of finely sliced salmon carpaccio, chicken consommé, chicken with rice and a very, very sweet dessert, even for me. Somehow, I manged to eat it all (and can, strangely, remember everything we ate without benefit of notes).

"I am so full," I said to S.

We were sitting relaxing in one of the lounges on board, drinking tea, reading, and watching the dark waters outside.

"I'm not at all surprised."

A red fox

The morning lecture today was about the indigenous tribes of the area. The subject was fascinating, but the speaker a little disjointed. I'd brought along Darwin's *Voyage of the Beagle,* and re-read his thoughts on the native 'Fuegians' as he called them. They make for uncomfortable reading.

'I could not have believed how wide was the difference between savage and civilised man. It is greater than between a wild and domesticated animal, in as much as in man there is a greater power of improvement.'

There were a large number of different tribes in the area. Many, according to Darwin, lived in, 'poorly constructed wigwams'; though he conceded the Fuegians were a tall, powerful race, well suited to the climate which the *Beagle* crew found uncomfortably cold.

'Whence have they come?' Darwin asked. 'What could have tempted, or what change compelled a tribe of men to leave the fine regions of the north, to travel down the backbone of America...and then to enter on one of the most inhospitable countries within the limits of the globe?'

That was an interesting question, and one to which we'll never know the answer.

Lunch was yet another extravaganza. The Asian fusion food was perfect for someone missing their Japanese favourites of miso soup and noodles. I even managed to limit myself to four puds.

"Do we get to walk on the glacier?" asked someone. We were boarding the Zodiacs for Pia Glacier that afternoon.

A red fox

"No. We'll be walking on the bedrock opposite the glacier," replied the guide. "Though it will be slippery on the rocks."

"Look!"

At that moment, a humpback whale breached the water, startlingly close by. I was pleased we weren't already floating in the flimsy-looking Zodiacs, and wished vehemently I'd had my camera at the ready.

"I thought the glacier would be whiter," I said, as we drifted to shore.

Most of the ice field was a dirty blue-white colour, reflecting the colour of the sky on that sunny afternoon, but one part was muddy-brown – like a dirt road.

I suddenly remembered my geology lecturer, Fiona, telling us how disappointed most students were the first time they set foot on a glacier in Iceland, where she studied. "They are often dirty brown or almost black as they've been there for thousands of years. Nothing like the pristine white snow you get after a new flurry."

I'd also expected Pia Glacier to be smooth – but it rose, jaggedly, out of the milky sea. As we photographed it there was an alarmingly loud bang. Snow rose into the air as a large piece of the glacier calved right in front of us.

"Wow! That was unexpected. Does that mean it's melting?"

"No," replied Marc. "Don't worry."

He unfurled a large map to show us the movement of Pia Glacier over the years. Although it flowed back and forth, there was little overall difference in size.

"Now, we will hike across the island and up to the viewpoint. Those who prefer can wait here."

Everyone set off, even the elderly chap I'd noticed earlier. With his cane and brown brogues, he looked more suitably attired for a walk in a city park than a hike near a glacier. Loud cracks and bangs followed us as the glacier continued to calve.

The viewpoint, overlooking the grey-green sea below, was worth every minute of the steep climb. The ship, sitting alone in the Garibaldi Fjord, looked like a toy against the splendour of the mountains behind it.

Hot chocolate awaited us on the shore today, heated by our catering staff. But something else had smelt the sweet-savoury scent of chocolate wafting on the breeze.

"Don't move," whispered someone. "Look!"

Not a dozen paces away, was a male Chilean red fox. One of the iconic breeds of Chile, this fox is a brighter orangey-red than its russet British counterpart, with a broad black stripe down its back and a black tip to its thick bushy tail.

Darwin describes this wolf-like native, called a culpeu, or colpeo, as being; '...well-known for their tameness and curiosity...They have been observed to enter a tent, and actually pull some meat from beneath the head of a sleeping seaman.'

This young dog-fox was certainly inquisitive. We watched mesmerised as he wandered our site, examining the bright orange lifejackets lying on the floor and generally having a good look around, oblivious to the startled humans.

"Where's he gone?" I asked, scanning with my camera.

"There!"

The fox had reappeared from the other direction. Bolder now, he walked right past our group and grabbed hold of the Chilean flag which was lying on a rock. Immediately, Donna took it upon herself to rescue the Chileans' honour, leading to a wonderful tug of war between her and the determined fox. Eventually, Texan cunning won the day and the flag was liberated. The fox turned tail and left, no doubt sulking.

"That is the funniest thing I've ever seen," I said to Donna, as we clambered back on to the Zodiacs. "You'll be a national hero, you know."

A red fox

"If you would like to make your way to one of the lounges, we will be passing through Glacier Alley shortly," announced the ship's tannoy.

Glacier Alley is part of the 120-mile-long (193 kilometre) Beagle Channel. The channel is straight and wide, bounded on both sides by mountains. Huge glaciers, each named after a country, come right down into the sea – sometimes accompanied by a half-frozen waterfall or cataract, spilling from the Patagonian ice field.

The blue-green, glass-like glaciers looked spectacular as we cruised slowly along the channel, watching transfixed through the floor length windows of the lounge. As we cruised, we were treated to music from the countries associated with each glacier and, unexpectedly, food and drink. Glacier Alemania (Germany) was accompanied by pilsner and sausages, Francia by champagne and brie, and Italia by a robust chianti and pizza. By the time our lecture on Cape Horn came round, I was rather merry from mixing my drinks.

That evening was the captain's dinner. Our host was a small compact man with grey hair and a neat beard. He was friendly and not at all aloof. On hearing we lived in Galicia, he chatted with us about his past journeys to A Coruña and Vigo ports on the west coast. It was all surprisingly relaxed.

Dinner was leek and potato soup, salmon steak with polenta, and a delicious chocolate brownie with vanilla ice cream. Our attentive server, Hoswald, even managed to procure six slices of birthday cake from another table.

And, as usual, I totally failed to photograph any of it.

Around the Horn

"There! I can see Cape Horn."

I was peering out of our cabin window into a spectacular sunrise. The sun painted the sky in stripes of pink, lilac and gold. The tip of Cape Horn was visible as a dark mound, poking out of the unruffled, calm sea.

Every night, our cabin steward insisted on closing our curtains when he turned down the bed, and every night I reopened them before we went to sleep. With no light pollution and no one to see us, I wasn't going to leave the curtains drawn against such a perfect view.

We'd been warned that we would only be able to land on Cape Horn if the captain deemed the conditions safe. I kept my fingers crossed as I dressed in full wet-weather gear – making that lengthy operation all the more awkward.

We disembarked early. Sea conditions were due to change mid-morning, and by 7.20am we were clambering out of the Zodiacs onto a tiny rocky shore. We climbed a set of wooden steps before heading uphill via a boardwalk. The beach was full of boulders, the gangplank slick with sea water, which surged over it at intervals. The crew helped us disembark as quickly as possible, standing chest high in the freezing water.

At the top of the steep climb, there was a T-junction. One way led to the lighthouse keeper's cottage, where a family were living, isolated on this uninhabited point of land. The other direction led to a viewpoint. There, the albatross monument, created in 1992 by Chilean sculptor José Balcells Eyquem to commemorate all the lives lost trying to sail around the Horn, flew above the waves. Over 10,000 seafarers are known to have perished making that hazardous trip.

Around the Horn

We were just heading for the lighthouse cottage when the call came; conditions were changing quicker than expected.

"Go to the albatross, then come back to the beach," said one of the crew, as we passed by.

I was sad we'd missed chatting to the lighthouse keeper and his family; his was a fascinating story, according to those who had landed first. But we got the iconic photos of ourselves by the huge metal silhouette of the albatross, and by the sign which says simply; 'parque nacional cabo de hornos', Cape Horn National Park.

Boarding the Zodiacs to return to the ship was slow; only one boat could land at a time on the tiny beach. We queued down the steep steps, being loaded fifteen or less to a boat. The calm sea of this morning was no longer. Waves were battering the beach and the gangplank with frightening force. The crew members who were holding the Zodiacs in position were soaked, despite their chest-high waders. They were both hefty young men, and one looked familiar.

"Isn't that one of the waiters from the lounge bar?" I asked S.

One of the crew members escorting passengers down the steps answered; "It is. Manuel has a diver's certificate and two jobs."

"I feel safe now," I replied, smiling. "He makes a mean cocktail too."

Back on board, after a late breakfast, we received our diplomas, 'for having reached Cape Horn, the southernmost point in the world on board the *Stella Australis*', then made our way to the lounge for a lecture about Shackleton's Antarctic quest.

Ernest Shackleton is one of my favourite explorers, and all-time hero.

In 1915, Shackleton's Imperial Trans-Antarctic expedition to complete the first land crossing of

Bento Boxes, Boomerangs & Red Foxes

Antarctica was in tatters. His ship, *Endurance*, had sunk off Elephant Island, leaving the expedition team stranded on an ice floe. Shackleton took the incredible, bold decision to set out in one of the small lifeboats, along with five crew members, to South Georgia island, 1,300 kilometres (800 miles) away across deadly seas.

I knew most of the material but particularly enjoyed the Imax documentary we were shown. In April 2000, three well-known mountaineers; Reinhold Messner, Conrad Anker and Stephen Venables, recreated Shackleton's nightmare 22-mile (34.5 kilometre) traverse of the South Georgian mountains and glaciers using full, modern gear.

Messner said of their journey; "We had crampons, ice screws, ice tools and super light climbing rope. On Crean Glacier, the situation was so hopeless that I thought we would be unable to get through."

Shackleton and his men had heavy leather boots, tweed jackets and no mountaineering equipment. They had already endured a long and dangerous journey through heavy seas before even reaching South Georgia. What Shackleton did have in spades was grit, leadership, and a determination to save his crew. His desperate gamble paid off, and not a single crewman lost his life.

A walk around the deck in a sharp breeze was invigorating. Less so for a large moth I found, exhausted on the deck. I warmed him in my hands then put him safe in our room, in a small pot, while we had lunch.

Today was a Chilean buffet. This was as unlike the meals we'd had in Santiago as a McDonald's burger is to Copenhagen's *Noma* restaurant's scallop steak, and I ate far too many desserts again (no, I'm not saying how many).

Our afternoon trip was to Wulaia Bay where *HMS Beagle* and its resident scientist, Charles Darwin, had also docked.

Around the Horn

Wulaia Bay was once home to the native Yamana peoples and was the most stunning location of the ones we'd visited so far. I would have been content to be a radio operator, 'stuck' on the island for months at a time. The large radio house, now a museum, was of sand-coloured stone with a red roof. It sat in the centre of a meadow, knee high with dried grasses and backed by low scrub-covered hills. In front, the bay spread out in a semi-circle and beyond were taller, snow-covered hills.

My first task was to release the recovered moth onto a patch of scrub, probably ruining the ecosystem of the area in one fell swoop. Still, the moth seemed satisfied with its new home.

"Look, a wigwam!"

Darwin likened the natives' home to; '...a haycock. It merely consists of a few broken branches stuck in the ground, and very imperfectly thatched on one side with a few tufts of grass and rushes.'

The reconstructed wigwam, outside which I posed in the sunshine, looked quite cosy to me. And certainly preferable to sleeping outdoors.

Our long walk around Wulaia Bay, had given me an appetite. This was our last dinner on board the *Australis*. The lamb was tender and delicious, the dessert, well, sweet.

The evening continued with the captain's toast, then an interminable slide show of passengers' photographs, and a prize draw to win the ship's flag.

"I think you ought to have got the flag – for your gallant rescue," I whispered to Donna.

Personae non gratae

I was woken on Friday morning by a bright light outside our bedroom. Thinking we were late rising, I jumped up, stark naked, to peer out of the window. A second later, I jumped back smartly, grabbed my specs and peeped out again. Yup, there were a large number of dockworkers walking around, directly outside our window.

"Oops. Maybe we ought to have drawn the curtains," I said, hopping back into bed. "We've docked."

"What time is it?" asked S, sleepily.

I checked my phone. "Unless we've changed time zones again, 3.30am."

I tried, and failed, to get back to sleep. The arc lights and the noise of the dockworkers was just too much after the peace of the dark ocean. By 6.30 we were up and dressed, ready for an early last breakfast and an 8am disembarkation. Our cruise was over.

Unlike the comfortable embarkation in Punta Arenas, where a luxury coach drove us the short distance from the check-in building to the ship, in Ushuaia we were unceremoniously dumped at the bottom of the gangplank with our luggage and instructed to walk towards the town – a kilometre away down a rather breezy, dock road.

"Is there a bus?" I asked, watching the party of Americans boarding a coach.

"No." was the curt answer.

I guess once we'd disembarked, no one cared any longer. It was a shame, as it had been a lovely cruise.

The dock road was level but seemed interminable, dragging Rosie and Blue behind us. The wind was so strong that at times I had to stagger sideways to stay on my feet.

Personae non gratae

The first thing I saw as we neared the end of the docks was a large poster; *'Prohibido el amarre de los buques piratas ingleses',* it read.

Since 'Gaucho Rivero's Law' was enacted, following the Falklands dispute, British flagged ships have not been allowed to dock or take on supplies in Ushuaia. In its none too subtle way, the Argentinian notice read; 'the mooring of English pirate ships is prohibited'.

In a green area next to the docks, a large statue of General Belgrano watched over two incoming Brits with scorn.

"I'm not feeling a huge welcome in Argentina, so far," I muttered, as we scurried past.

The tourist information office was not yet open, but a kindly German couple outside gave us a spare street map and we headed off towards our accommodation. It was heavy going, dragging the cases. The sun was warm, and our accommodation appeared to be at the very top of a steep hill. They didn't mention that on Booking.com.

It was, though, an interesting walk. The Ushuaian architecture was eclectic: wooden boarded chalet type homes nestled next to large stone mansions, and gingerbread cottages with gnomes outside snuggled up to multi-storey dwellings with large bay windows.

The view back down the hill, took in the sweep of the docks and the whole of the bay. By now, we were level with the snow-capped mountains behind the town; mist coated the tops of the hills around the bay and both sea and sky were steel grey. But thick clouds were amassing, even as we sweated in the unexpected sunshine.

"Nearly there," I puffed. "I think it's this one."

Having seen the passion with which the Argentinians seemed to loathe Brits, even forty years on from The Falklands War, I was nervous of our welcome as *personae non gratae*.

As luck would have it our hosts were Chileans, and exceedingly friendly.

"¡*Bienvenido! ¡Venga! ¡Venga!*" our host cried, opening the door wide.

We were dragged over the threshold and offered tea; an odd brew beloved of Chileans and Argentinians called *yerba maté*. This caffeine-rich herbal tea is made in a lidded mug and drunk through a communal straw. Topped up with hot water and honey on a regular basis, it is both bitter and pungent. Drinking *maté* with friends is as much a social event as a thirst quencher.

Our accommodation was not yet ready, but our hosts were happy to store our bags, and heavy woollen jumpers, while we explored the southernmost city in the world. (Author's note: Since our trip, Chile has redesignated Puerto Williams, a city. This tiny town of 3,000 people is half a minute (in latitude) south of Ushuaia, meaning the Argentinian city is now relegated to a miserable second place. But I'm almost sure that wasn't due to any rivalry between the countries.)

It was a relief to walk downhill into Ushuaia, unburdened. The city was clean and tidy. Shops seemed to be thriving, and the people happy and smiling. We had a huge pizza for lunch, wrapping up a third of it to take back to the accommodation, before going shopping for our dinner.

"Oh look, real orange juice."

I was delighted. Chilean supermarkets only seemed to stock sweetened '*nectar*' rather than pure orange juice. It was puzzling and, to my palate, quite disgusting.

We'd planned to visit a couple of museums, but quite unexpectedly the wind rose and an icy squall sent us shivering into a café. The temperature seemed to have plummeted twenty degrees and I wished my woolly jumper wasn't still at the accommodation.

"Shall we head back?" S asked, looking at me shivering in my thin waterproof.

"Good plan, I don't fancy getting pneumonia before our coach trip tomorrow," I replied.

Personae non gratae

Our accommodation was a neat ground floor apartment attached to the owners' main house. There was a large, well-equipped kitchen, a double bedroom, and a bathroom off to one side.

Dinner was a triumph. Four sausages, six eggs and a tin of peas between us, with a tin of peaches for dessert, meant we were replete once more. It might not have been the high cuisine we'd become accustomed to on board the ship, but it made a suitable farewell meal to our brief side trip into Argentina. I felt sure I would sleep better that night.

Poor man's burger

Sadly, that was not to be.

I'd forgotten, once again, the Latinos' enjoyment of loud music and late nights. Being once more in a city, even one as small as Ushuaia, was noisy and I slept poorly. Still, we needed to be up early to catch our coach back to Punta Arenas, and I could always snooze on the long coach trip.

I thought.

The previous evening, our host had insisted he would drop us at the bus terminal on his way to work. We ate cold pizza for breakfast, washed down by hot tea, packed our ham butties (courtesy of the ship buffet the previous morning) and were standing outside in the half-light by seven.

I was pleased to see our Texan friend, Donna, already seated opposite as we boarded the coach.

"Yeah! I hoped you'd be here," I said, letting S have the window seat and settling in for a chat.

It was a picturesque journey – or would have been had the windows not constantly steamed up in the warm, humid atmosphere. The driver seemed to think we were all hothouse flowers. He kept the heat cranked right up, there were no opening windows and the skylights were all firmly closed.

We drove through flat countryside seeing my first guanacos (a camelid native of this region, related to the llama and vicuña), rheas, cattle, geese, and large, white herons. Occasionally we'd spot a small settlement of white, red-roofed houses in the distance but the coach didn't stop until we reached the Argentinian-Chilean border.

By now it was 1pm and I was feeling peckish. We'd long since eaten our ham butties; Chile was strict about

Poor man's burger

the import of meat and dairy products and we didn't want them confiscated.

"I hope there's a café at the border."

No chance.

On the Argentinian side we all trooped off the coach and through a long shed-like building, carrying our luggage. This was scanned through an x-ray machine and we were all zapped with a metal detector rod before trooping obediently back to the coach.

A young Dutch couple unwrapped their cheese sandwiches, sensibly left on the coach, and ate yoghurt with a shared spoon while we edged towards the Chilean border post one hundred metres away.

Once more we trooped off, subjected ourselves and our luggage to x-ray machines and trooped back to the coach. It was the only exercise we'd had for over five hours and I was glad to stretch my legs.

"It's a bit bumpy, isn't it?" said Donna, as we re-joined the bus.

"It is. I'm wobbling as if I've been at sea for days. No, scrub that, the Straits weren't this bad."

"I'm feeling seasick," admitted Donna.

It was true that the journey was anything but smooth. A combination of the driver's erratic swerving and the potholed roads were making us all feel a bit worse for wear and I had no chance of catching up on my sleep.

"I can see the sea!" I shouted, poking S in the ribs.

"I know, so can I," he replied, calmly. "I think we're near the ferry port."

The ferry terminal at Bahía Azul was our last stop before Punta Arenas. We were to cross the northernmost point of the Magellan Straits to Punta Delgada, literally the 'narrowest point' of the channel. We were leaving the Tierra del Fuego behind. To the north was the bulk of the South American mainland, whilst further east was the mighty Atlantic Ocean.

I'd assumed the bus would drive onto the open-decked roll-on-roll-off ferry with the passengers on board; it was only a twenty-minute ride across the choppy bay. But, no. We were once more ushered off the coach and ordered to make our way up the ferry ramp on foot.

"*¡Rapido! ¡Rapido!*" the ferrymen yelled, as we dodged cars, coaches and trucks driving up the ramp alongside us.

The red and white ferry looked old and dilapidated. The wide, open deck was given over to vehicles, while a two-storey structure on the port side held the conning tower and a small, cramped passenger lounge – making the boat look lop-sided.

We were directed up steep external metal steps to the dismal 'lounge'. With ripped leather seats and grimy windows, it had seen far better days. There was a café, but it was closed and there were no signs of refreshments. Still, the windows blocked the wind which whipped up over the bay and it made for a change of scenery.

The sun came out and the sandy dunes across the bay glowed in the low, southern light. It was another ninety kilometres to our destination, but we knew the journey was nearly at an end.

"Oh god, I feel sick," panted Donna, as we alighted in the centre of Punta Arenas at five o'clock that afternoon. She did look a tad green around the gills. "I think I'll go for a lie down," she said.

I gave her a quick hug, almost falling over as the earth tipped beneath me. "Whoa. That feels strange." I shook my head and took a deep breath. "Hope to bump into you again, *chica*."

I'd pre-booked our accommodation in Punta Arenas some nine months earlier – a pretty looking wooden cabin with 'excellent' reviews and a surprisingly reasonable price for a city, even one as remote as this.

Poor man's burger

Just two weeks before our departure, the accommodation had cancelled our booking with no explanation. Apparently, it was something that could be done on Booking.com. By then all the reasonably priced apartments were long gone. I'd found a bed and breakfast with 'pleasant' reviews, an alleged short walk from the city centre.

"It should be over the railway line and to the left," I said to S, following the directions I'd written down.

That road must have been the longest in Punta Arenas, and of course we were at the wrong end. As we traipsed down the never-ending pavement, the houses became poorer and more broken down. Paint peeled, and fences lay broken in tattered heaps. Cars, which looked like they'd last been driven twenty years earlier, were parked in weed-strewn yards.

"This is starting to look dodgy," I remarked, sidestepping an abandoned motorcycle, lying half across the pavement. Weeds grew through the paving slabs, which were broken and uneven – as if laid by a drunk.

Eventually we came to a dark green wooden building which proudly announced it was the hostel we were looking for. Inside, our hostess, a large lady with bottle-black hair, greeted us like long-lost friends.

"Breakfast is served in here," she said, dragging us through their living-come-dining room and down a long corridor.

The corridor seemed to be an afterthought, tacked onto the house by a cowboy builder some years after the original structure. The floor was bulging chipboard and I could see daylight through gaps in the panelled wooden walls. A bright lounge, halfway down, was full of bohemian youngsters, smoking pungent herbs and sipping beer.

Our room was at the very end of the corridor.

Inside, it was a vision in dark, institutional green. The carpet behind the door was sticky and loose, rising to trip the unwary – just in front of four steps down to the bedroom area. A pine-framed double bed and a bunk bed shared the space. The bedroom walls were the same institutional green and the only window was set high up, near the ceiling. Even that ceiling was dark green. The overall effect was of being underwater, deep below the ocean waves.

The bathroom was at the top of the steps, opposite the main door. It was clean, but again the lino floor was warped and peeling. Nothing looked at all like the photos on Booking.com.

"I can't stay in here all evening," I said, shivering. "I feel like I'm drowning."

"Let's go and explore then," said S. "We could do with stretching our legs."

As we left, our host asked if everything was okay and I, being British, said it was fine.

"Breakfast is from eight," she said.

"Ah, we need to be at the airport by eight. We fly to Santiago tomorrow."

"No problem. I leave your breakfast here. You want me to call taxi?"

"Oh, thank you. That would be wonderful. We are going out to eat. Can you recommend anywhere?"

Listening to her instructions in rapid Spanish, I said to S; "Apparently there are a number of cafes nearby to choose from. Other than that, I was lost."

In the end, we chose a café simply by the expediency of it being open. The menu was mainly burgers and pizzas.

"The burger '*a pobra*' is on a two for one deal. What do you think?" I asked, perusing the menu.

"What's *a pobra*?"

"It's a poor man's burger. *A pobra* usually means with eggs. This says it's meat patty, fried eggs and onions. We could get a chips to share too, if it's not very big?"

"Sounds good."

Poor man's burger

"Dos a pobras y una porción de patatas fritas, por favor."

The waiter looked at me a little strangely, but I assumed it was my odd accent. After so many years in Galicia, I have an English/Galician twang to my Spanish – as well as the mainland habit of lisping my c's and v's.

We sipped on colas and passed the time chatting, until a large white plate was placed in front of each of us, closely followed by a great tureen of crispy fries.

"You have to be joking," I said, my eyes bulging.

The waiter was smirking far more than I felt was kind, given the circumstances.

Our burgers *'a pobra'* were on bread buns the diameter of a dinner plate. Each bun was smothered in ketchup and mayonnaise and topped with three standard sized meat patties, three fried eggs and at least two large onions, chopped and fried.

"We didn't need the chips," said S, helpfully.

The burger was so well sodden with relishes, and so unwieldy, that it was impossible to lift; I had to cut it in a ridiculously ladylike manner. Halfway through I messaged my niece, Belle, another foodie, for encouragement.

I'm not going to manage this, darling, I texted, sending a photo of my burger.

Gosh, that is huge, Aunty Lisa. I have faith in you, though, came the reply.

Three quarters of the way through, I hit the wall.

Failed, I messaged my niece, adding a sad emoji.

The two burgers, chips and colas came to 15,500clp, around 15$ – expensive for Chile, but not for the sheer quantity of food.

"No wonder it's two for one. One burger would have been plenty," said S, as I waddled out of the café.

"And without the chips," I added.

It was only 9.30pm, but we'd had a couple of broken nights and were bulging with fast food and fizzy pop. It was time for bed.

West side story

Our room seemed cosier in the dark. The yellow glow of the single centre light was too dim to read by, but I was happy to turn in for the night. It was surprisingly quiet and peaceful in our little underwater room and I slept until the alarm stridently announced it was time to get up.

"I don't fancy that shower anyway," I said, rolling over for a five-minute snooze until S pushed me, none too gently, out of bed.

In the living room/dining room, a table had been laid for us. There was a jug of the incredibly sweet Chilean '*nectar*'; some interesting looking, very heavy and dense, bread; a glass dish of tasty homemade jam; a few slices of cheese and ham, two yoghurts, and an apple each. We waded through most of it, making a couple of butties for the journey with the cheese and ham and pocketing the apples for later. Our taxi arrived just as we finished eating and we were soon on our way back to the tiny Aeroporto Presidente Carlos Ibez del Campo, which served Punta Arenas.

Oddly, our taxi was far cheaper on the way back. Maybe it was a shorter route, or maybe it was because our host had booked it. I didn't care. I'd enjoyed our cruise, and exploring two new cities, but was looking forward to going 'home' to Santiago. There were still some things on my to-do list.

Our flight arrived at Santiago Airport at 1.30pm, and the bus to the city centre was outside as we emerged back into the heat of a somnolent Santiago afternoon. The journey by now was as familiar as home. We walked slowly through the park in the centre of the dual carriageway, watching the Chilean flag drawing closer as we neared our aparthotel. It felt like coming home too;

West side story

walking through the streets below the apartment building, talking to the street fruit sellers, and buying grapes from a stallholder. Rodolfo had our rucksacks and our new door code ready when we arrived. He had even given us a quieter, rear-facing room, for which I was grateful.

I was raring to go and explore more of Santiago, but, for once, S was happy to relax in the room with his book, and a shower.

I wandered to the museum of pre-Colombian art alone, enjoying the bustle of the streets and admiring the architecture in the centre of Santiago. The museum, when I arrived, had just closed its doors for the day so I went into the Plaza de Armas to sit and people watch. There was a clown performing in the centre of a large crowd of people. He was doing a lovely line in slapstick and I giggled along with the rest, before deciding I too needed a shower.

I'd discovered that the Moneda Palace Gallery was free to enter after 3pm and there was a J W Turner exhibition on. It was a rush; the museum closed at 4.30pm and it was already nearing four when we arrived, but I enjoyed the exhibition – seeing the gradual changes in Turner's work through the years.

That evening, I wanted, desperately, to visit the street food market we'd stumbled on before our cruise. We headed up to the area where the market had been, but I was disappointed to find it deserted.

As we walked further along the streets, we began to meet groups of people heading our way. It was a strange parade – made up of wooden carts, bicycles, and metal supermarket shopping trolleys. All were laden with blankets, goods to sell, or cooking equipment.

"Good grief. Look at that one!" I cried, as a woman bustled past pushing a supermarket trolley.

The trolley held a large wok full of sizzling oil. The wok was heated by a gas burner below and that in turn was fed from a fifteen-litre gas bottle strapped to the side of the trolley. A wooden tray over the trolley's child seat held chicken drumsticks ready to be deep fried, while paper plates were tucked into spare corners.

By now streams of shopping trolleys were crossing the busy main road, dodging between cars in their race into the centre of town. It was just 8pm. The shops had closed and the evening was given over to the street vendors.

The aromas of frying food were overwhelming, and I couldn't decide where to go first.

"Oh, Wow!"

At one end of the long street, a sheet of flame rose into the air, along with the aroma of frying noodles. Around one of the ubiquitous trolleys was a large crowd. A short stocky man was throwing noodles into a wok then tilting it into the flame of his gas burner. The burning oil caused a tall golden flame to erupt from the wok. Once the air cleared, the noodles were ready.

For 2000clp (2$) he filled a large polystyrene tray with noodles and chicken, and even threw in a couple of wooden forks. This was not just street food, but street theatre.

The idea of street theatre grew a few moments later when a fight broke out between stall holders. It was very *West Side Story*. Suddenly the street was filled with uniformed *carabineros* carrying guns and truncheons. A police van appeared and the two combatants were whisked away. The market carried on as if nothing had happened.

I got chatting to a tall, good-looking African stall holder. He gladly posed for photographs and told me his ambition was to emigrate to mainland Spain.

"But you won't be able to do this," I said, taking in the trolleys and the impromptu market with a wave of my arm. "In Spain, it is more regulated. Less free."

West side story

After being in and out of Santiago so often, I was starting to see a different side to the city. The rose-coloured lenses were falling from my glasses.

In one of the main pedestrian streets, I noticed, for the first time, the men living on benches, beneath piles of cardboard boxes. I saw that many of the once proud buildings were graffitied on the lower floors – not in an artistic, Valparaíso street art, way but scrawled names; 'Kisa', 'Bracs', 'Nocto', they cried. Paint was peeling from the lilac, buttercup yellow, and powder-blue coloured walls of the old buildings, but the upper storey windows still gazed out onto stone balustrades. Colonnades still stood proudly and the first-floor cornices were intricately carved with vines or flowers. Santiago gave me a distinct feeling of a society split in two, and these buildings reflected that.

My feeling was to prove prophetic those six short months later, when students rebelled and forced a billionaire president to resign.

The Chilean virgin

Our last full day in Santiago dawned hot and humid. We had a lie-in for the first time in over a fortnight, before breaking our fast with muesli, grapes from my favourite stall-holder, and pure orange juice – found after much searching in a supermarket the previous day.

My aim today was to climb to the top of Cerro San Cristobal – at 860 metres (2,280 feet), the highest of the hills around which Santiago is built.

Actually, I lie.

My aim was to walk to the base of the *cerro*, then catch the funicular railway to the top before ambling back down. As with many of my plans on this holiday, this one fell apart as soon as we arrived at the base station.

"It says the funicular doesn't start 'til one."

"Shall we walk then?"

"Why not," I sighed. It was still relatively cool for Santiago, and it didn't look too far to the top.

The path began with a few steps, then a nicely concreted walkway with wooden slatted rails which took us past the entrance to the zoo. We walked along the smooth path beneath the shade of the trees which rose up the hillside.

"This is easy," I said, far too quickly as it happens.

After the zoo entrance, which the walkway had evidently been constructed for, the track deteriorated into an eroded, steep, exposed, sandy path which wound uphill under a ferocious sun. We climbed and climbed, then climbed a bit more, slowly drawing closer to the blindingly white, fourteen-metre-high (46 foot) statue of the Virgin Mary which watched over the hillside.

As we climbed, we paused frequently to gaze down on the city scape below. All around the green hills rose tall skyscrapers, looming through the smog clinging to

The Chilean virgin

the city streets. From one side of the hill we could peer down on the *cerro* of Santa Lucia which we'd climbed on our first day in Santiago, a lifetime ago. It seemed but an ant hill from up here.

At the top of the *cerro*, we sat on one of the many benches in the amphitheatre – a semi-circular open-air theatre of tiered benches for the faithful to pray in front of the Virgin. Spiritual music blared out from hidden speakers as we tucked into a couple of Virgin Airways Australia biscuits, found serendipitously in a rucksack pocket.

The views from the feet of the Chilean Virgin were spectacular but I was surprised to find a small chapel inside the hollow base of the statue, cool and dimly lit. The sun was slowly turning my shoulders the same shade as my dark red vest top, despite the sunblock I'd added, and I was pleased to shelter beneath the virgin's skirts.

"Shall we go find the funicular and ride down?" I asked. "I think I saw the sign somewhere."

It was, in the end, easy to find the funicular with its little wooden hut. A wooden hut which was firmly shuttered. To those wooden shutters was pinned a notice, which told me that the funicular would not run at all today.

"Could've told us that at the other end," I said, with a sigh.

"Ah, but then we might not have bothered to walk up here."

I smiled. "That's true. And this way I'll be earned my lunch by the time we get down."

I did earn my lunch.

The sun seemed to be getting hotter, the air more humid, with every step we descended. By the time we reached level ground at Pio Nono, I was ready for a cool drink and a stiff lunch, in that order. There were a number of restaurants along the road and we chose one with smiling waiters and tables laid outside in the shade. We ate fried fish, and chicken and rice. It was, with the exception of the street food and the cruise, the best meal we'd had in Chile.

Replete, we wandered back to Moneda Palace to see the Turner paintings we'd missed the previous day and some of the other exhibitions and artisan works on the upper floors. A display of hand-woven fabrics in bright, primary-coloured stripes caught my eye, and I took some photographs of cleverly designed wicker baskets, flowers, and even chickens for my basket-weaver friend, Debs.

Back outside we walked along the familiar streets, dodging the stalls and vendors set up seemingly at random in the centre of the footpath. Despite my new found understanding of the inequality of the city, I still loved the chaos of Santiago. It seemed a free-spirited place, full of interesting, and conflicting, ideas and thoughts.

Our last night beers were dark and delicious and there was no comment from the waiter about my lack of a tip. As we sat on an outside terrace, a duo performed for patrons from the street beyond. Afterwards they sent a hat round, to which we happily contributed. It was the perfect way to enjoy the end of our mammoth trip around the world.

Sweet home, Galicia

We were up, dressed, showered, and breakfasted by 9.00am the following morning, in time for our last walk to Los Héroes and our final journey to Santiago Airport. The bus was once more bursting at its rickety old seams with passengers by the time we arrived, so we waited for the next one. In a scene of *déjà vu*, many, many more passengers were squeezed on board than the seating notice declared to be the maximum number. I worried whether the driver would actually be able to see around his passengers.

Squeezed but unharmed, we literally fell out of the coach doors at the airport and straight into a queue for check-in. In yet another *déjà vu* moment, Iberia's self-service check-in machines didn't work. We queued at the desk, where we were awarded seats which bore no resemblance to the ones I'd already booked online. The overworked and hostile check-in crew just shrugged and we obediently moved along, directly into a queue for customs.

Thankfully, this time we were processed quickly and were soon in the final queue of the morning, the one to board our flight home to Spain.

Iberia had not improved much since our flight to and from Costa Rica, five years earlier. The inane 'muzak' on take-off and landing, far from relaxing me, made me want to stab someone; the orange juice was the sickly-sweet Chilean '*nectar*' and the food was Iberia's finest.

"What's in this?" I asked at lunchtime, poking the grey potato salad.

"The black forest gateau is good," replied S, tucking into his meal backwards.

Afternoon tea was the standard Iberia sandwich with ham and cheese which had caused so much trouble on our Costa Rican flight, where we had (briefly) gone vegetarian. The single slice of sweet, white-sliced bread (called *pan molde* in Spanish to my never-ending delight), cut in half, was at best a snack.

We ate the remains of our Qantas Tim Tam biscuits and snoozed until breakfast. By then I was hungry, having only had a half-sandwich since the previous lunchtime.

"Oh, yuk," I said, biting into a sickly-sweet croissant.

The soggy pastry was accompanied by a slimy wet slice of ham, a saccharine-sweet muffin, and sweetened yoghurt. Is Spain the only country to add sugar to natural yoghurt? It's one of my bugbears in the supermarket, attempting to find a natural *unsweetened* yoghurt. If you order yoghurt in a restaurant, it even comes with a sachet of sugar to add. Refusal leads to an offer of *sacarina* instead.

Even S was unimpressed with the offerings. Thankfully, I discovered a tasty chocolate biscuit hidden beneath the inedible breakfast. I dined on that and stewed tea.

"Which airline d'you think's been the best on this trip?" I asked S, trying, and failing, to distract him in order to filch his choccy biscuit.

"Qantas," he said instantly, moving his biscuit out of reach.

Sweet home, Galicia

"Tim Tams?"

"Definitely. And the space."

"That's true. The old jumbos do have a lot more space. I was impressed with Aeroflot to be honest. Other than them leaving Rosie behind, of course."

"A lot better than I expected. The food was good."

"And no mid-air disasters."

"And no wodka," replied S, grinning.

"Iberia are at the bottom of my pile again," I said, eyeing S' biscuit enviously.

"They are cheap."

"Apparently, they're starting a new, no-frills route to Santiago de Chile. No food, and no luggage allowance other than cabin bags, but only 299 euros return. I read it in the magazine."

"Good for a weekend away. And no food could be an advantage," he added, swallowing the last of his chocolate biscuit.

The flight landed early at Barajas Airport, Madrid. By 6.30am we were already through customs. In fact, customs appeared non-existent as we pushed our way through the doors into the terminal building.

"Isn't it funny? We've been subjected to so much prodding from customs along the way and when we get home…'*nada*'."

"Welcome to Spain."

Our coach to Lugo wasn't due until 10am so we had time to kill. We grabbed sandwiches and colas from a kiosk, then sat on the carpet inside the airport building, reading. We climbed aboard our luxurious coach, settling into our clean (and not peed-on) seats.

Yes, I checked – carefully.

The luxury coach lasted until the first stop. At the main bus station in Madrid, we were all ushered from the spanking new bus to a much older version for the remainder of our ride.

"Nice while it lasted," I said, cautiously settling onto my new seat. "Smells okay. I think."

At our first comfort break there was a change of drivers, and a welcome cup of hot tea at the nice Spanish price of a euro each. It even came with a free *tapa*.

"I love how even service stations don't rip you off in Spain," I said, settling back into my seat.

The man in front turned round. "Hey, are you English?" he asked, in an American drawl.

"Yeah. But we live in Galicia," I replied.

"Wow! That's great. Say, do you speak the lingo?"

"Er, yes, why?"

"I need to get off at a place called Ped *rafita*. Can you ask the driver to tell me when we arrive?"

"Pedra *fita*," I repeated, putting the emphasis back in the right place. "You'll know when we get there. It's the highest spot on the A6. Always snows."

"Really? I'm supposed to be meeting friends. They have an apartment in the hills. We're walking the Way of St James."

"Oh right. That'll be great. Are they collecting you?"

"No. I'll grab a cab."

I doubt that, I thought, remembering the small town of Pedrafita through which we'd passed the previous year.

I wandered down to the front of the bus.

"The American is worried about missing his stop at Pedrafita. Will you tell him?"

"He'll know," replied the driver.

"I told him that," I said, and shared a complicit smile with our driver before returning to my seat.

"Sorted," I said to our new friend.

Fat flakes of snow were falling as the coach climbed ever higher towards the mountain peaks bordering Galicia. The American had his mouth open.

"Highest spot on the route," I said helpfully, as the coach slowed to a halt.

Sweet home, Galicia

"Pedrafita do Cebreiro," yelled the driver.

The tourist gulped. "Where's the cab stop?" he asked, glancing fearfully at the deserted streets, white with fresh, unsullied snow.

"Doubt there is one," I replied. "If you ask in the bar, they'll call you a taxi." I pointed at a tiny doorway. Above it, the sign read 'Bar Antonio'.

"I don't speak any Spanish."

"Say '¿*hay taxi?*'," I offered. "I'm sure they'll help."

The poor man climbed down and recovered his bags. As we drove away, he was still standing at the side of the street, a forlorn figure in a snowdrift. I hoped his friends would come and rescue him soon.

We were back in our beloved Galicia. The snow storm which had arrived with us at Pedrafita dispersed as we descended towards Lugo. A sun's ray broke through the clouds, and suddenly a rainbow appeared directly outside my window.

"Home sweet home, Galicia." I sighed, then turned to S. "I think I'm cured," I said, as the bus sped along the A6 towards home.

"Of what?"

"Planning everything so carefully."

S lifted his eyebrows.

"Look at all the things that went wrong that I'd planned: pee on the coach seat, no time for showers at Moscow, Rosie ending up coming with us round Japan, the Nullarbor..."

"Even you couldn't plan for a bush fire and a broken alternator," reasoned S.

"No. But that proves planning doesn't work." I thought a moment, then added; "That was my favourite part of the trip, you know."

"What breaking down?"

"Nooo. The Nullarbor. The adventure. The peace. And the way we could stop where and when we wanted. The surprises."

"You hate surprises."

"Exactly. It was so far out of my comfort zone. I loved the whole trip but that was the most unusual. What was your favourite?"

"The cruise," replied S, unhesitatingly.

"That was special. Not rediscovering all your old haunts?"

"Ha. I didn't recognise a thing, did I?"

"It was over fifty years ago. I suppose everything was bound to have changed."

"Yes. But a new city in Japanese paddy fields, and extending the docks in Valparaíso into the water. Who'd expect that?"

"True. We'll have to rediscover more of your old haunts. There's the rest of the Pacific coast of South America to go at yet. Then there's Fiji and all the other places you went."

S smiled and went back to his book.

"It was a holiday of contrasts, wasn't it?" I interrupted a second time.

"Go on," said S, laying his book down.

"Well, Japan was so polite and clean, and punctual. And quiet. Chile was a contrast in itself; Santiago, noisy and dirty and chaotic, the Magellan Straits, peaceful and calming. Singapore was a city of sights and smells and sounds. It assaulted the senses. So ordered and safe. Australia was laid back and incredibly friendly. The Nullarbor was vast and empty. There are more than twice the number of people in tiny Singapore than in the whole vastness of Western Australia. Isn't that incredible?

"Then there was the food."

"A lot of noodles."

I laughed. "There were, weren't there? Japanese noodles, Chinese noodles in Singapore…"

"Noodles for dinner most nights in the camper," interrupted S.

"Haha. Not every night. Then there were the noodles at the street food market in Santiago. And even on the cruise."

"We've had noodles in every country."

"And McDonald's, bizarrely. Isn't it weird how each country had a different McDonald's menu?"

"To fit in with the local tastes, I guess."

"That's where they're missing out in Galicia. McDonald's should do a *pulpo* burger," I said, remembering a thought I'd had, weeks earlier.

"Octopus? Hmm. It's a million to one chance."

"But it might just work." I finished the quote, as S knew I would.

"Then there were the gardens," I said after a while.

"We did see a few."

"The Japanese idea of gardens was a little strange. It seemed to be mainly gravel, interspersed with neatly planted shrubs."

"It was winter."

"True. I'd love to go back at cherry blossom time."

"We saw the plum blossoms though."

"Oh yes. In Kanazawa. It was much milder than normal, wasn't it? And I loved the botanic gardens in Singapore. So colourful."

"Things grow and flower all year there, don't they?"

"Especially the orchids. Amazing."

I lapsed into silence, thinking of all the places we'd seen, and the people we'd met, over our two-month trip. I was full of excitement for everything we'd experienced. I looked forward to getting home, but at the same time I was eager to see more of this amazing world.

"You know we could hire an RV to tour New Zealand next," I said, after a pause.

"Mmm."

"I promised Jenny we'd go. After all, they made the effort to fly all the way to Australia to meet up with us.

If I looked online when we get home, I bet we'd get a good price. Tickets will have just gone on sale for next year."

S said nothing.

"Do you think we could do North *and* South Island? Or would that be too much in one trip? We could Workaway again; we enjoyed that."

"We did," said S.

"You've not been to New Zealand, either."

"I haven't, true."

"So, maybe a Workaway or two, and an RV to visit Jenny and…"

S raised his eyebrows again. I must teach him to raise just the one, I thought, inconsequentially.

"Yup," he said at last. "No more planning for you."

COMING NEXT

Far from putting our intrepid pair off travelling, their action and disaster packed round-the-world trip was such fun that when opportunity knocks, they leave their home in the remote northwest of Spain a second time. This time they journey to New Zealand, at the very beginning of a pandemic which was set to rock the world.

Oblivious of the future, Lisa and S once more sign up to Workaway. Using their building skills, they volunteer their way around the beautiful North Island, meeting new friends, and discovering old ones they didn't know they had, as serendipity follows them across the globe.

Chasing the last flight out, our adventurers finally return to their beloved Galicia and a locked-down Europe, stranding mum, Iris, a thousand kilometres from home.

Look out, Slugger Stewart and Slammer Wright are on their way.

Want a sneak peek? Join my subscribers' list for offers, photos and more
https://lisarosewright.wixsite.com/author/

For updates follow me at
http://www.facebook.com/lisarosewright.author
http://www.twitter.com/galauthor_lisa

If you'd like to see some photos from our travels, download this free album
https://online.fliphtml5.com/ojyvt/zrrk/

Acknowledgements

So many people have helped bring this book to fruition. I thank you all.

To my beta readers, Pat Ellis, Julie Haigh, Beth Haslam, Val Poore, Simon Michael Prior, and Alyson Sheldrake. Thank you for daring to read the first draft and for your incredibly helpful comments. You are all five-star heroes.

Bjørn Larssen for rescuing me from the perils of formatting disasters. Bjørn writes great books too.

To all our fabulous Workaway hosts around the world, thank you for making this a holiday of a lifetime – and giving me something to write about.

To Sho & Michiru, our lovely Couchsurfer hosts who spent their precious time off escorting us around Japan, *arigato gozaimasu.*

To the guys at Curtis New Holland – without you, I may not have been here to write this book of our adventures. You are my heroes!

To the friendliest group on Facebook, We Love Memoirs, for support, and lots of fun-filled hours when I should have been working but was instead online. If you love reading memoirs (or writing them), enjoy competitions and chatting with like-minded people, then I highly recommend this wonderful group. Find us at: http://www.facebook.com/groups/welovememoirs

To S, my blue-eyed husband, for alpha, beta and omega reading, and for always being by my side in any adventure, wherever in the world we are.

And to you, my readers – without you this book would be just another dream.

About the author

In 2007, Lisa left a promising career as an ecologist catching protected reptiles and amphibians, and kissing frogs, to move to beautiful green Galicia with her blue-eyed prince (now blue-eyed husband).

She divides her time equally between growing her own food, helping renovate two semi-derelict houses and getting out and about to discover more of the stunningly beautiful area she calls home.

Lisa is happiest outside in her *huerta* weeding, watching the antics of her chickens, or in her kitchen cooking interesting recipes on her wood-burning range.

You can read about Lisa and Stewart's adventures buying and renovating *A Casa do Campo*, their ancient, derelict stone farmhouse; defying Spanish bureaucracy to marry in Galicia; and their continuing adventures when 'Mother makes three', in Lisa's *Writing Home* trilogy.

In 2022, Lisa published *Pulpo, Pig & Peppers – travels around Galicia*. Her fourth, full-length travelogue memoir, *Pulpo* follows the adventures of Lisa, Stewart and mum, Iris, as *Los Tres* travel around this beautiful region discovering its secrets, and its gastronomy.

All Lisa's books are available in hardback, paperback, eBook, and free with Kindle Unlimited at Amazon stores worldwide. *Pulpo* is also available as a large print book.

A short story prequel to Lisa and S' adventures in Galicia, *Camino – a peanut butter, marmite & banana butty* is just 99p/99c in Amazon stores or FREE to subscribers to Lisa's newsletter, along with other exclusive goodies.

Join Lisa's subscribers' club, read more about her books, and check out her photo gallery and monthly blog at: https://lisarosewright.wixsite.com/author

Lisa also has stories featured in Alyson Sheldrake's fabulous travelogue anthologies which can be found at: https://www.alysonsheldrake.com/travel-stories-series/

https://lisarosewright.wixsite.com/author

If you have enjoyed this book, please consider leaving a review on Amazon or Goodreads. Every nice review makes me smile and helps others find my books.

Thank you
Lisa

APPENDIX I

Lisa's multi-weather packing list

Clothing: I aim to have a week's worth of clothes before we need to find a washing machine, but often wash smalls etc by hand as we go along. This was especially true in the Nullarbor, where we were sweaty almost instantly but where washing would dry to a crisp in an hour.

One set of working clothes for Workaway placements to keep separate: washed between venues. Cargo pants with lots of pockets, which is good unless one leaves a penknife in there while going through customs. I use zip-off trousers so I have shorts and trousers in one. Two polo shirts (with collars), one fleece jumper, two pairs of socks, I worked in my short wellies or sandals.

Two sets of cold weather clothes: Fleece-lined cargo pants, fleece leisure trousers (for evening), fleece jumper, plus my Mexican agave hoodie (I travelled in this, it's my favourite comfort blanket, unless it gets pee on it!). Two to three vest tops for underlayers, thin puffa jacket (this folds up to fist size but is surprising warm, especially in conjunction with the Mexican hoodie), two long-sleeved Ts, two pairs of socks (one day, one evening).

For the cruise, in addition I packed: waterproof trousers and jacket, scarf/snood, waterproof gloves and woolly hat, plus sunblock and sunglasses, as advised by the company.

Two sets of hot weather clothes: Two pairs shorts, one sundress, three to four vest tops (as above) one long-sleeved silk shirt as a cover up/mozzie guard, sandals and trainers, two pairs thin socks, baseball cap, bikini/swimsuit.

I always wear the bulkiest stuff to travel. This was easy coming from a snowy Galician February: short wellies (comfy and waterproof), Mexican hoodie (I can pull the hood up and sleep), cargo pants (lots of pockets for documents etc), T shirt (in case it gets hot on the plane).

I had a small, fold up bag within my hand luggage for our two-night, Singapore stopover: shorts, two vest tops, sundress, two pairs of knickers, long-sleeved silk shirt, sandals. I planned to change at the airport once we landed.

Toiletries: I take small bottles of toothpaste, shampoo, conditioner and gel, which can be topped up as we go. On this trip I put the larger versions in the hold bag, in case I couldn't find the products I needed or they were mega-expensive. Moisturiser and sun cream (we use P20 which is a thin, varnish-like, oily product that binds with the skin to help tanning whilst giving a sun protection factor of 20. It is waterproof and only needs to be applied once a day. Useful if you are in and out of the water).

First aid kit. This is a small, waterproof bag which holds enough of everything for emergencies: plasters, steri-strips, anti-histamines, ibuprofen, aspirin, rehydration sachets, anti-diarrhoea tablets, Germolene antiseptic cream (pink medicine as we call it) and Germolene 'new skin' (amazing stuff for minor cuts, like a layer of superglue...which works too), tiger balm (brilliant for insect bites and headaches), small scissors and penknife (not to be confused with the one left in the cargo-pants pocket).

Printed in Great Britain
by Amazon